Dear David:

Just a little token of
my appreciation for you
leading our worship

PERSONAL HOLINESS

IN TIMES OF

TEMPTATION

ministries! Not only do
I appreciate it, but I

BRUCE H. WILKINSON

Know that our Lord
sees and is blessed
    Your friend,
        Dan
            Hebrews

HARVEST HOUSE PUBLISHERS
Eugene, Oregon 97402

6:10

Cover by Design Point, Salem, Oregon

PERSONAL HOLINESS IN TIMES OF TEMPTATION
Copyright © 1998 by Bruce H. Wilkinson
Published by Harvest House Publishers
Eugene, Oregon 97402

Library of Congress Cataloging-in-Publication Data
Wilkinson, Bruce.
    Personal holiness in times of temptation / Bruce Wilkinson.
      p. cm.
    ISBN 0-7369-0153-1 (softcover)
    ISBN 1-56507-943-4 (hardcover)
    1. Holiness. 2. Temptation. 3. Spiritual life—Christianity.
I. Title
BT767.W55 1998
234' .8—dc21

Printed in the United States of America.

99 00 01 02 / BP / 10 9 8 7 6 5 4 3 2 1

For more than 20 years, I have been serving the Lord shoulder-to-shoulder with the most outstanding team of committed and godly leaders I have ever known, the Walk Thru the Bible Executive Team. These servant leaders have faithfully built the ministry of WTB into the widespread and effective ministry it is today through fervent prayer, exhilarating teamwork, innovative leadership, and diligent management.

Together we have seen the Lord multiply the ministry so that Walk Thru the Bible conducts more than 10,000 Bible seminars and training conferences around the world each year; publishes ten devotional guides each month (having recently surpassed the 100 million cumulative circulation total); distributes numerous video courses to thousands of churches and dozens of denominations, Christian organizations, and missions; broadcasts the WTB television program into hundreds of thousands of homes each week; ministers to the ever-growing WTB support team through the President's Councils and Prayer Team; and now ministers actively in more than 70 countries and 50 languages.

Whenever I am around these outstanding men and women, my heart beats more deeply for the Lord and His commission to teach His Word to the whole world for lasting lifechange. Whenever I am with these godly leaders, my heart is more resolute to continue in my commitment to "be holy, for I am holy." When I considered to whom this book should be dedicated, I found myself with only one choice—thank you to the Walk Thru the Bible Executive Team for the honor of serving the Lord at your side and for His glory:

Bill Watson: Executive Vice President
John Hoover: Vice President for International (1950-1997)
Jim Kinney: Vice President for Seminars and Training
Jill Milligan: Vice President for Video
John Nill: Vice President for Publications
Robert Westfall: Vice President for Ministry Advancement

ACKNOWLEDGMENTS

As the last page of this book worked its way through my trusty ink-jet printer just moments ago, I felt the immense weight every author knows all-too-well slide from my weary shoulders. How good to finally say "Finished!"

The next emotion that flooded over me was one of deep gratitude for those who have run this race with me or cheered from the sidelines. The Harvest House Publishing team under the superb servant-leadership of Bob Hawkins proved to be excellent at every turn—what a pleasure working with Harvest House!

Senior Editor Chip MacGregor provided immeasurable guidance and leadership in the entire publishing process. His expertise, genuine encouragement, and kindred spirit proved to be the highlight of the entire process. Thanks Chip—you are a true pleasure to work with! Carolyn McCready, Julie McKinney, and Bill Jensen all brought their expertise to bear, for which I am deeply grateful.

At the source of this book stands a small cadre of good friends who constantly nudged me to put these concepts into print. Without Bill Watson, Jill Milligan, Jim Kinney, John Nill, Bob Westfall, Terry Sparks, Phil Tuttle, Frank Wilson, and Norm Clinkscales, this book would only have been available in video series form!

Deep gratitude to the Board of Directors of *Walk Through the Bible*, who have long weaned me from operational responsibilities to the delightful focus of developing new and creative biblical seminars, videos, and books—this book finds its deep roots in your twenty-year dreams. Thanks to Paul Johnson, Robert Boyd, Howard Hendricks, John Van Diest, and John Isch.

For those who labor under the reality of deadlines, rewrites, and galley-proofs, we always reserve our deepest appreciation and affection. For my family, who stood loyally with me while I seemed to forever sit before a competing computer screen, thank you Darlene and Jessica for sharing me with the book. I could never have done it without your understanding, patience, and prayers. Now all that remains is to follow the ancient words of a fifteenth-century monk:

"The book is finished! Let the writer play!"

CONTENTS

ME? HOLY?

Picture yourself interviewing for the ideal job. Each part of the interview process has gone well, and today is the final test: a meeting with the president. After the normal small talk, he asks an unexpected question, "If you were to describe yourself with just five words, what would they be?"

Your heart pounds as you search for the best answer—how can someone summarize himself or herself in only five words? As you scramble for the answer, you notice the president reach across his desk to a small stack of 3" x 5" cards with lists of words on them. Sensing your discomfort, he slowly shuffles through the cards and says, "Don't be so tough on yourself, just pick five words. Our personnel department already spoke to a number of your friends, family members, and a few of your previous work associates and asked the same question. We're just curious to see if your responses line up with how everyone else sees you."

Reflect on that for a moment. What words would others use to describe you? If the president slid those cards across the desk for you to read, what words would you see on them? Even more important, would any of those people have put the word "godly" on the list? Would you have selected the word "holy" to describe your life?

If you are like most people, the thought of calling yourself holy probably never entered your mind. The concept of being "holy" seems to be one of those qualities reserved for Sunday mornings and to describe saints and missionaries, not people like you and me.

On a recent Saturday morning, I tried this experiment with a couple dozen men from my home church. After requesting they write down the five words which best describe their lives, I asked if any had written the word "holy." The answer was an embarrassed silence. A few rocked back on their chairs, some folded their arms, and most looked around the room, trying not to make eye contact.

When I asked why they felt uncomfortable describing themselves as holy, the men had no problem relating their reasons: "Being holy is for preachers! I'd use it to describe a martyr or a missionary, but not me! It's for saints, not sinners. Maybe when I'm dead I can be holy, but right now I'm just a normal guy." In the minds of most "normal guys," holiness exists "out there" somewhere—with dusty, distant, or dead saints; not riding around in trucks, wearing boots, and working 9 to 5.

Wanting to understand their attitudes about holiness more fully, I asked the men to describe a holy person. They offered examples like: "*Holiness means stern people, wearing dark colors and high black stockings, walking in rigid strides—the women bound by tight corsets!*"

"*People who would write 'holy' on their sheets live hard lives, with hidden troubles, carrying big black Bibles around to remind them what they shouldn't be doing.*"

"*To be holy is to live in the Valley of 'NO'—no to everything that has color, joy, spontaneity, humor, variety, creativity, football, music with a beat, and a thick, medium-rare T-Bone steak!*"

Then one guy, the wit in the group, gave this answer: "*Holiness is like that famous painting of the old couple, standing sternly next to their red barn, holding a pitchfork.*" At that, everyone exploded with laughter, because in their minds, his answer nailed it. We define holiness with words like sober, sad, boring, tight, and super-religious, but don't define it as real or recent.

The more I listened that morning, the easier it was to understand why no one put "holy" on their list. Who wants to stand stiffly, looking severe, pitchfork in hand?

WHAT IS YOUR HOLINESS "ATTRACTION QUOTIENT"?

The deeper I probed, the more depressed I became. I knew these men weren't alone—in fact, they revealed the normal reaction to being called "holy." *Holiness seems to be a welcome discard from the previous generation.* People seem almost relieved that holiness finally lies buried in the dim past, and most don't want to return and dig up its tattered, undesired remains. Think about yourself for a moment...are you attracted to holiness?

In the business world, marketing experts describe how a person feels toward something as the Attraction Quotient (AQ), and they rate it on a scale of 1 to 100. The more a person is drawn to a product or concept, the higher its AQ; the more a person avoids that product or concept, the lower its AQ. Now imagine the Holiness Marketing Firm has hired you to research the Attraction Quotient of holiness. First, you research how people feel about holiness within a one mile radius of your home, rating them on their perceived AQ score. Second, you narrow your research to those who are members of churches and rate their AQ. Finally, you conduct a historical comparison of the AQ of holiness during the last three generations.

What do you think the scores would be? Your generation's Attraction Quotient toward holiness? Your parents' generation? Your grandparents' generation? What is the trend—have people become more or less attracted to holiness?

Now let's say the Holiness Marketing Firm wants to know if there is any clear relationship between holiness and quality of life. In other words, as holiness decreased dramatically, what happened to the foundations of society? For example:

1. As holiness declined, what has been the trend in marriages and families—has the rate of divorce increased or decreased, has the relationship between parents and children become stronger or weaker, and has abuse become more or less prevalent?

2. As holiness declined, what has been the trend in the lives of children—have youth become more wholesome, honest, self-disciplined, and respectful, or more dishonest, selfish, and disrespectful of authority?

3. As holiness declined, what has been the trend in the media—have movies, television, radio, and magazines promoted solid values, sexual fidelity, and integrity in relationships and business, or have they hyped sexual immorality, greed, and violence?

4. As holiness declined, what has been the trend in the prison population—has the percentage of incarceration, the average age of inmates, and the level of violence in society increased or decreased?

5. As holiness declined, what has been the trend in physical illnesses—are more people healthy or sick, are psychological problems increasing or decreasing, and are individuals using more or less drugs in order to escape their problems?

6. As holiness declined, what has been the trend in society's morality—how do people feel about leaving their doors unlocked? Are our cities safe? Are alcohol and drug addictions increasing or decreasing? Are lawsuits becoming more or less prevalent?

7. As holiness declined, what has been the trend in the overall quality of life—have people enjoyed a more balanced life with growing peace and contentment, and has general kindness and goodwill become more or less prevalent?

What would you find? The trends are unmistakable. Although you may never have related the concept of "holiness" with such things as marriage, family, media, prison, physical illnesses, psychological well-being, addictions, morality, and quality of life; the Bible not only links them, it relentlessly presents an unmistakable cause-and-effect relationship between holiness and the routines of everyday life. Since that is true, can you now begin to see the devastating result of the widespread negative attitude toward holiness?

REPOSITIONING HOLINESS

In recent years, one of the buzz words of the business world has been "positioning." How is a given product or service "positioned" in the mind of the public? When a product is "repositioned," people respond in a dramatically different manner. A well-known example is the repositioning of the words "made in Japan." Back in the 60s, those words left the impression of poor quality merchandise, but today, something "made in Japan" is perceived as being of the highest quality. The Attraction Quotient, which used to be very low, has been raised substantially—the public's purchasing of those products proves it.

It's amazing that in only 30 years everything changed. Not many of us wanted to purchase a Datsun in the old days, but today the names Toyota, Nissan, Honda, Lexus, and Infinity nearly monopolize the lower and middle automobile markets. As positioning changed, so did purchasing. In a similar way, the title "President of the United States" used to carry the utmost respect—it stood for freedom, integrity, honesty, leadership, and moral uprightness in our nation and the nations of the world. Today that title seems to have been significantly repositioned.

As you consider holiness and its influence on your life, how you *feel* about it right at this moment exerts dramatic power over your choices and your life. If a given concept is genuinely harmful, then an emotional aversion provides a helpful safety net and keeps you away from it. But if a concept perceived as negative is actually something beneficial and helpful, it needs to be repositioned. Otherwise we would end up avoiding the very thing which is best for us. In my view, the Bible reveals our mistaken perceptions of the word "holy."

The enemies of holiness have purposefully and relentlessly strategized to deceitfully reposition holiness until it stirs only negative emotions in people. The holy ones are not just stern people wearing dark colors. Those who see themselves as holy don't necessarily live in the Valley of "No." As the great Christian writer C. S. Lewis put it, *"How little people know who think that holiness is dull. When one meets the real thing, it is irresistible!"*

Do you suppose Lewis is correct? Could it be that when you meet a person who thinks holiness is dull, it proves that individual doesn't know very much about holiness? And could it be when you meet a person who is genuinely holy, he or she is one of the few who are genuinely happy? In this current generation, holiness has been repositioned in most minds as something undesirable, even harmful, when in fact it is something beneficial and filled with joy. So I had to tell those good Christian men in my church who felt uncomfortable with holiness that they have paid dearly for their mistake. Over the years, I've come to believe that C. S. Lewis was correct.My attitude toward holiness has been repositioned. I've come to believe what the Bible says about holiness, and this book unabashedly seeks to reposition holiness in your mind.

If I'm successful, at some future time when you are asked to describe yourself, you could find yourself using the word "holy"! Perhaps friends and family will think of the word "holy" when asked to describe you. Hold on, my friend, for we are going after holiness in your life. Holiness is the center of God's will for you, and it is the theme of this book.

The Holy One Himself wants you holy.

The Purpose of This Book

This book has one clear goal in mind: your personal holiness. It is my fervent prayer that by the time you have finished reading, your heart and habits are turned toward holiness. This book divides into three sections, with four chapters in each section. Each part can be read independently of each other, although the sections follow each other logically.

Part One deals with the biblical concept of holiness and introduces you to the three stages of holiness. The first chapter presents an overview of what holiness is and is not. The second chapter focuses on the first stage of holiness and unveils the secret of how to become a "saint" in God's eyes. You'll find out what the Holy Spirit does for you in this stage and what you can do to attain the first level. The third chapter focuses on the holiness of your heart, and prepares you to enter into the Ceremony of Consecration. The last chapter treats "progressive holiness" by unboxing the theological boxes, unmasking the major misconceptions about holiness, and equipping you to evaluate your holiness by a "Holiness Chart."

Part Two transitions to the "dark side of holiness," and prepares you to deal victoriously with the "unholy" problems in your life. Chapter five trains you to use the "Ten-Step Deep Cleanse" for major sin problems, and chapter six marches right into the enemy's camp and reveals his basic strategy to defeat you: your temptations. The following chapter strengthens you by revealing your Temptability Quotient and describing the seven stages of every temptation. The last chapter deals boldy with our culture's toughest temptation: sexual immorality. If Christians can't break free from this bondage, holiness will remain only a desired dream rather than an enjoyed reality.

Part Three moves to the "bright side of holiness" and prepares you to strengthen yourself in the inner man through the exercise of holiness habits. Chapter nine introduces you to these habits and reveals the sowing-reaping principle. Then chapters ten through twelve survey the six major Holiness Habits practiced by the church throughout the centuries.

This book focuses on the practical and the usable—so enjoy the discovery of many biblical insights and practical tools to encourage you in your personal pilgrimage toward holiness in these times of temptation.

Bruce H. Wilkinson
Atlanta, Georgia
1998

PART ONE

TURNING YOUR
HEART TOWARD HOLINESS

1

PERSONAL
HOLINESS

*"How little people know who think that holiness is dull.
When one meets the real thing, it is irresistible. If even 10
percent of the world's population had it, would not the
whole world be converted and happy before a year's end?"*

—C. S. LEWIS

The theology professor walked into the lecture hall for the last class in his fifty-year career. As usual, the vast auditorium buzzed with anticipation for his series entitled "The Life of Holiness," but throughout the semester an undercurrent of argument and debate had marred the class. Some insisted holiness meant one thing, others argued it meant something else. One faction claimed holiness had to be lived one way, while others claimed it couldn't be lived at all. Even after a half century's experience at the podium, the cagey old professor couldn't break the harsh and divisive attitudes of this group of graduate students. Everywhere he looked across the tiered lecture hall, pockets of students sat in isolated groups.

What he had feared most had occurred. No matter what he said about holiness, the conflicting theological divisions in the auditorium dogmatically and harshly argued with each other, to the point that they now were physically and emotionally separated from each other. Every group touted their verses, and nobody backed down

> "THE DESTINED END OF MAN IS NOT HAPPINESS, NOR HEALTH, BUT HOLINESS. GOD IS NOT AN ETERNAL BLESSING MACHINE FOR MEN. HE DID NOT COME TO SAVE MEN OUT OF PITY; HE CAME TO SAVE MEN BECAUSE HE HAD CREATED THEM TO BE HOLY."
>
> —Oswald Chambers

nor genuinely listened to another group's verses or perspective. For nearly the entire semester, he had labored to break through their judgmental attitudes and independent spirits without success. After pacing for days in his book-lined basement library, searching for a possible solution, he came up with one last idea. It was a long shot, but perhaps it was the necessary cure.

Instead of beginning class his normal way, he slowly wrote one solitary word on the middle of the blackboard and stared at it, focusing every eye in the classroom on the word: *"Trunks."*

He turned to face the class and delivered each measured word: "This session may be the most challenging of your entire graduate career. With the students around you, please define this word and give every reason why you believe you are correct. Do not discuss your thoughts with another group, nor will any questions be entertained at the lectern. In ten minutes, be prepared for your group's official spokesperson to stand and read your written answer." A long pause followed. "Let me advise you from the outset, students, there is only one correct answer to this question, and your written answer will weigh heavily on your final grade for this class." With that sober revelation, he calmly turned on his heels and walked resolutely from the room and toward his office. The corners of his mouth twitched upward, though ever so slightly, as he walked down the hallway, wondering about the debates raging in his classroom.

Ten minutes passed. As the second hand reached the top of its arc, he strode back into the room, opened his grade book, faced the class, and asked for a group to volunteer. No one spoke. Confusion reigned in the most unexpected place on the entire university campus: his classroom. The professor waited for what seemed an eternity. "Then, if no one will volunteer, this option is hereby closed. Please pass forward your written statements with the name of each person in your group signed at the bottom."

From the back of the room came a rumbling. "This isn't fair! Besides, what do 'trunks' have to do with personal holiness?" Without even acknowledging the accusation, the professor turned to the blackboard and in front of the word "trunks" added three more: "*The big gray.*" Then he looked back at his class.

"After further consideration, I've softened my previous position and decided to give you a second chance. Follow the same instructions precisely. Let me advise you again, there is only *one correct answer* and your written answer will weigh heavily on your final grade for this class." With that, the classroom nearly exploded in frustration. But the professor quietly departed, with nary a word or a backward glance enroute to his safe haven at the end of the hall. Ten long minutes passed before he returned, once again requesting a volunteer. This time some of the more committed students hung their heads, sensing failure in the eyes of their esteemed mentor. Once again, the papers were collected and stacked neatly on top of the previous ones, deliberately placed next to his grade book.

For the third time, the professor's shoulders turned toward the words on the board, and he added six words: "The big gray trunks *bounced down the dusty African road.*" With an exaggerated emphasis, he placed the period at the end of the sentence.

"After further deliberation, I have elected to provide you a third opportunity. Follow the same instructions precisely. Let me advise you again, there is only *one correct answer* and your written answer will weigh very heavily on your final grade." He paused for a minute before adding, "Oh! And because of the importance of this paper on your theological future, after you have completed your answer, please debate your findings with the groups around you in order to consider all perspectives."

As the professor left the room, furrows crossed his brow. "How," he wondered to himself, "will students perform under such an assignment, considering their strident defensiveness and dogmatism as displayed in their discussions of holiness all semester long?" This time, he turned to the right after leaving the lecture hall, circling back upstairs to the sound booth in the far corner. He wanted to observe first hand the results of his plan.

Chaos reigned as the students vented their pent-up frustrations. Debates and arguments flooded the room, not only between groups but within groups. Voices were raised and arms waved. Finally, after 15 minutes of discussion, the professor knew it was time to cut off debate. For the final time, he entered the auditorium. Never had he felt such division within a class, yet never had he felt such a responsibility to deal uncompromisingly with an issue. Addressing his class, he began to challenge their thinking. First, he asked the various groups to list on the board what the word "trunks" meant. There were four different interpretations: (1) the trunk of a car; (2) the trunk of an elephant; (3) a trunk like a suitcase or chest; and (4) the trunk or body of a person from Africa. Next, the professor asked them if they had changed their minds in the course of the debate. Almost everyone admitted they had changed their answer at least once. The professor repeated again the earlier revelation that there was only one correct answer before asking the groups if any would like to risk their entire semester's grade on their response. No one moved. "Why won't you risk your grade?" he questioned. "Aren't you *sure* you know the answer?"

The students in the class nearly yelled back, "No, because we don't have all the necessary information!"

Slowly the professor nodded in affirmation and turned yet again toward the board. With great care, he touched his chalk to the period at the end of the sentence and dramatically added a long tail, making it a comma. Still facing the board, he turned his face back toward the class and scanned the faces, heightening the implications of his unexpected action. Then he finished the sentence: "The big gray trunks bounced down the dusty African road, *as the boy who was wearing them ran by.*"

Everyone groaned. Not one group had come up with the correct answer. With the first smile of the day, the professor asked a pivotal question: "Now how many of you would be willing to risk your entire semester's grade on your answer?" Every hand shot up. "And what changed to make your confidence so complete?"

The oldest member of the class, who spoke only on rare occasions, summarized for everyone: "We finally have all the parts we need for the answer. Before we had only one word, and we were wrong. Then we knew only fragments, and still we were wrong. Then, when you wrote about 'bouncing down an African road,' most of us changed our minds, thinking we finally had the answer. It was only after you gave us the complete sentence that we knew the whole truth."

The professor nodded. He knew his class was on the brink of a strategic lesson. "Good. Now let me ask you a question: What percentage of you were mistaken about your earlier answers?"

The reply came flooding back: "100 percent!"

"That's right—all of you were mistaken. Even though I heard your intense debates, all of you were wrong! Even though some of you were sure of your position, you did not have adequate information to feel so. We can't be dogmatic about things unless we have all the information." Then, turning back to the board, he added, "Now let me ask you what another word means." With that the professor erased the sentence on the board and wrote the word "holiness" in place of "trunks." A flash of insight flooded the classroom. At that very moment, the bell rang. The professor laid down his chalk and said, "Make sure you have all the information before making your decision." Then he smiled gently and walked toward the door. The only noise to be heard was the growing thunder of applause by the students, whose hearts had been touched by the truth.

Now that you're pursuing holiness, do you know where you are going and what you're looking for? Will you know when you have hit the target—not in your eyes, but in heaven's eyes? After all, holiness is not a human thought, it's a supernatural thought, right from the very throne of heaven.

If you are a bit unsure, then perhaps you may decide to stick around after class for a few moments. I'm sorry to say the wise old professor is nowhere to be found, just a guy who likes to "Walk Thru the Bible" now and then....

I. HOLINESS MEANS "SEPARATION"

The first step in pursuing holiness starts with a clear understanding of what God means by "holiness." Holiness has been defined by individuals and denominations in all kinds of ways—with as much emotional baggage as the professor experienced. The root concept of holiness is unmistakable, however, and is first exposed in the Bible through the drama of the burning bush:

> When Moses saw it, he said to himself, "I will now turn aside and see this great sight, why the bush does not burn." So when the LORD saw that he turned aside to look, God called to him from the midst of the bush and said, "Moses, Moses!" And he said, "Here I am." Then He said, "Do not draw near this place. Take your sandals off your feet, for the place where you stand is *holy ground*" (Exodus 3:3-5).

Holy ground? How could "ground" be holy? If Moses had taken a handful of "unholy" ground and compared it with the holy sand at the burning bush, would he have seen the difference? If the previous week Moses shepherded his flock through that same patch of the desert, would it have been holy then? Or if Moses would have taken a few grains of holy sand back to his tent and studied it carefully, would he have discovered the nature of the sand changed or that it was still just plain old desert sand? Since nothing in the nature of the sand changed, why did the Lord label it "holy"?

1. Holiness Can Be in the Mind of the Believer

If you had one of those big Hebrew dictionaries like I do sitting within arm's reach, you could soon find the answer. You'd quickly discover that the root concept of holiness lies in the word "separation." The ground became holy simply because God separated it as the unique place that He would reveal Himself to Moses. In a sense, all the rest of the desert re-mained unholy because God didn't choose it as the location for His conversation. If God would have moved a stone's throw to the north and spoken there, that particular part of the desert would have been holy.

Extend your understanding of holiness a bit further through a second hypothetical illustration. Imagine, after one of the massive feasts conducted during King Solomon's reign, one of the temple priests went home to his wife with this request: "Sweetheart, I need a new holy knife for the temple. None of the knives remain sharp, so would you mind if I took one of ours?" The instant the priest dedicated the knife to the Lord's service, that unholy kitchen knife became the holy temple knife.

> "HOLINESS IN US IS THE COPY OR TRANSCRIPT OF THE HOLINESS THAT IS IN CHRIST. AS THE WAX HATH LINE FOR LINE THE SEAL, AND THE CHILD FEATURE FOR FEATURE FROM THE FATHER, SO IS HOLINESS IN US FROM HIM."
>
> —Philip Henry

Holiness can describe the "separation" in a person's mind regarding a knife, sand, a city, or many other things. I call this "mental holiness" as the separation occurs only in the person's thinking. For example, not only didn't the nature of the sand change, but no one would have known the ground was "holy" unless God revealed it to them.

2. Holiness Must Be Both "from" and "unto" or It's Not Holiness

Holiness requires *separation from* one thing and *separation to* a different thing. Think about that for a moment and it becomes immediately obvious as you can't have one without the other. For that knife to be-come holy it must be *separated from* the house and *separated to* the temple. Once again, notice that the *nature of the knife didn't change to make it holy, only its separation made it holy*.

Holiness requires division. Up to the moment the temple priest took the knife *from* his home, that knife couldn't become holy. Why not? Because it was with all other knives and not distinct. Until the Lord set that particular part of the desert apart from the rest of the desert, He couldn't call it holy. Holiness then, requires withdrawal. Holiness requires disconnection. For a person to become holy in this sense, he must depart from something or holiness is impossible.

The second side of separation requires that the knife becomes *united to* something else. The priest took that knife from the kitchen and *placed it into* the temple. Holiness requires reconnection.

Holiness requires addition. New people or new practices or new pursuits must be added into your life to replace the old, unholy patterns. We *abandon* our old, unholy ways, and *pursue* His holy way. Without both sides of this separation, biblical holiness is not possible. To separate "from" without separating "to" is not biblical holiness. Biblical holiness must have a "stop" followed by a "start."

The believer must flee from something and then follow after something else. Notice these two distinct parts in 2 Timothy 2:22:

> *Flee* [separate yourself from] also youthful lusts; but *pursue* [separate yourself to] righteousness, faith, love, peace with those who call on the Lord out of a pure heart.

Whenever a person only seeks one half of this equation, imbalance and error will eventually invade their life. So much of the negative baggage in people's minds about holiness is a result of the harsh focus on "fleeing." Holiness is not living in the world of "no" but leaving the world of "no" in order to enter the world of "yes!"

If you can't look back over your shoulder to identify some areas of your life which you have fled or departed from as well as some other areas of life which you have added or pursued, you may be sorely lacking in holiness at this time.

Throughout the Old Testament and the New Testament, the root word "holy" and all its related words are translated by such terms as set apart, dedicated, consecrated, sanctified, holy, separated, and saint. Whatever context these words may be part of in the Bible, they are all rooted in the concept of "separateness."

The theme verse for this book is taken from 1 Peter 1:15-16:

> ...but as He who called you is holy, you also be holy in all your conduct, because it is written, "Be holy, for I am holy."

Captured in this verse is the call of the Lord God to you personally: The Lord calls you to be holy. He beckons you to come out from the people and be separate from and to Him, to depart from everything that isn't like Him, and to devote yourself fully to Him and His glorious life. In essence, practical "holiness" for the Christian occurs as we leave behind the patterns of this world in order to become more Christlike in our character and conduct. May your heart discover the incredible power of release and reattachment. May you depart from all that isn't holy and pursue all that is.

II. HOLINESS HAS STANDARDS

Every culture in the world honors some type of holiness. In some cultures, certain places are described as "sacred" while other items are called "taboo." Both of these terms describe the issue of separation from that which is secular to that which is sacred.

For separation to be categorized as holy, it must take two additional steps. For instance, when a husband and wife experience trauma in their lives and choose to separate from each other and separate to independent lives, no one would call them "holy" would they? Why not?

1. Holiness Requires Separation from the "Secular" to the "Sacred"

First of all, separation which is holy must include the separation from that which is "secular" to that which is "sacred." Deity must be included in holiness or there cannot be any genuine holiness. Pagan cultures have "holy men" who have separated and devoted themselves to the pursuit of their tribal deities and their supposed powers over nature, sickness, crops, and enemies. But believers are called to leave that sort of unholiness behind and pursue the truth of God. As you think about your holiness, whatever you choose to separate *from*, you must choose to separate yourself *to* the Lord.

This insight provides the foundation to understand many holy things in the Bible such as the Holy Temple, Holy Sabbath, Holy Altar, Holy Place, and Holy Assembly. In these cases, the nature did not change, but instead they were separated from the natural and devoted to the supernatural, from the service of man to the service of God.

At various times in my ministry, I am asked to publicly dedicate a room or building to the Lord. In a true sense, that room or building becomes sanctified, or set apart to the Lord, His work, and His glory. The building becomes "holy unto the Lord."

Darlene and I devoted our home and all our belongings to the Lord. First we walked around the plot of ground we purchased in the country and dedicated it officially to the Lord and His glory. Then we stood together and specifically dedicated our home and everything in it to the Lord and His service. Up to that point, I wouldn't have considered our home to be officially devoted to the Lord. It still remained a regular "home" in our minds—but when we devoted it to Him, it transitioned into the realm of holiness. Now we are but stewards of His asset and workers in His home.

Perhaps you've attended the sacred ceremony of the ordination of an individual to the Lord as a minister. At the most solemn moment in the service, the individual will be asked to kneel before the congregation and the elders will lay their hands on him and officially dedicate and devote him to the Lord and His service. You would be correct in thinking it is a holy ceremony, in a holy place, for a holy purpose, resulting in the official devotion of a holy person. Individuals then, may devote themselves to the Lord in a certain manner which heaven would describe as holy.

Therefore, separation not only occurs in the tangible but also the intangible, in the seen and the unseen. A knife can be made holy by devoting it to service to the Lord. Likewise, a man or woman can choose to devote their heart, soul, and might to the Lord, thereby separating themselves to the Lord in their own heart and mind.

The Old Testament in particular is full of examples of this devotion and separation. When the nation of Israel agreed to be God's holy nation, the Lord outlined some rather unusual ways He wanted them to separate themselves from all the other nations. These specific "holiness regulations" constantly reminded the Jews and everyone who was around them that they weren't just any nation; they belonged to the Lord, a fact which practically influenced everything in their lives. Consider two illustrations from Leviticus 19:19:

You shall not sow your field with mixed seed.
Nor shall a garment of mixed linen and wool come upon you.

In other words, for a Jew in the Old Testament to be ceremonially "holy," he could not sow two different kinds of seeds in his garden or wear a blended shirt. He would have to wear an all-wool shirt.

Now, think about it: Is wearing a shirt with two different kinds of threads unholy for me today? Absolutely not! Why? Because these specific and unique "laws of holiness" were for the Jews at that time to distinguish and separate them from everyone else. Every morning as they dressed they were forced to remember that because they were the Lord's nation, they were separate from the rest of the nations and were called to practice separation. In other words, the wearing of an unblended shirt didn't change the character of the individual, it was merely an external sign of the covenant with the Lord.

Another interesting illustration of "holy behavior" is found in Leviticus 27:30: *"And all the tithe of the land, whether of the seed of the land or of the fruit of the tree is the LORD's. It is holy to the LORD."*

How could "seed of the land" or "fruit of the tree" be holy? Only because the Lord revealed that the "tithe of the land" or 10 percent of all seed and fruit were His and must be "separated from" them and "separated to" Him through dedication and donation.

2. Biblical Holiness Is Defined by the Lord and His Revelation

The pinnacle of biblical holiness, however, is not merely separation, or separation from in order for separation to, or separation from the secular to the sacred, or separation through devotion in the heart, but *specific separation as revealed by the Lord God Himself.* In other words, those "holy men" in many cultures of the world worship neither the Lord God nor His Son Jesus but instead interface with an unseen spirit world. The Bible would describe them as the "anti-holy men" because they have devoted themselves to serve the enemies of the Lord.

Likewise, many of the cultures of the world practice specific rituals and religious practices which they consider to be the height of holiness, but heaven would consider them to be either worthless or anti-holy. "Holy men" who walk for miles on their knees to a holy temple are not performing the will of God nor in any manner pleasing Him.

"Holy cows" who ravish the poverty of people and eat while humans right next to them die of starvation are a travesty to heaven. The Lord of heaven never revealed that cows are holy or should be treated as holy. In fact, the Bible expressly reveals that those who teach that one must abstain from certain foods to be "holy" are actually giving heed to deceiving spirits! Just read for yourselves these pointed words in 1 Timothy 4:1-5:

> Now the Spirit expressly says that in latter times some will depart from the faith, *giving heed to deceiving spirits and doctrines of demons,* speaking lies in hypocrisy, having their own conscience seared with a hot iron, *forbidding to marry,* and *commanding to abstain from foods* which God created to be received with thanksgiving by those who believe and know the truth.
>
> *For every creature of God is good, and nothing is to be refused* if it is received with thanksgiving; for it is sanctified [made holy] by the word of God and prayer.

This principle is absolutely crucial for biblical holiness. The Lord sets the standards for what is holy, not man! If the Lord didn't reveal objective standards for His holiness, imagine the confusion and distortion that would reign as everyone did "what was right in their own minds"! The Bible is absolutely clear, my friend, regardless of how sincere and devoted individuals may appear, if they have established standards of holiness out of their own emotions or minds or other literature outside of the Bible, their standards do not reflect biblical holiness.

For instance, many cults forbid the practice of marriage. They teach that higher levels of holiness or service to the Lord require they do not marry. Yet God reveals in 1 Timothy 4 that the standard which "forbids to marry" is not only not from the Lord, it is from actual "deceiving spirits."

3. Manmade Holiness Is Worthless Holiness

Do not miss this crucial point: Holiness is defined by the Lord, not by man. Holiness which is manmade is worthless! If you have invented nonbiblical standards or methods of holiness, you probably have opened yourself unnecessarily to suffering and eternally worthless behavior. Listen as Colossians 2:20b-23b outlines this issue:

> ...why...do you subject yourselves to regulations—"Do not touch, do not taste, do not handle," which all concern things which perish with the using—according to the commandments and *doctrines of men?*
> These things indeed have an *appearance of wisdom in self-imposed religion,* false humility, and neglect of the body, *but are of no value....*

As I have traveled widely across this world, my heart has been broken time after time by false and manmade "self-imposed religions" and doctrines of men which cause great pain and suffering but are of "no value." What then must we do if we are seeking the appropriate and effective methods of personal holiness? Just listen to the answer revealed by the Lord in Exodus 19:5-6a:

> Now therefore, *if you will indeed obey My voice* and *keep My covenant,* then you shall be a special treasure to Me above all people; for all the earth is Mine. And you *shall be to Me* a kingdom of priests and *a holy nation.*

For people to be holy in God's eyes, they must "obey His voice" and "keep His covenant." The Lord is the One who must define the boundaries of what is holy and what is not. A religion cannot, a cult cannot, a "holy man" cannot, a denomination cannot. Only the

Lord God Himself has outlined the standards of true, biblical holiness. Any new additions or deletions to the Bible must be guarded most carefully as they may be considered "doctrines of man" or "traditions of man."

During the life of Jesus, the Jewish leaders and preachers taught and prescribed their particularbrand of holiness widely. Listen to Christ's strong confrontation in Matthew 15:1-3, 7-9:

> Then the scribes and Pharisees who were from Jerusalem came to Jesus, saying, "Why do Your disciples transgress the tradition of the elders? [Note: not the Bible.] For they do not wash their hands when they eat bread."
>
> He answered and said to them, "*Why do you also transgress the commandment of God because of your tradition?*... Hypocrites! Well did Isaiah prophesy about you, saying: "These people draw near to Me with their mouth, and honor Me with their lips, but their heart is far from Me... *Teaching as doctrines the commandments of men.*"

Therefore, the "commandments of men" are often taught as "biblical doctrines" when in reality they are not. In many churches and religious groups around the world today, this is precisely what is happening. Personal preferences and personal standards are taught as biblical holiness and usually by more emotional fervor than accompanied Scripture.

Read the above passage most carefully for it reveals the natural tendency: Our traditions become more important than God's commands. In other words, we disobey true biblical holiness *because of* our traditions! Be extremely careful about defining the standards of true biblical holiness beyond the boundaries of the Bible! All of us know individuals who are greatly deceived in their pursuit of holiness through man's teachings and traditions.

4. External Holiness Without Internal Holiness Is Not Biblical Holiness

The final standard of biblical holiness is also revealed in this same passage. After calling them hypocrites, the Lord tells them "their hearts are far from Me." For a person to be holy, his or her heart and motives must be pure before the Lord or the action cannot be holy. In other words, it is possible for a person to do something that the Bible clearly defines as holy and yet not fulfill biblical holiness. Holiness can be faked, but heaven calls faked holiness nothing less than unholiness! Not only must one's behavior be holy, but one's heart as well.

When a Christian seeks holiness in their life and practices specifics which the Bible would affirm, yet permits their heart to remain aloof or even rebellious to the Lord, He would call such behavior unholy—even if that behavior appears externally to be holy. For the Lord to evaluate something as holy, both the habit and the heart must be separated unto the Lord. One without the other only breeds destructive unholiness:

> "WHEN WE THINK OF HOLINESS, GREAT SAINTS OF THE PAST LIKE FRANCIS OF ASSISI OR GEORGE MUELLER SPRING TO MIND—OR CONTEMPORARY GIANTS OF THE FAITH LIKE MOTHER TERESA. BUT HOLINESS IS NOT THE PRIVATE PRESERVE OF AN ELITE CORPS OF MARTYRS, MYSTICS, AND NOBEL PRIZE WINNERS. HOLINESS IS THE EVERYDAY BUSINESS OF EVERY CHRISTIAN."
>
> —Chuck Colson

External holiness without internal holiness breeds hypocrisy.
Hypocritical holiness inevitably degenerates into the bondage of legalism.

Internal holiness without external holiness breeds emotionalism.
Emotional holiness inevitably degenerates into the bondage of fanaticism.

*Biblical holiness does not drift into the dangerous waters of
legalism and fanaticism.*
*Biblical holiness defines internal and external separation
by biblical standards.*

May you have a clear picture of what biblical holiness is all
about—and may you long for a heart and habit full of genuine, balanced holiness.

III. HOLINESS HAS STAGES

Last week, my wife's parents were visiting with us in our home
in Georgia and spent hours putting together a very large and difficult jigsaw puzzle with over 2000 pieces. Her parents are truly sea-
soned "puzzle people." After glancing over the hundreds of pieces, I
realized that this one had to be one of the most difficult I had ever
seen. Nothing was distinct. The sky and mountains and meadow
and lake all blended together. When you picked up one piece, you
immediately saw that it could fit almost anywhere! But, ultimately,
each piece could fit in only one place.

When you come to the subject of holiness, you immediately recognize its vast scope. Holiness pieces are scattered throughout all 66
books of the Bible! But, unlike my in-laws' single picture, I am convinced that biblical holiness has a number of distinct pictures in its
puzzle! In other words, I believe that biblical holiness is one unified
subject with very different meanings, depending upon the biblical
context.

Return for a moment to the professor's classroom. The reason
his students were all separated and isolated and even opposed to
each other was because of their different perspectives of holiness.
Each group selected a certain part of the holiness puzzle (each had a
distinct and complete picture in it), set up walls around their particular picture, and then emotionally and denominationally defended
their picture. Obviously, when they considered their picture, there
were numerous pieces (passages in the Bible) which could fit only
in their picture and nowhere else. They were absolutely correct—
and since their perspectives were biblical, anyone with differing
views must not only be wrong, but potentially even heretical.

No wonder holiness is so "puzzling"! After reading and studying many passages in the Bible on the subject of holiness, I realized how very massive and extensive it is. When I read certain passages, I could hear my Presbyterian friends applauding, other passages my Methodist and Wesleyan friends, other passages my Baptist friends, others my Pentecostal or charismatic friends. In other words, depending upon which group of "biblical pieces" of the holiness puzzle you focus on, your understanding will be influenced and ultimately controlled.

Throughout this process, I set aside all my own preconceptions. In order for this book to have biblical integrity, it must reveal what the Bible teaches, not what I may or may not believe. So, I began afresh looking through passage after passage with only one question: What does this passage actually say? As best I knew how, I set aside those "theological boxes" with all of their boundaries, and held onto only one boundary: the words and phrases and verses and paragraphs in the "biblical revelation" directly relating to the subject of holiness.

How frustrating this became! No wonder there are so very many different groups proclaiming they have the "truth" about holiness. My conclusion? For the most part, I believe that many are absolutely correct, they do have the truth.

They have the truth, but perhaps not the *whole* truth.

For instance, were those students correct in defending their position that "trunks" means an elephant's nose? Yes. Were other students correct in defending their position that "trunks" means the back of a car? Yes. If they surveyed all of American literature, they could prove that "trunks" indeed means the back portion of a car.

But, does "trunks" always mean the back of a car? Not at all.

In other words, one can have the truth, but not the whole truth. *One can be fully within the boundaries of what the Bible teaches in one passage, yet outside the boundaries of what the Bible teaches in all its parts.* It is my conclusion that most of the confusion regarding this most vital subject is due to the sincere error of defining holiness in too small a puzzle.

Could it be that holiness indeed fits into one puzzle but has three different and distinct pictures within that same puzzle? Then perhaps all parts would indeed fit within one whole without contradiction. In the next three chapters, three distinct yet interrelated parts of biblical holiness will be presented.

These three parts are actually three different stages of holiness. Before you are finished reading these three chapters, you may discover, perhaps for the first time, where you are in this life of holiness.

2

THE HOLINESS
OF SALVATION

*"He who created us without our help will not save us
without our consent."*

—Augustine of Hippo

S cattered over the top of my worktable were pages of verses
on the subject of holiness taken from throughout the Old
and New Testaments. After serious consideration, I had
decided to set aside everything I believed about holiness and start
all over—with just the Bible and a fresh slate to make sure that I let
the Bible talk for itself instead of me talking for it.

These pages listed all the Bible verses translated from the root
word "holy" regardless of how they were translated into the English
language. As I read these verses, words such as holy, holiness, sanc-
tify, set apart, and separated threaded their way through the pages.
For some reason, I had expected this to be a relatively easy step in
the developmental process, but my expectations were far afield
from reality. Little did I anticipate this task would create more frustration and confusion than insight and clarity.

The problem surfaced almost immediately: How could this root
concept of holiness be revealed in the Bible as something that had
already happened, in other verses as something that should happen

in the present, then in still other verses as something that will happen later? How could holiness be something Jesus did for me totally, in other verses something the Holy Spirit does in me, and then in other verses a commandment to be holy and live in a holy manner? I discovered the four tenses of holiness:

- Holiness described in the past tense.
- Holiness described in the present tense.
- Holiness described in the future tense.
- Holiness described in the future tense referring to the eternal state of believers.

The more I read, the more confused I became! Was I already holy or not? If I was holy, then why did the Bible command me to live holy? How could believers who were called "holy" in one verse, later *in the same chapter* be strongly exhorted to stop living such sinful lives? How could they be holy if they were unholy?

Time after time I felt waves of frustration and confusion. Instead of holiness being a biblical subject easy to unravel and present in a logical, helpful form, it was rapidly becoming a tangled mess of fishing line. By this time, I could take a handful of these verses and prove to you that you are already holy—so live what you are. Then I could take another handful of verses and prove that you will be holy one day, so you'd better keep working to grow in holiness. How can you grow in holiness if you are already fully holy?

No wonder there are so many different viewpoints and theologies built around this intriguing and intricate subject. At this point, my mind flooded with serious thoughts about letting someone else write this book! Why write a book about a subject on which so many godly people disagree? We at Walk Thru the Bible have worked extremely hard over the past 25 years to teach the Bible openly and clearly in a nondivisive, nondenominational, nonsectarian way. The Lord has blessed this approach, and Walk Thru ministers widely across scores of denominational and cultural barriers in 71 different countries and 52 languages.

So why risk offending someone now? If the Lord hadn't taught me so deeply regarding personal holiness in the past decade, I can assure you I would have dropped this project. If the men and women who'd been a part of the early teaching of this material hadn't responded so profoundly to what the Lord did in their hearts because of this material, I would have abandoned it on that worktable.

> "A PERSON MAY GO TO HEAVEN WITHOUT HEALTH, WITHOUT RICHES, WITHOUT HONORS, WITHOUT LEARNING, WITHOUT FRIENDS; BUT HE CAN NEVER GO THERE WITHOUT CHRIST."
>
> —John Dyer

Through this process of clarification, I became convinced that this book shouldn't be a book on the theology of holiness; in fact, you purposefully won't even find a single footnote. You won't find me evaluating someone else's viewpoint, nor working hard to exegete all the fine points of a certain passage. Why not?

Because I have some very clear goals in mind, and those goals have been the guiding lights for everything that's been written: First, by the end of this book your heart will have been stirred so deeply regarding the Lord's personal call for you to be holy that you will solemnly turn your heart toward holiness. Second, that you understand exactly what the Bible teaches and doesn't teach about holiness and what to do in order to achieve the Lord's goal for you to be "holy as I am holy" and to be "holy in all your conduct." Last, that you are equipped with three sets of tools to experience holiness—tools to break you free from the bonds of unholiness in your life; tools to enable you to overcome the temptations that assail you; and tools to pursue personal holiness through the habits of holiness used by the Lord's people throughout the centuries.

In other words, this book purposes to equip you to take major strides in personal holiness. Instead of focusing on the Lord's holiness, this book will focus on your holiness. Instead of majoring on head knowledge, this book majors on deep life change. Instead of pursuing theological systems, this book pursues personal transformation. With that introduction, let us begin with an investigation of how I finally made sense of all those pages of verses.

THE THREE STAGES OF PERSONAL HOLINESS

When I began preparing this course in earnest, none of my "rough draft" concepts about holiness had anything even remotely to do with "stages" of holiness. Instead, I suppose it would be safe to say I accidentally stumbled over the idea while trying to make sense of all those seemingly contradictory verses on holiness. Each single verse wasn't usually difficult to understand in isolation, but when two or more verses were compared that seemed to teach the exact opposites, I knew I was surely missing something foundational. Finally, I began to pay very close attention to the tense of the verbs in each verse and then arranged them into the various categories of past, present, future, and eternal.

As you could anticipate, when the verses *within* each category were studied, they made perfect and logical sense. But *between* categories, things didn't seem to fit together in any logical way. With further study and considerable meditation, I began noticing:

- Past holiness had certain characteristics and truths.
- Present holiness had different characteristics and truths.
- Future holiness had different characteristics and truths.
- Eternal holiness had yet different characteristics and truths.

Because this book focused on holiness in the here and now, the category of verses on "eternal holiness" was set aside. The verses in each category were studied carefully and the three stages of holiness soon became an extremely helpful framework to understand personal holiness. All this may seem a bit unclear at this point, but in the next few chapters, you will find your understanding about holiness deepening quickly. So let's get started.

THE FIRST STAGE OF HOLINESS

Read carefully the following verse and see if you can locate the two words that are both translated from the same root word for holiness:

> To the church of God which is at Corinth, to those who
> are sanctified in Christ Jesus, called *to be* saints, with all
> who in every place call on the name of Jesus Christ our
> Lord, both theirs and ours... (1 Corinthians 1:2).

The first word from the holiness root is "sanctified" and the second is "saints." You may have been surprised to discover that "saint" comes from the same root as holiness, but it does and opens new vistas of understanding. Notice that this verse describes the "church of God which is at Corinth" in two different ways.

First, they are the ones "who are *sanctified* in Christ Jesus," which means they have been made holy (or separated) in Christ through His death and resurrection. Second, they are "called *to be* saints," a title which the apostle used to describe who they are.

Did you notice that in the verse there are only two italicized words? When the Bible italicizes a word, it means the original Greek or Hebrew doesn't contain that word(s), but the translators added it seeking to make the meaning clearer to the English reader. Now you know that "*to be*" isn't in the original text but is instead the translators' addition. In the vast majority of times that my Bible includes the translators' additions, I find myself appreciating and benefiting from their insights. Unfortunately, in this case, I feel they threw me completely off track as I studied holiness. Track with me and see what I discovered.

If the Bible meant to communicate "called *to be* saints," I realized a "saint" represented something these Christians should grow into, or hopefully "be" sometime in the future. This interpretation of "called *to be* saints" beckons Christians to live a holy lifestyle at the highest level so that perhaps one day they may achieve that rare label of "sainthood."

On the other hand, if the Bible meant to say "called saints" as in the original Greek, then the Christians in Corinth would realize, much to their surprise, they already were "saints." *Instead of saint-hood being a future goal, it would be a present state.*

If "called *to be* saints" represented the best translation, then undoubtedly very few of the Corinthian Christians had attained that lofty state, but if "called saints" were the better translation, every single Christian in Corinth had already attained the title "saint." Mull over these next verses and seek further clarification in your own mind:

> Paul and Timothy, bondservants of Jesus Christ, *to all the saints* in Christ Jesus who are in Philippi, with the bishops and deacons (Philippians 1:1).

> To all who are in Rome, beloved of God, *called to be saints* (Romans 1:7).

> Paul, an apostle of Jesus Christ by the will of God, and Timothy our brother, to the church of God which is at Corinth, *with all the saints* who are in all Achaia (2 Corinthians 1:1).

When these similar verses are placed next to each other (others could be added), it's not too difficult to discern that the Bible is referring to the Christians as saints, not as Christians who should seek *to be* saints. In fact, as you follow this "saint" thread throughout the entire New Testament, you'd discover to your surprise that the New Testament refers to born again believers as Christians only 3 times but as saints 62 times! Now, what are the implications of being a saint?

The root word for holy, holiness, or sanctification is the Greek word *hagios.* As you read in the earlier chapter, holiness carries with it the basic meaning of separation. When *hagios* is used in noun form in the New Testament it is translated by the word "saint," which literally means the "separated one" or "the called-out one." The word "saint" doesn't represent a state of elevation of godliness but rather a state of separation to God.

Much of our confusion in this matter stems from the practice of some in labeling certain notable Christians as "Saint John" or "Saint Mary." Church history openly records that the designation of sainthood only occurred many years after the close of the New Testament and death of the apostles and disciples. Sainthood wasn't a New Testament practice as it isn't specifically a New Testament teaching but an ecclesiastical practice.

Interestingly, each one of those 62 times "saint" is used in the New Testament, not one of them in the original language is singular; they're always plural. Never once does the Bible say, "Saint Paul," using instead the "saints in Rome" or Corinth or Philippi. To use the word "Saint" as a title would be like using the word "Christian" or "Believer" as a title:

The "Christian" Paul
is the same as
the "Believer" Paul
who is the same as
the "Saint" Paul.

The New Testament uses "saint" to describe every single born-again believer in Jesus Christ. If you are born again, *you already are a saint* or a separated one. If you aren't born again as of yet, you are not a saint or a separated one.

The term "saint" introduces us to the first stage of holiness, which is the *holiness of the past tense.* At what moment did this "separation" take place so that believers can properly be called the separated ones? Notice these two verses which translate that same root word for holiness with the English word "sanctified."

> And such were some of you. But you were washed, but *you were sanctified*, but you were justified in the name of the Lord Jesus and by the Spirit of our God (1 Corinthians 6:11).

> By that will *we have been sanctified* through the offering of the body of Jesus Christ once for all (Hebrews 10:10).

"You *were* sanctified" and "we *have been* sanctified" clearly reveal that a certain type of holiness takes place in the past. The

Bible doesn't teach that only some of the believers "were sanctified" or were "saints" but everyone: *all* the saints…in Philippi" or "with *all* the saints…in *all* Achaia."

A great deal of confusion surfaces at this point across the landscape of the church regarding holiness—and it's not difficult to see why. Since the Bible teaches that all believers are saints and "have been sanctified," then any who don't live like "saints" or act "sanctified" certainly can't be Christians, can they? That may be a logical question, and other verses in the Bible may raise that issue, but the Bible teaches openly and repeatedly that a "saint" may indeed live for a period of time very "unsaintly." It's at this very critical point most believers become a bit hazy about the dramatic differences between the three separate stages of holiness.

How Does the First Stage of Holiness Make You Holy?

The first stage of holiness begins with your act of trusting the Lord Jesus Christ as your personal Savior. At that moment, you become a "saint" and "have been sanctified." Does that stage of holiness—when you become a saint and have been sanctified—mean that your behavior reflects what is true about you?

Think about the church of Corinth for a moment. Paul called them *"those who are sanctified in Christ Jesus"* and *"called to be saints."* Yet within a few short chapters, he delivers strong words against many of their sins including gross immorality, law-suits, widespread divisions, bitter envy, and others. Of all the churches in the entire New Testament, the Corinthian church was obviously the most sinful and "still carnal" (1 Corinthians 3:3). Yet as you read through Paul's first and second letters to them, he doesn't invite them to become Christians but to change their behavior. He doesn't tell them that because of their "unsaintly" behavior they couldn't be "saints." Instead, he argues that because they are "saints" they should live as "saints." The Bible is undeniably clear: Christians are saints who can choose to live like

> "I REMEMBER TWO THINGS: THAT I AM A GREAT SINNER AND THAT CHRIST IS A GREAT SAVIOR."
>
> —John Newton

sinners for a period of time. If Christians live like sinners, they are to be confronted and challenged to repent from their ways, depend upon the Holy Spirit, and walk in holiness.

What I'm driving at here is clear differentiation of *"past sanctification"* from *"present sanctification."* All believers have been sanctified, but not all believers live sanctified lives. Are you fully convinced that this perspective is completely biblical? I believe many passages support this concept including 1 Peter 2:9-12 which underscores much of what I am seeking to make clear. Note the three different steps in his argument:

> But *you are* a chosen generation, a royal priesthood, a *holy nation*, His own special people, that you may proclaim the praises of Him who called you out of darkness into His marvelous light;

> who once were not a people but *are now the people of God*, who had not obtained mercy but now have obtained mercy.

> Beloved, I *beg you as sojourners and pilgrims, abstain from fleshly lusts* which war against the soul, having your conduct honorable among the Gentiles, that when they speak against you as evildoers, they may, by your good works which they observe, glorify God in the day of visitation.

When people accept Christ as their personal Savior, as Peter states, they are brought "out of darkness into His marvelous light." Up to the point of their salvation, they "were not a people [of God] but are now the people of God." Until the moment of the Lord's forgiveness, they "had not obtained mercy" [by the Lord forgiving them of their sins and saving them from eternal punishment in hell] but now have obtained mercy [by the Lord giving them eternal salvation and a rich inheritance in glory].

Since no one would doubt that these very people were clearly born again and therefore "saints" and "having been sanctified," *then why in the very next verse does Peter have to "beg you" to "abstain from fleshly lusts"*? Only because at that very moment, they were indulging in fleshly lusts and sinning against the Lord and not having their "conduct honorable among the Gentiles." The point should be clear: The sanctification that occurs because of the belief in the finished work of Jesus isn't equal to or the same as the sanctification that occurs in the behavior of the believer.

If your behavior doesn't become holy during the first stage of holiness, then exactly how does a person become holy? How do other "things" that the Bible describes as "holy" become so? Take that famous passage of Christ's temptation in Matthew 4:5, "Then the devil took Him up into the *holy city*...." In answering that question, how could anyone call Jerusalem at that time anything remotely holy? Would you say that the behavior of Jerusalem could be characterized as godly and morally pure? (Remember when Moses took off his shoes because of "holy ground" yet nothing in the nature of the sand changed one bit.)

When something is "set apart" from the secular to the sacred, it is biblically called holy regardless of its nature or behavior. When the Lord selected Jerusalem and separated it to Himself as the "apple of His eye" and the location of "David's throne," the city became holy. When the Lord selected that part of the wilderness to speak to Moses and separated it to Himself, the ground became holy. Both were described to be holy not because they changed in their behavior or nature, but only because they were "separated" unto God and His purposes.

Not only can a "thing" be holy without the nature of the thing changing, but so also can a "person" be described as "holy" in one sense without the nature of that person changing. Think back to the Old Testament and you'll remember the words "holy priesthood." Flip through many of the Old Testament accounts of prophets and you'll see them repeatedly denouncing the wickedness of the priesthood—and yet they are still the "holy priesthood."

Wicked holy priests. Think about that for a moment: holy priests living as unholy people. Sounds to me like the same problem of Corinth hundreds of years later: saints living unsaintly lives.

Therefore, the essence of the first stage of holiness isn't in the change of the behavior of the person, but in the change in the Lord's mind about that person. The sand became holy only because the Lord decided to use it for His purposes. The city of Jerusalem became holy only because the Lord selected it for His purposes. The tribe of Levi became the holy priesthood only because the Lord appointed it as His priesthood. In identical fashion, the Lord separates to Himself every single person who believes in Jesus Christ as His personal Savior. At the moment of faith, the person (not his behavior) becomes "holy" or "sanctified" and even a "saint" in the mind of God.

That's why every single born-again believer is a saint, sanctified, and holy. If they weren't then they couldn't be truly saved because the essence of salvation is what happens in the Lord's view of us, not our view of Him. We believe in Jesus, and He separates us to Himself.

HOW TO ENTER THE FIRST STAGE OF HOLINESS

Becoming a saint is an instantaneous event rather than a progressive improvement of godliness. In order to deepen your understanding about the remarkable "rest of the story" about this first stage of holiness, the roles of the Holy Spirit, Jesus Christ, and the believer will be explored:

1. The Role of the Holy Spirit in the First Stage

Second Thessalonians 2:13 is most helpful in understanding what the Holy Spirit does in this first stage of holiness:

> But we are bound to give thanks to God always for you, brethren beloved by the Lord, because God from the beginning chose you for salvation *through sanctification by the Spirit* and belief in the truth....

The Holy Spirit is the agent through which this first stage sanctification is instituted:

> for salvation through sanctification by the Spirit....

At the moment of saving faith, the Holy Spirit sets us aside unto God. The Holy Spirit regenerates us so that we become born again (John 3:3-8), He seals us until the day of redemption (Ephesians 4:30), He is sent forth into our hearts by the Father crying out "Abba Father!" (Galatians 4:6), He indwells us (Romans 8:11), He baptizes us into the body of Christ (1 Corinthians 12:13), He gives us spiritual gifts (1 Corinthians 12:7,11,18), and bears spiritual fruit (Galatians 5:22ff.).

This incredible process of first stage sanctification is primarily the work of the Holy Spirit. All these blessings are granted instantaneously to the believer by the sanctifying work of the Spirit whether or not the believer even knows it. You'll notice that the Spirit does these works, and not the believer.

2. The Role of the Lord Jesus Christ in the First Stage

The work of sanctification is accomplished by the Holy Spirit on the basis of the work of salvation accomplished by the Lord Jesus Christ. Note how this is underscored in 1 Corinthians 6:11, "...you were washed, *but you were sanctified*, but you were justified *in the name of the Lord Jesus* and by the Spirit of our God."

A person is sanctified and justified only by means of the Lord Jesus. If Jesus hadn't finished His work, then the Spirit couldn't do His work. Hebrews 10:10,12-13 offer profound insight into this amazing work of Jesus:

> By that will [this is the work of the Father in salvation] *we have been sanctified through the offering of the body of Jesus Christ once for all.*

> But this Man, after *He had offered one sacrifice for sins forever,* sat down at the right hand of God, from that time waiting till His enemies are made His footstool.

Such a profound statement in so few words. A human being can be accepted by God and separated to Him for His purposes only because of the once-for-all sacrifice of Jesus. Christ died once—for all sins, for all people, for all time.

God considers all mankind to be on one side or the other side of this first stage of holiness. Either man is unholy or man is holy. *If man is unholy he is separated from God; if man is holy, then he is separated to God.* The reason why unholy men are separated from God is due to their sin and rebellion against God and their rejection of the sacrifice of Jesus. The penalty for such direct disobedience against God is the death penalty, including both physical death and eternal death in hell.

When Christ died, He offered His life as full payment for our sins. Unless Christ had paid for the sins of mankind, all of us would have no other option except eternal damnation. Out of grace and mercy and love, God sent His only begotten Son to die so that others like you and me may live.

Too many today are confused about the nature of salvation and the work of Christ. Think for a moment, when were your sins paid for by Jesus Christ? Christ paid for your sins by His death on the cross 2000 years ago. The Father accepted Christ's payment as sufficient for all your sins at that moment in time or your sins would still be on Jesus, yet unpaid for, and He wouldn't have been permitted back into heaven.

Now, where were you when Christ died for you and your sins 2000 years ago? Since you didn't exist except in the foreknowledge of our omniscient, all-knowing God, you couldn't have been present at the cross when Christ died. God laid on Christ all of our sins and Christ paid for every single one of them. When Christ died 2000 years ago, how many of your sins had yet to be committed? Every single one of them, since they were all in the future as you weren't even born yet! Sins you committed last year, then, were just as much in the "future" to Christ on the cross as the sins you commit today, tomorrow, or 20 years hence. *All your sins were paid for before you committed any of them.*

Your salvation was the complete work of Jesus Christ and you and I had absolutely nothing to do with it. Because it happened 2000 years ago ("It is finished")

> "IT IS NOT YOUR HOLD OF CHRIST THAT SAVES YOU, BUT HIS HOLD OF YOU!"
> —Charles Haddon Spurgeon

and it never has to be repeated ("He has offered one sacrifice for sins forever"), it would be foolish and arrogant to say that we have a part in our salvation. Since Christ finished the work of salvation on the cross 2000 years ago, no one living today has anything to do with that ancient act of sacrifice.

3. The Role of the Individual

Christ's work finished everything necessary for your salvation; the Spirit's work applies Christ's work to you. *So what is the work you must do to be saved? Absolutely nothing! There's absolutely no unfinished work remaining for you to do.* The well-known passage in Ephesians 2:8-9 captures the essence of the "no work" wonder of your salvation: "For by grace you have been saved through faith, and that *not of yourselves;* it is the gift of God, *not of works,* lest anyone should boast."

The Bible can't be any clearer than that can it? Salvation is "not of yourselves" and "not of works." Salvation can't be something you do, since Christ did it. Salvation can't be a work that you achieve, since Christ already achieved it.

Since your works have nothing to do with Christ's work, then never again let yourself become confused about these two major issues: First, the notion that "I must *start 'good works'* in order to be saved." Second, the idea, "I must *stop 'bad works'* in order to be saved."

"Good works" is merely another way of describing "works"— and since Christ's death on the cross was the only "work" which God the Father would accept as payment for your sins, your "good works" are totally irrelevant to Christ's work of the cross. And besides, your "good works" are just 2000 years too late to make any difference!

The other problem with attempting to find a solution to the problem of sinning against God by doing "good works" is that God didn't decide public service projects could be an acceptable payment for disobedience against Him. Instead, God said from the beginning (even in the Garden of Eden) the punishment for disobedience is the death penalty. Good public service projects may be acceptable payment for speeding or drunkenness, but they don't even count toward the death penalty, no matter how many hours you may collect.

"*Bad works*" is merely another way of describing "sins"—and since Christ's death on the cross already paid for every single "sin" you have, are, and will ever commit, stopping your "bad works/sins" won't change anything regarding your salvation. Whether or not you sin tomorrow will not change the finished death of Christ 2000 years ago!

When you have fear in your heart about "what happens if I commit this big, terrible sin in the future...will God forgive me?" you have forgotten that every single one of your "big, terrible sins" were all future to Christ when He died for you. A terrible sin committed 20 years ago and a terrible sin committed 20 years into the future have both been paid for by the death of Christ almost 2000 years ago!

Therefore, regarding your salvation, you should feel entirely *helpless*. No matter where you turn, there's nothing you can do to fix the problem. Not by trying harder and doing more good things. Not by trying harder and avoiding more bad things. You can't do one single thing to fix the problem of your sin or earn forgiveness from God.

So what must you do to be saved? Once again: Absolutely nothing!

Well, then, let me help you rephrase the question: "Since I am a sinner, and have willfully disobeyed God and rightly earned the eternal death penalty, how can I connect with what Christ did for me on the cross and know God's forgiveness and be given eternal life?"

The beloved Apostle John had your question in mind when he wrote John 1:12: "But as many as *received Him*, to them He gave the right to become children of God, to those *who believe in His name*...."

Since there's absolutely, unequivocally nothing you can do, and since Jesus has absolutely and unequivocally finished everything for you, all that's left is merely to believe that He did it all for you, and receive Him as your Savior.

Nothing more will work. And nothing less will work.

THE GIFT OF SALVATION

You mean that's all? It sounds like something so simple, so easy. Like merely reaching out your hand and accepting a gift being offered personally to you. Paul said it this way to the church at Ephesus: "For by grace you have been saved through faith, and that not of yourselves; it is the gift of God" (Ephesians 2:8).

> "A MAN CAN ACCEPT WHAT CHRIST HAS DONE WITHOUT KNOWING HOW IT WORKS; INDEED HE CERTAINLY WON'T KNOW HOW IT WORKS UNTIL HE'S ACCEPTED IT."
>
> —C.S. Lewis

John said it this way to the church at large: "He who believes in the Son has everlasting life" (John 3:36).

Paul and Silas said it this way to the Philippian jailer: "Believe on the Lord Jesus Christ, and you will be saved" (Acts 16:31).

Philip discussed it this way with the Ethiopian treasurer: "Then Philip opened his mouth, and beginning at this Scripture, preached Jesus to him. Now as they went down the road, they came to some water. And the eunuch said, 'See, here is water. What hinders me from being baptized?' Then Philip said, 'If you believe with all your heart, you may.' And he answered and said, 'I believe that Jesus Christ is the Son of God' " (Acts 8:35-37).

Jesus said it this way to Nicodemus: "For God so loved the world that He gave His only begotten Son, that whoever believes in Him should not perish but have everlasting life" (John 3:16).

So, my friend, how many more in addition to Paul, John, Silas, Philip, and Jesus must say the identical thing before we realize that our salvation is fully the work of Christ and only requires our full faith in His finished work on the cross? He shed His precious blood as full and complete payment for the death penalty for our sins against God.

If you have never knelt before the King of Glory and received His matchless gift of eternal life, then now may be your time to kneel and say to Him with all of your heart:

Lord, I kneel in humility, confessing that I am a sinner and rightly deserve the death penalty You have declared as just payment for all who sin against You. I confess that nothing I can do is able to pay for my sins except my physical and eternal death. I hereby accept Christ's death and resurrection for me and receive His wonderful gift of eternal life. I accept the Lord Jesus Christ as my Savior. In Jesus' name, Amen.

If you've just received God's gift of salvation, then you are truly born again and have entered into the first stage of holiness!

3

PRESENTING
YOURSELF TO GOD

*"Consecration is handing God a blank sheet to fill in
with your name signed at the bottom."*

—M.H. Miller

My heart was still pounding and sweat dripped down my back. The intensity of the past 35 minutes of speaking had just about worn me out. The Lord had moved mightily in the stadium, and thousands of men streamed forward in genuine repentance and heartfelt recommitment. Now I was being ushered down a long corridor in the bowels of the stadium, to a little room at the end of the hallway for the last radio interview of the day. I'll never forget the moment that door opened, revealing *seven* radio microphones all pointed directly at me, like spears in a hostile jungle. Each of the interviewers wanted to ask the first question, but the man to my right took over by asking, "Dr. Wilkinson, you don't actually believe those men are going to be changed do you? We all know that men don't change just by coming forward and making an emotional decision at a conference."

This was a moment for someone as articulate as my friends Tony Evans or Joe Stowell—what was I doing here? "That's a good question," I ventured, "and let me respond to it by asking you a question: Are you married?"

"What difference does *that* make?" he answered defensively, before adding, "But yes, I am married."

Without breaking eye contact, I continued, "When you got married, did you come forward? Did you walk down a middle aisle? And at that moment, were you as emotional as most guys are when they get married?"

His defensiveness lightened just a tad as he replied, "I suppose so...but so what?"

"When you came forward that day, and made that one big commitment, would you say that emotional decision literally changed the rest of your life?" The hostility drained from his face. He softened as the truth penetrated his unbelief.

Think about it: Can a single decision change a person's life? Of course it can—not only can a decision change your life, but that's exactly how *every* person's life is changed! In fact, if you looked back over your life, you would find it has been determined precisely by the decisions you made. Each decision was a turning point—a moment that influenced your future, shaped your career, molded your family, and even determined your eternal destiny. Never underestimate the significance of a decision, especially a major decision. Decisions change your life.

At the end of this chapter, I'm going to invite you to make a decision that, as you'll soon see, may change your life forever.

THE SECOND STAGE OF HOLINESS

Have you ever stumbled on something you already knew, but surprisingly rediscovered it in a different context? That's exactly what happened to me as I traced through every reference in the New Testament where "holiness" appeared. I stumbled onto Romans 12:1—an old friend for many years. My first inclination was to pass it by in search of a new and yet unconsidered idea, but fortunately I decided not to allow anything to be overlooked and retraced this well-worn path.

Much to my surprise, Romans 12:1 revealed a distinct second stage of holiness. Not only did Romans 12:1 not fit into the first stage, it logically and biblically followed that stage. Consider the following seven-part outline of this verse:

1. I beseech you therefore,
2. brethren,
3. by the mercies of God,
4. that you present your bodies a living sacrifice,
5. *holy,*
6. acceptable to God,
7. which is your reasonable service.

As you can immediately see, *this* holiness had nothing to do with becoming a believer in Jesus Christ. The Apostle Paul is talking about "presenting" your body as a living sacrifice to the Lord,

> "THE GREATNESS OF A MAN'S POWER IS THE MEASURE OF HIS SURRENDER."
>
> —William Booth

an action which follows the decision to become a Christian. Since the word "holy" means separation, this second stage requires a believer to "separate" himself to the Lord in such a way that is "holy" to God.

Understand what I am saying: A second stage in the holiness process takes place when a believer makes the decision to "present" himself or herself to the Lord. It is a commitment to God, separate from the decision to put your faith in Christ, and it moves the believer down the path toward personal holiness. Unfortunately, the majority of Christians today seem not to understand this second stage of holiness, and underestimate its significance in the pursuit of practical holiness. Not only does the Bible clearly relate its pivotal power, but the experiences of leading Christians throughout church history bear witness to the strategic significance of this second stage.

Romans 12:1 invites individuals who have progressed through the first stage of holiness to take the next step. Through 30 years of ministry around the world and in many varying settings, I have discovered only a small percentage of believers have done this. Without understanding and breaking through this second stage, you will find yourself repeatedly floundering in your pursuit of personal holiness.

THE INVITATION TO PRESENT YOURSELF

This chapter will explore the issue of "presenting" ourselves to God. There are really three parts to this: an invitation, a motivation, and a presentation ceremony in which a believer decides to present himself or herself fully to the Lord. As we look at what Scripture has to say about presentation, it is my prayer you will decide to join the ranks of those who understand and choose to make that pivotal decision of personal presentation.

1. The Request to Present Yourself Is Not a Command but an Invitation

"I beseech you therefore" sets the tone for the rest of the verse. Instead of a command, the Apostle Paul "beseeches" his audience—which means to "plead," or "beg" them to take this action. Whenever you plead with a person, you are seeking to touch their heart and mind. Paul recognizes that for the presentation of oneself to God to be meaningful and life-changing, one's heart must be in it. However, Paul doesn't ask his readers to force themselves to presentation; he would have commanded such an action if he had wanted more obedience.

2. The Request to Present Yourself Is Offered to Born-Again Christians

Romans is easily the most profound book in the New Testament. Paul outlines the major doctrines of the Christian faith and presents them in the most logical, compelling fashion anywhere in the Bible. In order to interpret Romans correctly and apply it properly, you must consider its structure and audience.

Romans is unmistakably written to Christians, not to non-Christians. Romans 1:7 states the book is written "to all who are in Rome, beloved of God, called *to be* saints." As you'll remember from the first stage of holiness, individuals who are called "saints" are born-again and set apart in the mind and heart of God. Not only are they born-again, Paul goes on to describe them in such glowing terms: "Your faith is spoken of throughout the whole world." Therefore, the original audience of Romans is not the unsaved, but the saved. In fact, Paul calls them the "beloved of God" in 1:7 and in 12:1 calls them "brethren."

It is no mistake that this verse is written to the believer in Jesus Christ for their salvation, because it is impossible for a nonbeliever to do what this verse teaches with any result except frustration.

If a person who is not a "saint" or "beloved of God" or part of the "brethren" seeks to devote himself to the Lord, the Lord is unable to receive him. His presentation as a living sacrifice is not "holy" or "acceptable to God." Why? Because as Paul has carefully outlined in Romans 1–5, the only valid and acceptable approach to God is through the shed blood of Jesus Christ. When individuals who have not believed on Jesus Christ seek to devote themselves to God, they are seeking to find favor with God through an act of personal sacrifice rather than through Christ's act of sacrifice.

God is very clear, salvation does not exist except through the death and resurrection of Jesus Christ. The presentation of oneself to God as a living sacrifice can only be acceptable to God because of the acceptance of the substitutionary sacrifice of Jesus Christ.

3. The Request to Present Yourself Is Separate From and Follows Salvation

Every generation encounters its own unique difficulties regarding biblical Christianity. Somehow the truth can get mixed with a little untruth, then it gets spread across the land and believed as the full truth. I ran head-on into this a few weeks ago. No matter how often this surfaces in ministry, it still catches me off-guard every time.

I had just finished three intense days of teaching on the issue of personal holiness to a group of key pastors and leaders. The Lord had broken through powerfully in numerous ways, and many expressed how deeply their lives had been changed. After the conference ended, I was at the back door expressing appreciation and encouraging the men to teach the material on personal holiness in their churches and organizations. One young pastor shook my hand and warmly expressed how he was touched by the course and was going to teach it widely. He told me he was going to show the

> "JESUS DID NOT SAY, 'COME TO ME AND GET IT OVER WITH.' HE SAID, 'IF ANY MAN WOULD COME AFTER ME, LET HIM TAKE UP HIS CROSS DAILY AND FOLLOW ME.' DAILY IS THE KEY WORD. OUR COMMITMENT TO CHRIST, HOWEVER GENUINE AND WHOLE-HEARTED IT MAY BE TODAY, MUST BE RENEWED TOMORROW...AND THE DAY AFTER THAT...AND THE DAY AFTER THAT...UNTIL THE PATH COMES AT LAST TO THE RIVER."
>
> —Louis Cassels

Personal Holiness in Times of Temptation video series for men, but then added, "Of course, I'm only going to show parts 2, 3, and 4. I just *can't* show part 1."

His comment confused me, so I asked, "Why not session 1?"

I shall never forget his answer: "Because in session 1, you presented the false gospel."

You could have picked me up off the floor! Never before in a lifetime of extensive ministry have I been criticized for presenting a "false gospel." In one of his letters, the Apostle Paul directly states, "...if we, or an angel from heaven, preach any other gospel to you than what we have preached to you, let him be accursed" (Galatians 1:8). I don't know of a more serious allegation. So I took a deep breath and asked him to explain what he meant. As I soon understood his point, my heart broke. He believed you have to present yourself as a living sacrifice in order to be saved.

What do you think is necessary for an individual to receive the gift of eternal salvation provided through the shed blood of Jesus Christ? Specifically, what must a person do in addition to genuinely believing in Christ's complete and total work? Must you consecrate yourself to Him in any way in order to be saved? Must you devote yourself to Him in order to be saved? Of course not—the Bible is clear: "Believe on the Lord Jesus Christ, and you will be saved..." (Acts 16:31).

Belief in a person and devotion to that person are different things. I can believe in a person without devoting my life to him. Is it a false gospel to teach that the act of *believing* in Christ is a separate and distinct act from *presenting* oneself to the Lord in full consecration and devotion? Although I have heard and read many arguments in favor of adding things to "believe on the Lord Jesus Christ and you will be saved..." I still find myself resolute in my conviction that the Bible teaches nothing will save anyone except genuine faith in Christ and what He did through His substitutionary death and resurrection 2000 years ago. Adding another step or another condition is antibiblical.

Presentation occurs when a born-again Christian voluntarily dedicates and consecrates himself to the Lord. Does he need to "voluntarily dedicate, consecrate, and devote himself to the Lord completely" in order to be eternally saved? No. This well-meaning pastor decided that since I purposefully separated "dedication to Christ" from "believing in Christ," I taught a false gospel. As far as he was concerned, unless a person commits himself totally to Christ at the point of salvation—including consecration and dedication—he cannot be saved.

WHAT DOES THE BIBLE TEACH ABOUT SALVATION AND DEDICATION?

Romans 12:1 presents a crystal-clear answer to this all-important question. "I beseech you therefore, brethren, by the mercies of God, that you present your bodies a living sacrifice, holy, acceptable to God, which is your reasonable service." Think of it this way:

1. The Book of Romans was written to *Christians*, not non-Christians.
2. Therefore, the *readers* of Romans were already Christians.
3. Romans 12:1 exhorts *Christians* to present themselves to God.
4. Based on that, *some Christians had not presented themseves to the Lord at that time.*
5. Therefore, presentation to God *is not required in order to experience salvation.*
6. Since born again Christians are exhorted to present themselves to God, *presentation can follow salvation and does not have to accompany it.*

7. Furthermore, since Romans 12:1 exhorts the Roman Christians as a group by using the plural term "brethren", *a number of Christians in that church had not yet presented themselves to God.*

8. The situation of Christians in a local church in which *a proportion of the believers still need to present themselves to God may be more the norm than the exception.*

9. Since Romans 12:1 is written to numerous Christians who had been saved for varying amounts of time ranging potentially from days to more than twenty years, *there can be an extensive period of time between the decision to trust Christ as Savior and the later decision to devote oneself totally to God.*

10. Although the text doesn't specifically state this, I believe that Romans 12:1 *permits a true, born-again Christian to live his or her entire Christian life in a state of "unpresentation."* Salvation is not dependent upon consecration or dedication, or Paul would probably have said, "Because you haven't presented yourself to the Lord, this proves you aren't born again!" Instead, he begs them as Christians to devote themselves wholly to the Lord.

In summary, consecration to the Lord does not necessarily occur at the same time as salvation and is not required for salvation. Consecration is a voluntary act of a true believer and may occur at the time of salvation, shortly after, or many years after the decision to trust Christ. *Or it may never occur!* Paul did not say the Roman Christians who had not consecrated themselves to the Lord were unsaved. Neither did he warn them that they would lose their salvation if they did not dedicate their lives to the Lord. Consecration and salvation are distinct from each other, separated in some cases by numerous years. Presentation (or consecration or dedication or whatever term you prefer) is therefore not required in order to be saved. Consecration occurs when a Christian decides of his own free will to dedicate himself to Christ in a deep and meaningful way.

> "HE IS NO FOOL WHO GIVES WHAT HE CANNOT KEEP TO GAIN WHAT HE CANNOT LOSE."
>
> —Jim Elliot

The concept of "mature faith" or "discipleship" must be separated as a distinct truth from "salvation" or the gospel is tragically blurred. Consider carefully these words by Oswald Chambers:

> Discipleship and salvation are two different things: a disciple is one who, realizing the meaning of the atonement, deliberately gives himself up to Jesus Christ in unspeakable gratitude.

> Jesus Christ always talked about discipleship with an "if." We are at perfect liberty to toss our spiritual head and say, "No, thank you, that is a bit too stern for me,"—and the Lord will never say a word. We can do exactly what we like. He will never plead, but the opportunity is there.

MAKING THE DECISION

The Bible is our ultimate authority, not opinions or experience. While our experiences should validate our understanding of Scripture as we live in obedience to its principles, whenever our teaching contradicts the norm of Christian behavior of the generations of godly men and women, it should cause us immediate concern. Either our understanding of Scripture is flawed, or our conduct is clearly disobedient and misdirected.

Here's the heart of the matter: Since Paul "beseeched" a whole church of born again believers to consecrate themselves, what is the norm for Christians in this matter of consecration? What percentage of born again believers have typically experienced this "presentation of commitment" in any given church audience? How many years normally pass after salvation until people have presented themselves to the Lord?

Before I reveal my findings, let me ask you this question: Have you ever fully and completely consecrated yourself to the Lord? And if you did, how long after you came to know Christ was it? When I was teaching this topic at a pastors' conference recently, I asked this question. The average age of the participants was approximately 40. Here's what we found:

1. Up to that time, a number of pastors and leaders admitted they have never consecrated themselves to the Lord as outlined in Romans 12:1. When I challenged these men to do so, some knelt in response.

2. When that part of the audience who had already consecrated themselves to the Lord (a group ranging in age from the early twenties to the mid sixties) was asked how many years existed between the moment of salvation and the moment of presentation, we discovered the length of time spanned from two years to more than twenty. For these pastors and Christian leaders, the *average* time between salvation and consecration was over 15 years.

A few weeks ago I was teaching this information to 100 men at our Walk Thru the Bible International Headquarters in Atlanta. After explaining the concept of presentation, I asked if any of the men knew Jesus Christ as Savior yet had not presented themselves to Him in full consecration and dedication. Over 75 percent of the men immediately raised their hands. Then, when I asked if anyone would like to present themselves to the Lord as a living sacrifice, more than 50 men stood up. It became a moving time as those men kneeled to present themselves to God.

Similarly, I was ministering to approximately 500 people in California not long ago, and after talking about presentation, I asked if anyone would like to present themselves to the Lord. All across the auditorium, men and women knelt in solemn dedication, many moved to tears. When asked how much time had transpired between salvation and consecration, the average answer was more than 10 years.

Presentation is not necessarily simultaneous to salvation, but rather a decision each believer must make and often occurs many years later. The Lord encourages all His children to present themselves to Him as living sacrifices from the moment of salvation, but for many—and even for believers in a New Testament church—that decision won't come until they have been Christians for years. One of my prayers for this book is that the Lord will use it as a tool to move Christians toward making this important decision.

THE MOTIVATION TO PRESENT YOURSELF

Matthew labored on a spiritual merry-go-round—around and around he went, but without progressing further in his spiritual life. He grew steadily as a new Christian but eventually floundered, plateaued, and began a slow decline. We met on a Friday night and he wanted to know if I could help him.

As I probed Matt with a few questions, his problem soon surfaced: he had never come to the place in his life where he dedicated himself fully to the Lord. This logjam of the heart inevitably breeds frustration, confusion, and spiritual decline. Unless the believer puts Christ first, he will be unable to enjoy sustained victory in his life.

Matt soon opened up and shared that although he wanted to dedicate his life to the Lord, every time he tried, he ended up slamming on his brakes and running into that proverbial ditch. Finally with a heavy sigh of resignation, Matthew confessed he didn't know what to do and only hoped to lick this problem someday.

Put yourself in Matt's shoes for a moment. Why has he experienced such long-standing failure? Is he merely to hope that maybe someday he will break through? I hope you haven't fallen into the trap of thinking that the spiritual life is just too complicated, too difficult, too haphazard, and that one must just drift rudderless on the ocean, hoping things will change. Doesn't the Bible give us any specific help?

1. The Motivation to Present Yourself Is Found in the "Mercies of God"

Since Romans 12:1 is the key passage on "presenting yourself a living sacrifice," the answer may lie right at our fingertips. What is the reason the Apostle Paul used to encourage the whole church at Rome to consecrate themselves?

> I beseech you therefore, brethren,
> *by the mercies of God,*
> that you present your bodies a living sacrifice....

The motivation to present yourself is found in the mercies of God, not in yourself. Unlike many areas of motivation, Paul reveals that consecration isn't caused by a sense of responsibility or duty but by a sense of appreciation. Instead of "I know I should..." it is "I am thankful He did, and therefore I want..." Do you see the difference? Paul isn't trying to motivate through promising a reward of some kind, or threatening discipline or pain, or relying on some sense of moral responsibility—he doesn't mention anything of the kind. The motivation to give yourself to God is solely based upon what God has done for you.

> "I NEVER MADE A SACRIFICE. WE OUGHT NOT TO TALK OF SACRIFICE WHEN WE REMEMBER THE GREAT SACRIFICE THAT HE MADE WHO LEFT HIS FATHER'S THRONE ON HIGH TO GIVE HIMSELF FOR US."
>
> —David Livingstone

The mercies of God provide the motivation for you to present yourself. Now, listen in as I apply this truth to our friend Matthew, and see if you can anticipate what will happen as the story unfolds.

"So, Matt, what are some of the things the Lord has done for you that mean the most to you?" Matt could only think of two before he began to struggle and become uncomfortable sensing that he should obviously know many more. But he didn't.

Of course he didn't. Why? Because this principle never fails: Christians who struggle to dedicate themselves always struggle to recall the many mercies of God in their lives.

The mercies of God and the consecration of the believer are always inseparable. The more the mercies, the greater the consecration. If you meet someone who is struggling to consecrate, you automatically know their "mercies memory bank" is very low on deposits. Likewise, if you ask a highly consecrated individual what the Lord has done for them, it's not unusual to be deeply touched with their sharing of many illustrations.

Therefore, what's the clear biblical answer to Matthew's predicament? Load his memory bank with the mercies of God! Since the mercies of God are the secret motivation to all consecration, what would you have expected the Apostle Paul to have done with those mercies for his readership? Exactly. He filled to overflowing their memory banks and touched their emotional strings with the mercies of God. Then, and only then did he request that they dedicate themselves.

Although some may not agree with me, I have come to the conclusion that the entire book of Romans builds to this very point. After salvation (remember, Paul wrote this book to Christians), the next most strategic step in spiritual growth is life "presentation." What would motivate a church to do such a remarkable thing? Only a deep and comprehensive understanding of what God has done for them and everyone in the whole world.

Think back over Romans 1–11 for a moment: In verse after verse, chapter after chapter, and section after section, Pauls lays out the incredible mercies of God in rapid and logical fashion until he climaxes in Romans 11:30-36. Notice the theme of these mercies we've been discussing as you read verses 30-32:

> For as you were once disobedient to God, yet have now obtained *mercy* through their disobedience, even so these also have now been disobedient, that through the *mercy* shown you they also may obtain *mercy*. For God has committed them all to disobedience, *that He might have mercy on all.*

Perhaps it's clear now why the fourth word in Romans 12:1 is "therefore." The "therefore" summarizes not the last few verses, but the entire book from Romans 1:1 to Romans 11:32. Everything builds to Romans 12:1 and all that follows is a result of the personal presentation as a living sacrifice.

2. The Motivation to Present Yourself Increases Until Becoming the Most Logical Step

Although the presentation of one's life can be a very emotional time, the root of the action must always be reasonable and logical to the person. It must not move merely the heart, but the mind as well.

The more mercies and compassions of the Lord the person knows and brings to the forefront of their mind, the more reasonable will be the action of presentation. The act of releasing oneself to the Lord should be the most logical and mentally defensible thing they will ever do. If the presentation is done through emotion rather than reason, the "life presentation" may be flawed. That's why Paul says, "I beseech you therefore, brethren, by the mercies of God, that you present your bodies a living sacrifice, holy, acceptable to God, *which is your reasonable service*" (Romans 12:1).

In the high Rocky Mountains one year, I watched this process condensed into two hours in the life of a businessman from the Colorado Springs area. Like Matt, he sought for that spiritual breakthrough as his lack of consecration surfaced. For two hours, I gently but relentlessly probed his heart, knowledge of the Word, and awareness of the Lord's personal involvement in his life. The more I opened his eyes to the truth of the Lord's mercies, the more he softened.

One by one, we dealt with his hidden hardness of heart toward God due to his misunderstandings of the truth. Over and over again, his hardness turned to confession and praise and adoration. Together we scaled the incredible mercies of God's redemption, propitiation, reconciliation, adoption, and gift of the Holy Spirit.

Finally, something broke deep in his heart, and he fell on his knees. "Lord, how can I remain away from You? How I have suffered by saying 'no' to You while saying 'yes' to me. How foolish I have been to fight You when You have fought for me and sacrificed Your Son for me. Is there any other besides You who is worthy of giving my life to? Lord, I humble myself before You and offer myself up to You—a living sacrifice!"

You see, my friend, when the whole truth is seen about the Lord and His love and care and compassions and loyalty for you, the only thing that is logical to you is to immediately and fully devote yourself into His loving arms.

3. The Motivation to Present Yourself Is to Be Nurtured by the Believer and the Church

Since I knew I would see Matthew the next day, I gave him an assignment in order to load his memory bank with the truth of the Lord's mercies with the hopes of setting his heart free. I asked him to read Romans 1–11, Ephesians 1–3, and Colossians 1–2 and list on a couple of sheets everything the Lord had done for him personally. We met the next night around nine at the frozen yogurt stand. Matthew brought numerous sheets crumpled around the edges. When I first saw him, I noticed his eyes had softened and his demeanor had become more peaceful. "Well, Matt, what did you find?"

"I had no idea...I mean, where have I been all these years as a Christian? Just look at this list, and I didn't have time to finish all the chapters. The Lord is just incredible!"

Matthew now had a memory bank filled with God's mercies, but the truth hadn't sifted down deep enough into his heart yet. "So, Matthew, tell me how you feel about the first thing on your list." Off he went, listing good information, but not embracing the truth with his heart. "Slow down, Matt, and let your heart interpret the truth in your head. How do you emotionally feel, for instance, about God adopting you as His son?"

That proved to be the cork I was searching for, and within minutes, Matthew's eyes overflowed with tears that had been trapped all of his Christian life. The goodness of God hit the fear of Matthew's heart—and just overwhelmed him. Soon Matthew was sobbing, his heart broken for the first time with the personal love the Lord had for him, and for all the incredible things the Lord had done for him. Guess what happened that night under the tall trees of northern California? Heaven shouted for joy as another struggling believer became a living sacrifice.

If I sense my own personal consecration is waning, what do I do to deepen it? Return to the mercies of the Lord in the Scriptures and stir up my heart with the truth. I pull out my personal journal and read of all the many mercies and compassions that I wrote after rereading the previous year's personal journals. The last time I did this was just a few weeks ago, and I ended up celebrating God's overwhelming and bountiful kindness and goodness to me. I open my prayer journal and slowly read through the hundreds of specific answers to prayer I have recorded in the past few years. I open my heart and flood the throne of heaven with my fervent praise and adoration. I won't stop until my consecration is complete. No matter how far my heart may have strayed, I know with full assurance that my heart must be mastered—and will be masterd—until it is fully and joyfully submissive to the Lord of glory!

Unfortunately, however, too many of us haven't known what to do with our hearts. It is my prayer right at this very moment that you will rise up and review the files in your mind marked "mercies of God" and pluck the strings of your heart until it plays in beautiful harmony with the melodies of heaven.

Although this book isn't written to the pastors and Christian leaders of our world, I feel constrained to reveal to you what I have discovered in the churches of America and virtually around the world. With rare exception, I have found God's church sorely taught and challenged with biblical consecration. Whereas 50 years ago the Lord's shepherds openly challenged their flock for Life Consecration, now it is seldom preached from the pulpit. And how the church has suffered because of it! Some pastors have resorted to inappropriate emotionalism, whereas others have withdrawn to theological lectures rather than powerful, anointed preaching that God uses to change lives.

The bright side of this, however, lies in the hearts of laymen and laywomen all around the world. Without exception, the believers of the world I have had the opportunity to minister to across America, South Africa, Russia, Singapore, Ukraine, Malaysia, and others are hungry and desirous of moving deeper into consecration. Yet for the most part they are under-taught and desperately need a shepherd to lead them through the process. Undoubtedly this wonderful openness may not always remain, but the Lord's church is presently very tender toward consecration—may we in leadership rise up and fulfill our calling!

THE PRESENTATION OF YOUR LIFE

Paul instructs us to "present" ourselves as "living sacrifices"—a notion most Christians today do not understand. How do we "present" our lives to God? And what does it mean to be a "living sacrifice"?

1. The Meaning of "Present"

The word "present" in Romans 12:1 carries with it both a general and specific meaning. Generally, the word means to offer or bring. As numerous Greek scholars point out, the word also is technically used to describe the sinner who offers or presents a lamb as a sacrifice for his sins. When this word is linked to a "sacrifice," as it is in this verse, the New Testament readers could immediately envision the official presentation of a lamb before the Lord.

When that person presented his sacrificial lamb to the priest to be slaughtered, it was an official, once-for-all act for sins committed up to that point in time. The lamb died once. Never did the Israelite come again to present that sacrifice as it had already been completed. The Lord seeks our major decision to present ourselves to Him as a "living sacrifice" and then to return over and over again and renew that one commitment.

> "IF JESUS CHRIST IS GOD AND DIED FOR ME, THEN NO SACRIFICE CAN BE TOO GREAT FOR ME TO MAKE FOR HIM."
>
> —C. T. Studd

In the Gospel of Luke, this same word "presentation" describes what Joseph and Mary did with the infant Jesus in the temple:

> Now when the days of her purification according to the law of Moses were completed, they brought Him to Jerusalem *to present Him to the Lord* (as it is written in the law of the Lord, "Every male who opens the womb shall be *called holy to the Lord*)" (Luke 2:22-23).

This illustrates the concept of presentation of a person to God in such a way that it was "holy to the Lord." When Joseph and Mary presented Jesus to the Lord, they offered Him back to the Lord and dedicated Him to the Lord's purposes. Because they devoted their child to the Lord and separated Him unto the Lord, he was "holy" unto the Lord. Believing parents can offer their children to the Lord as "living sacrifices" through infant dedication—with the realization of the Lord's pleasure. However, each individual must later come to know Christ and then choose to devote himself or herself fully to the Lord.

2. The Meaning of "a Living Sacrifice"

Although everyone understood a "living sacrifice" at the time of this Roman epistle, several factors must have literally shook the audience. First, the Lord called for a sacrifice of a person and not an animal. Under the Old Testament, all animals sacrificed were to be alive, healthy, and without blemish, or the Lord would not accept them. Nothing new was revealed in the actual terms "a living sacrifice," but what broke through instantly into their sensibilities was that the Lord switched the animal for a person. Paul selected, under divine inspiration, an incredibly graphic picture of how completely the Lord sought the life of the believer.

Second, consider who brought the sacrifice. In the Old Testament, the Israelite brought a sacrificial animal which he offered to God. In the New Testament, the believer brings himself as the sacrifice and then offers himself to God.

The more mature in this church in Rome must have immediately recalled the only other living human sacrifice requested by God in the Bible: Abraham's sacrifice of his beloved son, Isaac. As Abraham brought down his knife to slay his son, an angel of the Lord stopped him and revealed the underlying reason for the sacrifice. "Do not lay your hand on the lad, or do anything to him; for now I know that you fear God, since you have not withheld your son, your only son, from Me" (Genesis 22:12).

The Lord brought Abraham to a crisis of consecration. Who would Abraham choose to be first in his life: his son or his God? How similar is this test of a living sacrifice. Instead of your son, however, the Lord requests your very own life. Once again, the underlying issue is who will be number one in your life—self or Savior.

The third distinction lies in what made the living sacrifice valuable. In the Old Testament sacrifice, the animal only had value at the very moment it died. Its life had no merit; its dead body had no merit. Instead, the very act of dying provided the atoning penalty for man's sin.

In the New Testament sacrifice, however, the real "value" of the believer occurs after the moment of presentation. The contrast is unmistakable. In the Old Testament, the value of the living sacrifice centered on the moment of death. In the New Testament, the value of the living sacrifice centers on the length of life. The believer dies to himself in order to live for the Lord.

3. The Meaning of "Holy"

The word "holy" in Romans 12:1 provides the clue for me which ultimately brought this concept of presenting oneself as a living sacrifice to a distinct and separate act from salvation and acts of daily obedience. As seen in this passage, consecration of one's life to the Lord occurs in the heart and mind of the believer as he separates himself wholly unto the Lord as His servant.

I personally believe that this presentation is very similar to the decision to follow Christ as a disciple and not just as a believer. Luke 14 presents conditions for discipleship which have absolutely nothing to do with eternal salvation but everything to do with obedience and service. In the midst of those powerful verses, the Lord exhorts those who are considering whether or not to become one of His disciples to carefully count the costs which one must pay to be a disciple. Both Luke 14 and Romans 12 present an invitation which appears to be a major life decision followed by actions which must be carefully considered and which carry lifelong results.

Because of the seriousness and consequences of this decision, many who make it experience intense emotion. The older the believer, the more traumatic the decision seems to be. Through counseling and mentoring many men to and through this crisis of consecration, I have noticed that it is not uncommon for the struggle to last upwards of 18 months to 2 years. The final act of consecration is made with such full knowledge of its implications that the believer frequently experiences almost spiritual birth pangs. This commitment to the Lord is often so dramatic and deep that numerous people seem to misinterpret what exactly happened.

Unfortunately, because some teach that until you consecrate yourself you cannot be saved, numerous adult believers incorrectly interpret this act of consecration and discipleship. Two weekends ago, I taught an in-depth series in Mexico on the *Seven Stages of a Pilgrim's Progress* which outlined the predictable stages all believers go through enroute to full conformity to Jesus Christ. Consecration is one of those seven stages and over half of the conference kneeled and presented themselves to the Lord.

After this happened, I warned the audience not to think that this act had anything to do with their eternal salvation. Many of these middle-aged adults accepted Christ as their personal Savior as children, but they didn't decide to give themselves fully to the Lord until their thirties, forties, or fifties. When the consecration is very intense and emotional, many people are tempted to "rewrite" their spiritual lives and erase their true conversion experience due to the depth of their consecration.

If as a child you chose of your own free will to accept Jesus Christ as your personal Savior and genuinely believed that He died for your sins and that only through His death and resurrection could you be saved, then you received eternal life at that very moment! Don't ever forget that truth, and don't ever allow anyone to confuse you: Salvation is only through the sacrifice of Christ, and consecration is only through the sacrifice of yourself to Christ. One was completed on the cross 2000 years ago, and one can be completed in your heart during your lifetime.

Before leaving the meaning of "holy" in this passage, one more issue must yet be discussed. Many teach today that in order to present yourself as a living sacrifice, your life must be fully obedient or the Lord won't accept your sacrifice. I realize that what I am about to share may trouble some, but I am convinced it is the correct biblical interpretation of this passage.

The meaning of the word "holy" must be determined by the context, not by our preconceived ideas, or we fall into the error of the "trunks." Remember, we become "holy" in God's eyes the moment we trust Christ—it is incorrect to interpret salvational holiness as behavioral holiness. Salvation holiness is the separation which occurs in God's mind, not in our mind or behavior. This would be similar to the holy ground which did not change in nature but only in God's thinking.

This is the second stage of biblical holiness, and many unfortunately force stages two and three into one and the same. Romans 12:1 invites the believer to separate himself in his mind to the Lord as a living sacrifice. Therefore both the first stage and the second stage are similar in that they occur in the mind and heart, and not in the behavior. The first occurs in the mind of the Lord and the second occurs in the mind of the believer. Romans 12:2 transitions quickly to stage three which focuses entirely upon the actions of obedience, godliness, and service: "And do not be conformed to this world, but be transformed by the renewing of your mind, that you may prove what is that good and acceptable and perfect will of God."

Therefore, must a person change all their behavior in order to become a living sacrifice? If he does, I believe he erroneously added conditions the Bible does not directly relate to becoming a living sacrifice! The order of the New Testament is so very clear: Present yourself to the Lord first, and then don't be conformed to the world but be transformed by the renewing of your mind. The order isn't "Don't be conformed to this world but be transformed by the renewing of your mind, and then, by the mercies of God, present yourself as a living sacrifice."

The whole point of Romans 12:1 is to encourage believers to voluntarily choose to give themselves to the Lord and abandon themselves under His leadership. After that decision has been made, the specifics of how to obey and serve Him are appropriate.

The only requirement for obtaining salvation is to believe in what Christ did for you. The only requirement for becoming a living sacrifice is to present yourself to Him. The requirements, however, for the third stage are many and varied and will be explored throughout the remainder of this book.

4. The Meaning of "Acceptable to God"

The last phrase in Romans 12:1 is one of the most inspiring in all the Bible. How can you be sure that the Lord will accept your sacrifice? I'll never forget counseling with a young woman who desperately sought to devote herself to the Lord but because of a long life of sexual immorality, was sure that God couldn't accept her and her desire. How wonderful to show her the Lord's "precommitment" to her! In Romans 12:1, the Lord reveals that all who would present themselves to Him as a living sacrifice would be "acceptable"!

5. A Genuine Heart of Consecration Is of Great Value to the Lord!

One final question yet remains: Why does the Lord want us to choose to present ourselves as a living sacrifice? What is to be gained by such an act? The answer to this question once again demonstrates the incredible grace of the Lord. Look what was true about you even *before* you present yourself to the Lord:

> Or do you not know that your body is the temple of the Holy Spirit who is in you, whom you have from God, and you are not your own? For you were bought at a price; therefore glorify God in your body and in your spirit, which are God's (1 Corinthians 6:19-20).

Who already owned your body from the moment you trusted Christ? The Lord Himself! Christ purchased your whole life with the price of His life. His death was the price tag of your life. Therefore, "you are not your own" but you may have been living your life as if you were your own up to this point!

Why then didn't Paul choose to announce the truth that they already were God's in Romans 12:1 and instruct his readers that they had better live that way? Only because the Lord always seeks for the voluntary service of His children. He knows that unless our hearts are committed, our actions will become uncommitted. So, even though you and I already belong to the Lord, He invites us to present ourselves to Him as a living sacrifice—abandoning our right to ourselves to Him.

THE CEREMONY OF CONSECRATION

This chapter must draw to a close with one question: "Will you now present yourself as a living sacrifice to the Lord?" If so, I ask you to set aside these next few moments as "holy" and dedicate them to the Lord. Set aside the place where you are seated as "holy ground," to undertake eternal business with God.

I wish I could be with you at this moment, right by your side, for I would kneel with you and lead you through the following prayer. If your heart beckons you to meet heaven's request, please kneel at this time with this book in your hands and pray this prayer with me:

> *Dear Heavenly Father,*
> *I hereby kneel in humility before Your Throne.*
> *I come into Your presence of my own free will and want to*
>   *be here with You.*
> *You are the most gracious and loving Person in the universe.*
> *Your kindness to me has no boundaries or limits.*
> *Your lovingkindness guides everything You do toward me.*
> *Your mercies are new every morning, great is Thy*
>   *faithfulness!*
> *Your love sent Jesus Christ to die in my place and give me*
>   *eternal life.*
> *I now respond to Your love and give myself to You in this*
>   *solemn moment.*
> *Forgive me for taking so long to come to this point of total*
>   *consecration.*
> *I hereby lift myself up to Your altar, and present myself to*
>   *you as a living sacrifice.*
> *I consecrate and dedicate myself to You for the rest of*
>   *my life.*
> *Thank You for accepting this sincere presentation!*
> *In Jesus' name, amen.*

Is this act truly a life-changing moment for Christians? Believe it or not, just this week I received a letter from a man who had written to me regarding what happened to him through a video series I produced earlier last year on this subject. How my heart rejoiced when I read of his presentation:

> When you asked if I had responded to the Lord by giving my life totally to Him and to die to myself while I am still living, it caused me to feel a thrill of anticipation. I'm sure the Spirit leaped inside me at that thought, for I couldn't wait to offer myself as a living sacrifice. It happened at 7:00 A.M., on March 18, on the floor of my family room. Praise our Lord! I now belong totally to Him!

Believer, your floor awaits your knees, and your Father awaits your life. Experience the incredible joy of giving your life away to the One who gave His life for you.

4

I WANT TO BE
MORE LIKE CHRIST

"It is the great work of nature to transmute sunlight into life. So it is the great end of Christian living to transmute the light of truth into the fruits of holy living."

—Adoniram J. Gordon

Every night after dinner, we met around the campfire under the incredibly beautiful wilderness sky. A rare contentment filled our lives those days as all of us once again became adventurous "boys" camping out along remote rivers and fishing from dawn to dusk for those incomparable salmon trophies. Our guide knew every bend and twist in the swirling waters and somehow knew where the secret "pockets" lay just waiting for our all-too-anxious lures.

Twenty close friends spent an unforgettable week fishing, but times we shared around that campfire became the real trophy memories. The nights were the high points. The Bible opened, and our hearts melted under the nightly movements of the Holy Spirit. Nary a man left for his bedroll who hadn't been touched and changed. On Thursday evening, I knew it was time to deal with some of the deepest struggles that men face with an open, transparent, and direct approach.

In talking about personal holiness, I asked the men if any of them had experienced a real breakthrough in one part of their life—where they used to sin "big time" and now no longer sin in that same area. Silence filled the tree-lined room until someone threw on a fresh log shooting sparks upward as tiny rockets.

Then one of the men sitting at the top of the circle said, "Well, I guess I can begin. I used to love money. *I mean really love money.* Money ruled my life—and it nearly destroyed my family and children. I was obsessed. Then God began breaking through about the fact that money was my god and I worshipped it more than Him. For about six months the Lord brought me through the ringer until I finally broke and confessed my heart of covetousness. Now I don't love money anymore: in fact, I finally broke the back of the love of money so much that now I love to give money away! I can honestly say that I'm a different person than I used to be—I don't love money anymore. It's great!"

Many heads nodded around that circle. I knew this man well— on both sides of this victory, and he was genuinely a different man and his family couldn't be any happier! But as I looked around that circle, I watched at least six men looking down at the fire nearly the whole time he shared. Why? Well, I knew all of them well, and none of those six could yet say they were free from the love of money. One of those men was right in the middle of the frying pan that very week—and we had a couple of deep and intense conversations.

Then the one who many of the group found themselves searching out for advice that week spoke up. "Well, this might surprise you, but for years I was hooked on pornography of one kind or another. To say that I was addicted would almost be an understatement. Now, I was never actually physically unfaithful to my wife with another woman, but I lived in sexual bondage and infidelity through magazines, videos, cable—you know what I mean." More than a few heads nodded, although not many were breathing at this point. Such honesty and transparency rivets one's fullest attention, doesn't it?

"Nearly ten years ago, the Lord and I had it out. I desperately wanted freedom from this bondage—I couldn't pray, I couldn't read my Bible much because it always made me feel guilty, and every time I served the Lord at church I felt like a huge hypocrite. I started confessing my sins to the Lord, and decided I couldn't do it alone, so I told everything—and I mean everything—to two of my best 'buds,' and they held me accountable!"

"But guys—" he became very quiet and solemnly looked into the eyes of each man, one at a time around that circle, "today, I am free from this sexual perversion! I haven't sinned in this area for almost ten years! You

> "IT IS TIME FOR US CHRISTIANS TO FACE UP TO OUR RESPONSIBILITY FOR HOLINESS. TOO OFTEN WE SAY WE ARE 'DEFEATED' BY THIS OR THAT SIN. NO, WE ARE NOT DEFEATED; WE ARE SIMPLY DISOBEDIENT. IT MIGHT BE WELL IF WE STOPPED USING THE TERMS VICTORY AND DEFEAT TO DESCRIBE OUR PROGRESS IN HOLINESS. RATHER WE SHOULD USE THE TERMS OBEDIENCE AND DISOBEDIENCE."
>
> —Jerry Bridges

talk about freedom in Christ! Can you imagine what this did in my marriage and in my sex life with my wife?" Then he began laughing, a laugh from deep down inside. "I'm free! And if you are in bondage, you too can be free! Just come to see me later or get in my boat tomorrow and I'll help you get started!"

Then after some remarkable discussion, I finally returned to teaching the Bible on the subject of personal holiness. "Men, that's exactly what the Christian life is all about! It's the utter joy of looking back over your shoulder and honestly saying to yourself, 'I used to commit this sin, but now I don't, I walk in holiness in that area.' If you have been growing in holiness in your life, you should have at least one major area of sin that no longer is true for you. That's what the work of Christ has provided for all of us—the promise of progressive holiness! And next year when we see each other, perhaps there will be one or two more areas where you have progressed to complete victory. How many of you could name at least one major area that used to be unholy but now is holy?" About 12 of the 20 men raised their hands while the rest found the fire too intensely interesting....

This chapter focuses on the third stage of holiness—called progressive holiness. Becoming more like Christ year after year. Less unholy, more holy.

STAGE THREE: "PROGRESSIVE HOLINESS"

Progressive holiness means that the Christian grows from one level of holiness to a greater level, and from one level of unholiness to a lesser level. Progressive holiness means you can and should move forward and onward in your spiritual life—that you can be more like Christ.

Progressive holiness begins at the moment of your salvation and concludes with the moment of your physical death. In that window of time, whether it is opened for a few moments or for over 100 years, progressive holiness is to be one of your life's greatest goals and passions. How you sow your life will result in what you reap, whether it is holiness or unholiness.

At the moment of salvation, we are all equally holy in the Lord's sight (remember positional holiness—that the Lord separates you to Himself in His own mind), but from that time forward, how much we become "holy as He is holy" is according to our response to His work in our life. As the Bible explicitly reveals that the Lord wants all of us to become holy as He is holy, a lack of holiness in any of our lives is not because of His failure but ours. God works continuously to conform us to His Son, and any lack of conformity is due to our resistance, not His lack of full participation. In the life of all Christians, therefore, unholiness is always due to resistance and rebellion against the Lord's call and work in our lives.

Not only does progressive holiness call us to be holy in the essence of who we are, we are also to be holy in everything that we think, feel, and do. "But as He who called you is holy, you also be holy in all your conduct" (1 Peter 1:15). A holy character ("be holy") will always produce holy conduct ("be holy in all your conduct"). Because these two verses are stated as directives, these two sides of progressive holiness are not automatically true, but must be obeyed in order to be true. Therefore, at salvation, my character is not completely Christlike, nor is my conduct completely Christlike.

Progressive holiness means that I continue to become more and more Christlike in my character and conduct. To the degree that I am Christlike in these two areas, is the degree that the Lord would characterize me as holy in my life.

Progressive holiness is seen and objectively noticed by yourself and by others. As your conduct changes, you will notice that you don't behave the way that you used to—and shouldn't! Others will also take note and express their appreciation for your growth. As your character changes, your motives and normal responses will be transformed. Instead of responding with anger, you will respond with patience and self-control. Instead of succumbing to selfishness, you will put others more and more ahead of yourself, caring for them even before yourself. Instead of gossiping and criticizing, you will guard your tongue and only speak that which edifies and builds up. Instead of bondage of immorality, you will live in sexual fidelity and loyalty. Those changes reflect transitions from "works of the flesh" to "fruit of the spirit," and as you grow in holiness, your life will transform right before your eyes into the image of Christ. Paul knew of progressive holiness when he penned these words in 2 Corinthians 7:1b: "…let us cleanse ourselves from all filthiness of the flesh and spirit, *perfecting holiness* in the fear of God."

Note carefully that Paul reveals that this kind of holiness requires that we "cleanse ourselves"—cleansing is an absolute requirement! Note also, however, that Paul reveals true holiness isn't a completed process but one which requires ongoing "perfecting." The Greek word translated "perfecting" means to properly bring to an end, to finish, to complete. Holiness has been birthed in the heart at conversion, and Paul exhorts believers to make every effort to complete it in all of its parts.

Not only does the word itself speak of an ongoing process, but under inspiration of God, Paul places "perfecting" in the present tense in Greek which normally describes the action as continuous rather than intermittent or once-for-all. Therefore, this verse clearly shows that the third stage of holiness must be progressive and continue throughout all of our converted life. You are holy, are becoming more holy, and will ultimately become as fully holy as Christ upon your death.

UNBOX THE THEOLOGICAL BOXES!

Even as I type these words on my trusty laptop in our friends' beautiful house in Colorado, I paused and prayed for you, that the Holy Spirit would open your eyes further and further into the biblical truths of personal holiness. The truth sets us free, and the lack of truth holds us in bondage. The more truth about holiness that you are able to understand, the more freedom and liberty you are released to experience.

The subject of holiness is among the most misunderstood subjects of the entire Bible, and because of that, many Christians suffer incredible bondage and live in continuous defeat. Consider the results of one man's confusion over what the Bible teaches about holiness.

Late one evening after an extensive and demanding meeting in the Midwest, I walked out of the conference center into the brisk evening air looking forward to my short drive to the hotel for a much-needed night of rest. Even as I finished walking down the front steps before turning left on the sidewalk to the parking lot, I saw him in the bright moonlight. His head hung deeply and his shoulders sagged with such discouragement that my heart went out to this person, even before I could see who he was. I sped up my pace—and then noticed that he had also seen me and immediately slowed his pace so we would hit the corner at the same moment. Then I saw who he was—a dignified Christian statesman of 72 years of age who served the Lord with such intense sacrifice and noble leadership that he garnered the respect of all who knew him.

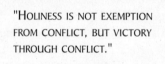

"HOLINESS IS NOT EXEMPTION FROM CONFLICT, BUT VICTORY THROUGH CONFLICT."

—G. Campbell Morgan

At the corner we stopped and greeted each other, commenting briefly about the meeting we'd been in all day long. As he spoke, I sensed the Lord may have crossed our paths for a moment of ministry, so I gently looked him directly in the eyes and asked, "My friend, I sense the Lord may have put us together on this dark corner for an important reason, is there any way I can be of service to you? Will you share your heart with me?" He breathed a sigh of heaviness and relief as the Lord must have alerted him of this unscheduled meeting as well. After a few awkward moments, he shared his grievous burden. Just a few hours earlier at dinner, a young woman had bent down in front of him to pick up her dropped fork and unfortunately, her blouse was very revealing. My respected friend confessed that he purposefully looked and then gave into lustful thoughts about her.

"Bruce, how could I have ever done that? I sinned with lust! This proves that I am not a true believer of Jesus. Unfortunately I did this once before about three years ago. I am a terrible sinner! And I've already consecrated my life to the Lord; how could I have ever done this?" Then he began to shake his head back and forth, "Now I know that I will never be saved!"

How my heart broke for my brother! If ever there was a true born-again believer who walked in holiness and served the Lord sacrificially and courageously, this was that man. Yet, here he was convinced that because of this sin, he couldn't be a saved man. Emotional trauma and internal fear plagued a mature Christian leader—all because of a deep confusion regarding salvation and sanctification. We spoke for about another 30 minutes and the Lord graciously opened his eyes to the difference between the "salvation of his soul" and the "perfection of his holiness." He prayed on that dark street corner, confessed his sin of lust and emotional disloyalty to his wife, and for the first time in his life experienced the joy of knowing that he indeed already had eternal salvation.

Did he sin? Yes. Did his sin prove he wasn't born again? Of course not! But it did prove he had sinned and this part of his life needed to grow considerably in holiness. Did this sin prove he wasn't truly consecrated to the Lord? Of course not! That man would have given everything he had for Christ at that moment, and if required, would have given his very life to Christ. How then could one say that this sin proved that he wasn't consecrated, because he was! His sin did prove that though his heart was truly devoted to the Lord, his eyes were not yet devoted to Him in all situations, nor was he practicing "taking every thought captive to the obedience of Christ."

Do you see how quickly we can get mixed up? We want to combine rather than clarify the three stages of personal holiness:

Positional Holiness (Stage 1)
is not the same as
Presentation Holiness (Stage 2)
is not the same as
Progressive Holiness (Stage 3).

The salvation of your soul
is not the same as
the consecration of your life
is not the same as
the holiness of your character and conduct.

God separating me to Himself in His heart
is not the same as
I separating myself to Him in my heart
is not the same as
I separating my heart and habits to Him in my lifestyle.

Believing on Jesus Christ as my Savior
is not the same as
presenting myself to Him as a living sacrifice
is not the same as
perfecting holiness in my character and conduct.

The more clearly you understand these three different types of holiness, the easier it will become to make sense of your spiritual life. How, then, would you answer these questions?

1. Can you be a "saint" and yet still act "unsaintly"?
2. Can you be truly born again and yet not be consecrated to the Lord?
3. Can you be consecrated to the Lord and yet still have parts of your life which are characterized as unholy?
4. Can you have parts of your character and conduct which are truly "holy" in the eyes of God and man

and yet at the same time have other areas of your character and conduct which are truly "unholy" in the eyes of God and man?

5. Can you come to know Jesus Christ as your personal Savior and live for years without growing hardly at all—and later experience a crisis of consecration where you genuinely dedicate yourself to Him and then serve Him in obedience?

6. Can you be a born-again Christian, having dedicated yourself to the Lord at church camp when you were 14, attend church semi-regularly as an adult, sing in the choir, seldom have meaningful personal devotions, rarely pray except for meals and at church functions, read your Bible twice a week, watch TV over 20 hours a week including numerous R-rated programs, sneak a drink when you're out of town, not really grow in holiness, attend a revival conference at your church and geniunely repent of your lack of true holiness in character and conduct because you haven't really changed much in decades, die on the way home and still go to heaven?

How Do People Think
Incorrectly About Personal Holiness?

Personal holiness is one of the most simple yet challenging truths in all of the Bible. It's been my observation that most believers become off-balanced in this area at least a couple of times in their lives, either in what they think about holiness, or how they try to behave in order to become more holy. Before moving into the meat of this chapter, a brief overview of the more common misconceptions may be helpful. As you read through them, see if you can identify with any of them (either in the past or present) or know of family or friends who are trapped in these holiness dead ends. Unfortunately, space limitations don't permit full answers to these errors, but merely a few general observations.

Misconception #1: "If I am truly born again, I will automatically live a holy life."

What bondage this places over people! The underlying thought is that salvation equals holiness and is usually caused by misunderstanding 2 Corinthians 5:17, "Therefore, if anyone is in Christ, he is a new creation; old things have passed away; behold, all things have become new."

As you'll see in the next section where the three stages of holiness are contrasted, salvation grants us eternal life and the gift of the Holy Spirit but does not grant us sinless perfection. Instead, the New Testament is filled with letters written to Christians who unfortunately are living as non-Christians. Over and over again, the Apostle Paul confronts their behavior and tells them to change it— by obeying Christ, not believing in Christ. If you want ample proof that born again men and women unfortunately still sin, just sit down for an hour or so and read 1 Corinthians.

The truth? If you are truly born again, you receive eternal salvation but do not become instantly sinless. If you are still wondering if salvation means you don't sin, just read 2 Timothy 2:19b, which absolutely proves that true Christians still sin: "Let everyone who names the name of Christ depart from iniquity."

Misconception #2: "Since all of us are sinners and sin all the time, no one can ever truly be holy."

This Christian has decided that holiness is impossible, so why even begin the process?

Whenever I meet a believer who has bought into this thought, they inevitably think that everyone sins all the time. Is this true? Do you sin *all the time*? Think about 2 Timothy 2:19b that you just read—do you think that all of us have an unlimited amount of sin that we must "depart" from in order to become holy?

If you began to obey this passage and many like it by departing from your sins and cleansing yourself of those sins one by one, do you think that you would never be finished? This is the opposite error of the previous one. The first thinks you automatically become sinless at salvation and this error thinks you cannot come to a place in your life that you aren't sinning all the time.

Consider our theme verse, 1 Peter 1:15: "But as He who called you is holy, you also be holy in all your conduct." Did you see those words "all of your conduct"? It is the will of God that you and I live lives which are holy in all our ways. Does this mean we never sin? Of course not—although we don't have to sin, we may still choose to sin.

Should you ever have periods in your life where you could honestly say before God and man that you are holy in all your conduct? Of course, that's the whole point! Progressive holiness means that by God's grace there are longer and longer time periods between your sins. Yesterday, while reading a biography of the famous preacher and author Charles Haddon Spurgeon, I received great encouragement through his words: "As I would not knowingly live even in the smallest violation of the law of God...." Heaven should agree that you sin less than you did last year, my friend!

Misconception #3: "I will finally be made holy when I have that crisis 'holiness experience.'"

There are many different names for this "crisis experience" depending upon your tradition of worship. For many, this crisis experience is actually the act of life consecration and dedication to live for Christ which we discussed as the second stage of holiness. Although presenting yourself to the Lord dramatically influences your ongoing life, it doesn't instantly erase all struggle with sin. Even the Apostle Peter, who was incredibly and honestly consecrated to Christ in the Upper Room, later denied Christ. Consecration doesn't provide instantaneous holiness.

Others link "baptism of the Spirit" or "filling of the Spirit" with the eradication of all sin. While no one would ever deny that the Holy Spirit holds the central place in any discussion regarding holiness, does an emotional and powerful "baptism" or "filling" fix all future problems of holy living? Once again the lives of the New Testament saints provide a ready and obvious answer. Of all New Testament churches, the church of Corinth undeniably overflowed with individuals "baptized, filled, and gifted." Yet of all New Testament churches, they exemplified the least holiness.

The truth? While genuine "crisis experiences" either of consecration or related to the Holy Spirit radically affect one's commitment and holiness, they do not bring us to a point of enduring holiness. That's perhaps the reason why the Apostle Paul commanded us to keep on being filled with the Spirit in order not to fulfill the lusts of the flesh.

HOW SHOULD I THINK OF MY HOLINESS TODAY?

Before seeking to answer that profound and strategic question, I would like to ask you a preliminary question. How holy would you say that you are in this season of your life? Be as honest as you can, and select the answer that you feel best describes your personal holiness:

- "Don't ask...I haven't made much progress toward holiness yet."

- "I think that I'm kind of average—like most of the church people I know."

- "Holiness has become more important to me and I've made some changes."

- "I'm a long way from saying I'm really holy, but my character and conduct are definitely more like Christ than two or three years ago."

- "Personal holiness is extremely important to me— I'm actively pursuing the Lord and have cleansed whole areas of my life that are now holy in God's eyes."

Holiness is one of those huge concepts that for most people seems so big, so overwhelming, and so complicated, that they leave it forever in that famous "Procrastination Box" that lies hidden in all of our closets. I have found that to make progress in any area of life, two things must be true:

First, the area must become simple enough that you easily understand it and can explain it to someone else after hearing it only once—and with no notes or help from the teacher. Second, the area must become obvious enough that you instinctively sense how it fits in your life, and know what you should do to enjoy significant progress in it—and with no one telling you what to do. This chapter seeks to accomplish both objectives about holiness for you. After reading this chapter and especially the next few pages, you'll understand the "big picture" of holiness so well that you could explain it to your ten-year-old neighbor. And as you sense where you fit in this holiness process, you will know exactly what you should do (without anyone telling you) in order to make major strides forward in your life. My hope is that you will desire it so deeply that you actually do it.

> "LET NO MAN THINK HIMSELF TO BE HOLY BECAUSE HE IS NOT TEMPTED, FOR THE HOLIEST AND HIGHEST IN LIFE HAVE THE MOST TEMPTATIONS. HOW MUCH HIGHER THE HILL IS, SO MUCH IS THE WIND THERE GREATER; SO, HOW MUCH HIGHER THE LIFE IS, SO MUCH THE STRONGER IS THE TEMPTATION OF THE ENEMY."
>
> —John Wycliffe

Unfortunately, mystery and intrigue seem to surround and cloud holiness. Holiness appears to be so large and complicated that most give up in frustration after even the littlest effort. When you ask people what their personal plan for becoming more holy is, the most normal reaction is the proverbial blank stare. Like you, I don't believe the Lord intends for us to be mystified or bewildered regarding personal holiness or to be frustrated about what we should do as individuals desiring a life of holiness. So, let's see if we can't make the "conceptual" more "concrete" and the "profound" more "practical."

One of the best ways to make a difficult concept understandable is to visualize it. How can you practically visualize your holiness in a way that represents what the Bible teaches about your holiness?

USE YOUR HOLINESS CHART AND "MAGIC MARKERS"

Summarize your entire life onto your "holiness chart"—one large piece of paper—by drawing a square box of 100 little squares,

10 boxes across and 10 boxes down. Each box is numbered and represents one particular part of your character (*"be holy as I am holy"*) or conduct (*"be holy in all your conduct"*). For instance, number 14 could be your "truthfulness" box, number 23 could be your "gossip" box, number 54 could be your "kindness" box, number 72 could be your "prayer" box, number 83 could be your "serve the Lord" box, number 92 could be your "anger" box. Therefore, everything that composed "you" is represented by one of those little boxes.

Then, do a little honest self-examination. Let's say the Lord gave you the power to step back from your life and instantly see how holy or unholy you were in each of those boxes. Take number 14, your "truthfulness" box and then number 92, your "anger" box. Instantly the Lord brought before you every single time during the past 12 months that you told the truth (holy behavior) or didn't tell the truth (unholy behavior).

To keep it simple, let's say that there were only 10 times that truthfulness occurred in your life during the past year (actually, more like 1000 times, right?). You mark each of these ten instances as either truthful/holy or untruthful/unholy and here's what you discovered for truthfulness and anger:

"Truthfulness" Box #14		*"Anger" Box #92*	
Truthful #1:	Unholy	Anger #1:	Holy
Truthful #2:	Holy	Anger #2:	Holy
Truthful #3:	Holy	Anger #3:	Unholy
Truthful #4:	Holy	Anger #4:	Unholy
Truthful #5:	Unholy	Anger #5:	Unholy
Truthful #6:	Holy	Anger #6:	Unholy
Truthful #7:	Holy	Anger #7:	Unholy
Truthful #8:	Holy	Anger #8:	Holy
Truthful #9:	Holy	Anger #9:	Unholy
Truthful #10:	Holy	Anger #10:	Unholy
80% Holy (20% Unholy)		*30% Holy (70% Unholy)*	

Therefore, you just discovered that regarding "truthfulness," you were 80 percent holy and 20 percent unholy. Regarding "anger," you weren't nearly as holy: 30 percent holy and 70 percent unholy. Remember, the Lord doesn't work in generalities; He keeps records even of the very words that we speak! Now, how could you record what you just discovered on your chart?

Perhaps next to you was a box of 100 magic markers of all different shades of gray ranging from black to white and everything in between. These "holiness markers" were numbered from 1 to 100 with the higher number representing the greatest holiness. Black was only 1 percent of holiness (or entirely unholy) while pure white was 100 percent representing complete holiness. Here's what a sampling of the 100 markers looked like:

Marker #	Description	Meaning	Color
1	Pure Black	1% Holy	
25	Dark Gray	25% Holy	
50	Middle Gray	50% Holy	
75	Light Gray	75% Holy	
100	Pure White	100% Holy	

Now, color in "truthfulness" in box number 14 with 80 percent holiness and "anger" in box number 92 with only 30 percent holiness and here's what you would instantly see regarding how close your conduct is to the Lord's command to be holy (total white—100 percent) in these two areas of your life:

Truthfulness	Anger
Box # 14	Box # 92
80% holy	30% holy

Then, the Lord opened your eyes to see what He recorded in each of the 100 parts of your life. After each revelation of your personal holiness, you selected one of the 100 markers and colored in the appropriate gray in each box. What a revelation you experienced! In some of your boxes, you had been holy the entire year and your box was all white. For instance, you colored your "stealing" box, number 17, with the white marker as you didn't steal once but always honored the belongings of others. In other boxes such as "perseverance," you had to use marker 15 because when things went hard for you, instead of practicing a holy behavior of long-suffering and perseverance, you were impatient and griped a lot.

With each box that you colored, you saw with your own eyes how holy the Lord truly considered you. Holiness no longer remained this big, religious term but now became easily understandable—in fact, you realized that holiness was just another way to describe how Christlike you were in each part of your life.

The longer you looked at your holiness chart, the more you realized that certain areas were far more holy than you ever expected! How encouraged you were! But others were almost all black—no wonder you felt defeated in those areas of your life. You wished for a bigger picture of your whole life, but didn't know how to find it. With a lingering curiosity, you picked up that holiness marker box and noticed in small print across the bottom of it: "If you want to see how the Lord sees you, just take ten steps back from your sheet and look at it again."

With your paper taped to a nearby bookcase, you started walking backwards, one step at a time—and you couldn't believe what you were seeing! The further away you walked, the less and less you could see the little boxes and the more everything seemed to blend together into one overall color. *Oh, that's how the Lord must see me.* Then you wondered how you could get a better handle on your whole life. So you just stood there thinking—until the answer became obvious! You brought the marker box back and opened the cover comparing the various colors of the markers until you selected the one marker which matched the overall color of your holiness chart. There it was—you were marker 62!

1	10	20	30	40	50	60	70	80	90	100

Then you thought you heard a voice from heaven say, "You have progressed further down the path of personal holiness than perhaps you ever expected—in My sight, you are 62 percent of the way toward My will for you." Now you can see that you are moving toward Christlikeness. You are beginning to be *holy in all your conduct!*" By this time next year, may you have taken further steps toward the image of Jesus Christ!

Does that make sense to you? Most Christians think that "holiness" is completely unfathomable, but our holiness is nothing more or less than the sum total of how holy we are in the various parts of our character and conduct. It's not complicated, in fact, when you look at holiness like this, you are both immediately affirmed and rebuked. Many areas of your life are "holy" in the Lord's eyes because you grow in grace in that area, stop sinning, and start living out Christ in that area of your life. Celebrate those areas!

On the other hand, many areas may be stuck halfway in between with your inconsistent behavior—holy at times and unholy at other times. Other areas are gray or totally black reflecting major failure and defeat. Sin reigns in these areas and needs a strong work of grace.

> "THE FIRST ARGUMENT SUGGESTS THAT THE NEW CREATURE DOES NOT NEED TO LIVE SO STRICTLY. THE MANNER OF VIGILANCE AGAINST SIN IS OVERLY SCRUPULOUS, IT ARGUES. THE SECOND ARGUMENT CONTENDS THAT WHEN SIN IS COMMITTED, IT IS NOT SO SERIOUS AFTER ALL. IT WILL NOT LEAD TO THE DESTRUCTION OF THE SOUL, BECAUSE IT WILL BE PARDONED BY THE GRACE OF THE GOSPEL. THE TRUTH IS THUS TWISTED INTO DECEPTION; AND IT IS A SOURCE OF TEMPTATION TO SIN ONCE MORE. IT BECOMES A DEADLY POISON WHEN IT IS THOUGHT TO BE A NOURISHING FOOD. THE MIND THUS BECOMES CARELESS ABOUT SIN, AND THE SENSE OF SIN'S VILENESS IS LOST."
>
> —John Owen

Last, holiness isn't merely that absence of unholiness, is it? Holiness means that in a particular part of your life, you have separated yourself from sin and have separated yourself unto the Lord. For instance, holiness in the Anger box doesn't mean you never get angry; rather, it means when your rights are violated, you respond with patience, forbearance, and speak the truth in love. The darker the box, the more flesh/self is in control; the lighter the box, the more Christ/Spirit is in control.

You know what? There isn't any experience which transforms you instantly from the dark to the light! Instead, the Bible reveals that this is a process of transformation in which we are changed from one amount of holiness to a greater amount of holiness. Another word which the Bible uses in describing holiness is "glory." The greater the holiness, the greater the glory. Read carefully Paul's comment in 2 Corinthians 3:18b, "But we all...are being transformed into the same image from glory to glory, just as by the Spirit of the Lord."

You see, my friend, Jesus Christ stands at the end of this Holiness Scale as He is 100 percent holy. He is the "same image" that all believers are being transformed into—all of us are in this process of transformation! So turn your heart toward holiness and pursue the goal of "perfecting holiness in the fear of God" (2 Corinthians 7:1b).

PART TWO

FINDING VICTORY
OVER TEMPTATION

5

How to
Grow in Holiness

"I have conquered an empire but I have not been able to conquer myself."

—Peter the Great

Gird up your loins," Paul might say. Or in modern terms, "Roll up your sleeves," because this chapter is a hands-on, practical approach to the most important issue of exactly what you should do to grow in holiness. No deep theology or highfalutin philosophy in this chapter, just straightforward, common sense communication about practical holiness.

By this time, I hope that holiness is no longer shrouded in mystery nor covered with confusion. I hope that holiness now has a powerful "Attraction Quotient" in your heart and that you are ready to learn the hands-on secrets of those who not only hunger for holiness, but know what to do to actually grow in their holiness! Hold in your mind the key principle of 2 Corinthians 7:2 that the Lord calls you to "perfect" (bring to full completion) your personal holiness.

THE TWO HALVES OF HOLINESS

When you come to the place in your life where you really want to pursue personal holiness, you must understand the principle methods you can use to actually grow in holiness. Holiness doesn't come naturally, does it? In fact, the Bible reveals that *unholiness* comes naturally! Therefore, prepare yourself to pursue holiness. Take purposeful steps in the right direction or you may end up heading in the wrong direction.

Imbedded in 2 Timothy 2:19b-22 lie the two halves of holiness. Read these verses as outlined below to discover what they are:

> "Let everyone who names the name of Christ depart from iniquity." But in a great house there are not only vessels of gold and silver, but also of wood and clay, some for honor and some for dishonor.

> Therefore if anyone cleanses himself from the latter, he will be a vessel for honor, sanctified (holy), and useful for the Master, prepared for every good work.

> Flee also youthful lusts; but pursue righteousness, faith, love, peace, with those who call on the Lord out of a pure heart.

Four key verbs reveal the actions the Lord requires from all who would be people of "honor" and "holy" and "prepared for every good work." Three describe the first half, and the last one describes the second half:

1. "Depart from iniquity" (i.e., leave sin)
2. "Cleanse himself" (leave your old, unholy ways)
3. "Flee also youthful lusts" (leave your selfish desires)
4. "Pursue righteousness" (chase after holiness)

We choose to leave behind the old ways, and pursue a new way.

Return to the holiness scale for a moment to picture these two halves a little differently. Remember when you evaluated your "truthfulness" (box #14) and "anger" (box #92) and noted how many times you acted holy and unholy in each? Those two actions reflect the two halves of holiness. The first half of holiness focuses on departing from iniquity, cleansing yourself from sin, and fleeing lusts. The second half of holiness focuses on pursuing righteousness.

Picture yourself standing on the timeline of your life. Look back over your shoulder to those areas which are unholy in the Lord's eyes—flee, depart, and cleanse yourself from them! That's the first half of holiness. Then, look forward in time to Jesus Christ standing at the end of your life, beckoning you to become exactly as He is in your character and your conduct. Now pursue righteousness. That's the second half of holiness.

Hebrews 12:1-2a is another passage which lays before us these two halves of holiness:

> Therefore we also, since we are surrounded by so great a cloud of witnesses, let us lay aside every weight, and the sin which so easily ensnares us, and let us run with endurance the race that is set before us, looking unto Jesus, the author and finisher of our faith....

Similarly, Hebrews describes the first half of holiness as "let us lay aside...the sin that so easily ensnares us" and the second half as "let us run with endurance...looking unto Jesus." Isn't it interesting that in both passages, the author clearly assumes that his readers need to cleanse themselves from present sin and pursue righteousness and Jesus. Don't ever allow yourself to believe—even for an instant—that you are an exception to these two admonitions!

Paul described these two halves differently in some of his books. You heard his description (cleanse/pursue) to his pastor friend, Timothy, now observe how he encourages a local church in Colossians 3:8 and 12b-13a: "But now you yourselves are to put off all these: anger, wrath, malice, blasphemy, filthy language out of your mouth...put on tender mercies, kindness, humility, meekness, longsuffering; bearing with another, and forgiving one another...."

Notice his order? First "put off," then "put on." Although each of these are separate acts from the other, they are both necessary for you to grow in holiness. You and I must continue to "put off" and then "put on" in order to grow in holiness. Never permit yourself to think you are an exception to His directions to do both!

THE STRATEGIC IMPORTANCE OF CLEANSING ONESELF OF ALL KNOWN SIN

Cleansing yourself from all known sin is one of the most difficult things for the believer to do. If you are the normal Christian today, you may not have thought a great deal about your sin. Personal sin doesn't seem to be at the top of our "To Do" list—unless, that is, you have decided that it's time for you to aggressively pursue holiness. Then you have no choice!

The threshold into all growth in personal holiness is always through the cleansing of personal sin. Why? Because your sin is nothing less and nothing more than personal unholiness. Therefore, any pursuit of holiness must begin by handling those areas of your life which you permitted to remain beyond the will of God. Up until this moment, you may have rationalized or been defensive regarding those areas of sin in your life. When you move toward holiness, you no longer seek to defend or rationalize your sin, you only want to cleanse it and get it out of your life. *The greater you desire holiness, the more willing you become to pay whatever the price tag to be fully cleansed, to have a clean conscience before God and man.*

> "WE MUST NOT PART WITH SIN, AS WITH A FRIEND, WITH A PURPOSE TO SEE IT AGAIN AND TO HAVE THE SAME FAMILIARITY WITH IT AS BEFORE, OR POSSIBLY GREATER.... WE MUST SHAKE OUR HANDS OF IT AS PAUL DID SHAKE THE VIPER OFF HIS HAND INTO THE FIRE."
>
> —Erwin Lutzer

Do you know what the Bible calls such movement toward personal cleansing? The stirrings of a personal revival. A biblical revival occurs when a born-again believer who has slid backward in the Christian life gets right with the Lord (previous generations knew that condition as a "backslider").

You will never experience any level of holiness if you choose to pursue righteousness without first asking the Lord to cleanse you from sin. That's why there are so many people who may have devotions on a regular basis but do not walk in holiness. They worship and praise the Lord but do not please Him due to existing sin. The believer must cleanse himself and commune with the Lord yet never deny the one in preference to the other. People who focus on cleansing their sin without learning to commune with God and pursue righteousness become harsh, judgmental, and legalistic.

Notice the strategic balance of positive holiness and negative holiness in the central passage of Scripture regarding revival (a corporate holiness) in 2 Chronicles 7:14. Most Christians read it this way:

> If *My people* who are called by My name will humble themselves, and pray and seek My face, *then I* will hear from heaven, help them turn from their wicked ways and will forgive their sin, and heal their land.

In other words, if we as the Lord's people do our part—"be humble, pray, and seek,"—the Lord promises He will respond with His part—"hear, *help us turn from our wicked ways*, forgive, and heal." In order for us to experience the turning from wickedness (according to this way of thinking), we must be humble, pray, and seek, and then the Lord will finally pour upon us the help we've always needed to "turn from our wicked ways!"

Have you ever tried that and nothing much happened? I have. Many times. After awhile, I became frustrated, then discouraged, depressed, and finally I gave up in total despair. Personal holiness and revival just wouldn't work. No matter how hard I tried to do my part, God didn't seem to do His part. I knew He heard. But He certainly didn't give me everything I needed to really clean up my life. I just remained the way I was, buried in the bondage of personal sin.

But then one day, I read that same verse again—and experienced the shock of my life! From my religious upbringing and from past teachings about revival and holiness, I brought my preconceptions about how holiness works along with me and read this verse exactly wrong. As you just did! Here's how the verse really reads:

If My people who are called by My name will humble
themselves, and pray and seek My face, *and turn from
their wicked ways* then I will hear from heaven, and will
forgive their sin, and heal their land.

Did you see it? "Turning from my wicked ways" occurs *before*
revival or holiness comes, not after it! The threshold to personal
holiness is always cleaning up the sin in your life.

The Bible teaches that I am the one who is responsible to turn
from my wicked ways. The Lord is not responsible for my turning—it is a choice that I must make in response to His command.
We go to Him, ask His forgiveness, and He cleanses us. Don't wait
for anything—just turn! One of the largest and most pervasive lies
of the enemy himself is that I am currently unable to turn from my
wicked ways right now. And, until God helps me really "want to" or
"have the power to," then I just cannot do it—it's too difficult for
me! (And by the way, since I prayed and asked the Lord to help me
and He didn't, then it mustn't be the time for me to cleanse myself
for some reason!)

THE ALARMING TRUTH ABOUT
THE AMOUNT OF SIN IN CHRISTIANS TODAY

Earlier in this book, I shared that my experience proved to me
without a shadow of a doubt the vast majority of Christians are not
actively pursuing personal holiness. Instead, only a very slim
minority of Christians are in any serious way seeking to become
"holy in all their conduct."

Think about all the Christians you know. Are many of them
seeking to become holy in all their character and conduct? During
the past six years, I had the privilege of serving in a massive missions movement that sends one-year missionaries to the former
Soviet Union. For the most part, these were the "cream of the crop"
of the laymen and laywomen of our best churches. They sensed the
Lord's call on their lives and sacrificially left everything behind to
serve the Lord.

The leadership team of this grand movement asked if I would minister to each group before they were sent over to the former Soviet Union, and so for 12 training conferences I directly ministered to these wonderful men and women. At each training session, I led these missionary recruits (average age was 35 to 45) who had been Christians for the vast majority of their lives (most had been Christians 25 to 30 years) through a session of personal cleansing of sin.

After teaching the biblical principles of cleansing, I had them pray and ask the Lord to reveal all the unconfessed sin that grieves Him and lies between Him and them. They wrote on a blank sheet all the specifics the Lord revealed during those convicting moments—whether they were broken relationships, immorality, lying, stealing, rebellion to authority, or anything else. Then I asked them to raise their hands if the Lord had brought at least three or four different significant things to their minds which He wanted cleansed. Do you know what percentage of this dedicated group raised their hands? Over 95 percent. Many had more than a dozen specific sin areas on their sheets.

Then I challenged them to do whatever it would take for them to have a clean conscience before they were officially commissioned in three days. When their list had been completed, they were to write the word "Done" on it—so others could encourage their obedience—and when noticing that someone in their group still hadn't finished, to pray and encourage them.

> "OSCAR WILDE, THE WELL-KNOWN BRITISH WRITER, SUMMED UP THE ATTITUDE OF MILLIONS OF PEOPLE WHEN HE SAID, 'I CAN RESIST ANYTHING EXCEPT TEMPTATION.' UNFORTUNATELY, 'RESISTING TEMPTATION' HAS GONE OUT OF STYLE. WE FORGET THAT WILDE ALSO SAID, '...I FORGOT THAT EVERY LITTLE ACTION OF THE COMMON DAY MAKES OR UNMAKES CHARACTER, AND THAT THEREFORE WHAT ONE HAS DONE IN THE SECRET CHAMBER, ONE HAS SOME DAY TO CRY ALOUD FROM THE HOUSETOP. I ALLOWED PLEASURE TO DOMINATE ME. I ENDED IN HORRIBLE DISGRACE.'"
>
> —George Sweeting

After leading this five or six times over the years with hundreds of adults, I finally asked this question of one group after they had gotten their lives completely cleansed of all known sin: "How many of you would say that this was the very first time in your entire life you experienced a completely clean life before the Lord and had no known sin that wasn't taken care of?" Over 70 percent of these committed Christians raised their hands.

Let that soak in for a moment.

Do you think I was exaggerating when I said the vast majority of believers are not walking in holiness? Ninety percent of the "cream of the crop" confessed to numerous known sins. Seventy percent of departing missionaries said this was the first time in their entire lives they were ever cleansed. Lest I miscommunicate at this moment, if a believer realizes he has three major sins between him and the Lord, would you say he is walking in holiness?

Wherever I have led an audience to make a list of their existing personal sins, more than 70 percent have at least 3 to 5 sins immediately surface on their list. How many are on your list right now?

Remember that "Attraction Quotient" from the Introduction was an easy test of how you felt toward the concept of "holiness" and becoming a "holy person." Apply what you learned earlier and uncover your "Attraction Quotient" as it relates to how you feel about your sin. Although this may not be comfortable, it will be extremely revealing to you. Obviously, your honest feelings about sin greatly influence whether you choose to sin or not to sin. Choose the level you feel is most true about you at this time in your life:

1. I actively pursue personal sin
2. I don't think much about it, sin just happens
3. I try to avoid sin most of the time
4. I feel regret when I sin
5. I become angry when I sin
6. I become deeply grieved when I sin
7. I hate and detest sin

Get in touch with how the Bible and the Lord "feel" about personal sin. If you are out of touch with where you should be, start asking the Lord to change your mind and mold your emotions to match His heart's response to your sin.

Evaluate Where You Stand on Personal Cleansing of Sin

After helping many Christians through personal cleansing of sin, I've observed five distinct seasons the normal Christian progresses through enroute to significant holiness through personal cleansing. As you read through these, identify which you feel best describes where you are and what needs to happen next.

1. Rejection of Cleansings Due to Hardness of Heart

During this season of the Christian life, the believer hardens his heart against the Lord due to the desire to continue in sin. The believer doesn't have any devotional life, doesn't feel close to the Lord, feels defeated, and is in bondage to at least one major sin which continues to dominate him.

2. Sporadic Cleansings Due to Powerful External Influences

During this season of the Christian life, the believer responds to the convicting work of the Holy Spirit in his life responsively but never purposefully. In other words, some painful experience, powerful preacher, or other personal experience touches his heart and he responds by genuinely repenting but not with a great deal of lasting lifechange.

3. Initial Deep Cleansing Due to Intense Internal Desire for the Lord

During this season of the Christian life, the believer has been growing spiritually, enjoying better daily devotions than ever before in his spiritual life, serving the Lord with more fulfillment and fruitfulness, and enjoying actual communion with Christ from time to time. Due to the unexpected pleasure, joy, and fulfillment of his relationship with the Lord Jesus, the believer now desperately desires more of the Lord and asks the Lord to show him the path to know Him more deeply.

Because the believer is unknowingly fulfilling all four conditions for revival (humbled himself, prayed, sought the Lord, and turned from some long-standing sins) the Lord responds at a deeper level than the believer has ever experienced. During this "initial deep cleansing," the believer will beg the Lord to reveal every sin that blocks a deeper walk with Him. It's not uncommon in this stage for the believer to make a list several pages long of specific sins that have never been dealt with properly. This will be the first time in the believer's life where the Lord opens his eyes to the breadth and depth of his personal sin. Depending upon the believer's response—either to pursue cleansing or run into the darkness and hide—the Lord will lead the believer through his first full cleansing experience. This experience is very humbling to the believer, and a deeper understanding of grace and humility always accompanies the Christian who has experienced this third level.

4. Repeated Deep Cleansings Due to Hunger for Holiness

After the initial deep cleansing, the believer will think that his heart is now fully cleansed before the Lord. In a sense, his heart has been significantly cleansed, but in reality, the Lord did not fully reveal the complete scope of sin in his life. The Lord knew that if the believer saw the full amount of suppressed sin that had accumulated over weeks, months, years, and in some cases even decades, that believer could become so overwhelmed, he might give up before even starting.

But as the growing Christian continues to seek the Lord, the Lord will put in his heart the desire for more and more Christlikeness. First, *the believer will plead with the Lord to make him more like Christ.* Second, *the believer will plead with the Lord to permit him to serve Christ more.* Third, *the believer will plead with the Lord for a more intimate walk with Christ.* As you already know, the Lord requires holiness for each of these requests. Therefore, once again without knowing it, the believer requests that the Lord work deeply in his life. The hindrance to all three of those answers lies directly in the deeper and more entrenched sins in the life of the believer. During this season, the Lord will expose to the believer deepening levels of sin so the person may cleanse himself.

As I teach in the *Seven Stages of a Pilgrim's Progress* series from Walk Thru the Bible, the cleansing moves from the external to the internal to the eternal. First, there is the *cleansing of conduct,* in which we ask the Lord to cleanse us of what we do. Second is the *cleansing of character,* in which we cleanse ourselves of

> "Every moment of resistance to temptation is a victory."
>
> —Frederick William Faber

who we are. Third is the *cleansing of the core,* in which we cleanse ourselves of why we do what we do.

The Lord surfaces these cleansings one level at a time for anywhere from a couple of months to a decade in duration, depending upon the believer's response and the depth and width of sin. The deeper the Lord cleanses us, the longer the time required. Not only that, but the deeper the cleansing, the more painful and difficult our sins are to deal with fully. Holiness has a tremendous price tag, and when you meet a truly holy individual, you can be sure their life has passed through numerous fires of purification.

If you have passed through the conduct cleansing, quite a number of external sins which others have known about are now passed and no longer a part of your life. If you have entered into the character cleansing, your "essence" has been transformed more into Christ's. Others will notice a kinder, gentler, more compassionate, tender, long-suffering, loving, and joyful countenance, and mention these treasured changes to you.

Last, the core cleansing deals with true motives. These may have been hidden from our true perception until the conduct and character cleansings were dealt with. Root issues such as selfish ambition, envy, jealousy, and desire for self-glorification surface and must be rooted out by the Lord's deep work in the life and heart and soul of the believer.

5. Regular Cleansings Due to the Deepening Relationship with the Lord

During this season, the believer has been humbled deeply and has learned the joy of walking with the Lord on an ever-growing scale and depth. Because the believer's heart has been so tenderized, he now knows he has become so utterly sensitive to any sin that he quickly and summarily cleanses himself through the principles outlined in 1 John. He or she becomes aware of the person of the Holy Spirit in a deeper way than ever before.

The believer grows in his or her intimate relationship with the Person of the Holy Spirit. He learns of the gentle nature of the Holy Spirit and His loyalty, kindness, compassions, and ever-enduring tenderness. This relationship with the Spirit is treasured greatly and the believer learns more and more what grieves and quenches the Spirit and responds quickly in personal cleansing in order to sustain the intimate relationship with Him.

During this season, the believer keeps close accounts with the Lord and confesses and makes restoration daily and moment by moment so that the larger and deeper cleansings are no longer necessary. Although for a period it may appear the cleansings will never end, there is a glorious end. How freeing and joyful is the believer who knows the freedom of walking in purity of body, soul, and spirit.

USE THE "TEN-STEP DEEP CLEANSE" FOR MAJOR CLEANSING

The greatest hindrance to holiness isn't a problem of motivation but of accumulation! The reason believers experience such frustration and defeat in their spiritual lives is due to the accumulation of unconfessed and unprocessed sins lying beneath the surface. Prepare yourself for this most strategic section on the "Ten-Step Deep Cleanse" by meditating on the secret of cleansing in 1 John 1:9: "If we confess our sins, He is faithful and just to forgive us our sins and to cleanse us from all unrighteousness."

Confession is the required component both for forgiveness as well as cleansing of all our unrighteousness. We choose to go to the Lord, and He chooses to cleanse us. In this passage, our confession is directed to the Lord and means we *agree with Him*—what we have done is sin against Him. Now, let me share a ten-step process which has helped literally thousands around the world to experience personal cleansing, many for the first time in their lives! Just think of the utter freedom and sense of joy you will experience at the end of this process.

1. *Sit alone in a quiet place* for at least one hour with a couple of blank pieces of paper, a pen, and your favorite Bible.

2. *Quiet your heart before the Lord* by sitting still, closing your eyes, and preparing your heart to seek the Lord. Put all distractions and worries and interfering thoughts out of your mind and remain at His throne long enough that you know you are finally quiet before Him. Don't be frustrated, this may take a few moments.

3. *Pray to the Lord and thank Him* for bringing you to this place in your life—where you desire to be cleansed before Him and His holiness. Ask Him to give you courage and grace as you humble yourself before Him. Commit to the Lord that you will not run away from His deep work in your life and that you will stay in the process until He reveals that you are fully cleansed before Him. Prepare your heart for this process and settle your conviction that you will complete the process regardless of the cost or consequences to you.

4. *Ask the Holy Spirit, "Please reveal to me the specific sins in my life*—even the ones I may have forgotten—which lie between You and me. In Jesus name, amen."

5. *List everything the Holy Spirit reveals to you.* Don't hesitate, and don't give into the temptation to skip some of the harder ones. When you can't think of any more, pray a second time, "Holy Spirit, I desire to confess all sins between You and me. Please reveal any additional sins—give me Your courage and grace." After you have listed everything, sit quietly for exactly five minutes—time yourself—and you may receive a couple more. When the list is completed, number them in the order of how difficult they will be for you to confess and make necessary restoration, with number "1" being the hardest.

6. *Confess your sins* one at a time before the Lord. Begin with the hardest first using words like these: "Lord, I hereby confess to You that I committed the sin of _____. Please forgive me for this sin and thoroughly cleanse me from it." Then, one by one, go through your list until you are finished.

7. *Anticipate the personal struggle you will face*, as you have not been willing to face these issues and confess them before the Lord until this point. Don't be alarmed at your strong desire to flee as everyone feels the same way, just proceed with your commitment. Give yourself a maximum of three days to make right every single thing on your list.

8. *Expect to have to humble yourself to at least one other person* in the process of restoration. Take the hardest first, and personally visit with that person. If that's not possible, telephone, if that's not possible, write him or her a letter. Perhaps you will have to confess or restore the situation. Sometimes you will have to return to a store and give them money for the items you stole, or confess to a teacher that you cheated on an exam or paper—always take the upper road and do more than what would be expected of you in order to satisfy the Lord and the offended person.

9. *Write "DONE!" across your sheet* after you have "confessed, made restoration, forgiven, and received God's cleansing!"—then burn your sheet as an act of assurance of the Lord's total and complete forgiveness. Never allow the Accuser to attack you on these issues again. If you are plagued with "I wasn't forgiven" or "I need to confess this again and again" or "I need to suffer something in order to be forgiven" realize that these thoughts are not from

God and you must stop them immediately. For tough cases, just pray these words out loud: "Lord, I have confessed this sin of _____ and I know You have forgiven me. I stand in Your forgiveness and cleansing."

10. *Thank the Lord* when you have completed your list. Praise Him for His forgiveness and thank Him for His cleansing. And if you would like to encourage one other person with your victory, I sure would appreciate a simple handwritten card with your name on it and the word "DONE!" That's all—just to encourage me that people like yourself are pursuing righteousness with their whole heart and are paying the price of humility and confession to cleanse themselves. You'll never know what your *"DONE!"* card will mean to me!*

Use the "Cleansing Cycle" for Regular Cleansing

Once this major cleansing is completed, you may be surprised to find the Lord leading you through two or three additional cleansings in the weeks and months ahead. Although you may have thought everything was handled in the first cleansing because you genuinely sought the Lord for all sins, He only revealed as much as He knew you could successfully handle. As your holiness increases, He will reveal other entire categories which you have forgotten from earlier days in your life. Don't be surprised by this! Instead, anticipate it. Take courage, prepare yourself, and then repeat the same "Ten-Step Deep Cleanse" to personal cleansing.

The "cleansing cycle" is preventative medicine and purposes to keep you out of the need for such major cleansings. Among those who walk with the Lord, this is often called "keeping short accounts with the Lord" and means that we are not to allow any time to pass between a sin and our confession of that sin.

---

* Bruce H. Wilkinson, Walk Thru the Bible Ministries, 4201 North Peachtree Road, Atlanta, Georgia 30341, Fax 770-986-9007.

Commit the sin	Crisis: "The Valley of Procrastination" How long after sin to confession?	Confess the sin

When you become committed to a life of holiness, one of the first things you must learn to practice until it becomes a virtual habit is to confess your sin the instant you commit one. Obviously, none of us desires to sin, but until we enter heaven's gates, we will sin. So consider the five "cleansing cycles" we can use in our lives.

1. The Moment Cycle

Anytime you commit a sin whether of commission or omission, instantly confess to the Lord your sin and make any restitution necessary. The more this is practiced, the more it will become a powerful tool in stopping you from sinning! If you practice the "moment cycle," as you may consider a particular sin for a split second, the realization that you are going to have to come before the Lord and confess it will certainly help your discipline!

2. The Daily Cycle

When you have your morning and/or evening personal devotions, always have a specific section in your prayer time that you quietly wait before the Lord and ask Him if there were any issues during the previous day needing your confession. Just this morning as the sun rose, I prayed through the previous day, and the Lord surfaced an act of impatience, so guess what I chose to do? Right. Confess it.

3. The Weekly Cycle

The Lord set the seasons and times of our lives, didn't He? From moments to hours to days to weeks to months to seasons to years to decades to lifetimes. All of these units are wonderful blocks of time to reevaluate and examine your life. Sometimes sins are noticeable the moment they are committed, at other times, they are only discernible with some hindsight.

It appears that throughout church history the Sabbath in the Old Testament and Sunday in the New Testament were utilized for deeper self-examination and confession. Perhaps the last hour of Sunday night would be a valuable time to be alone and review the past and upcoming week—but from the Lord's eyes and not yours. You may be surprised how the broader perspective will surface areas needing your attention and confession differently than the "moment method" and the "daily method."

4. The Monthly Cycle

On the first day of each month, I always read back through my journal to "harvest" life lessons the Lord is currently working in and with me. For instance, I have been working through some deep issues in my life which are slow in conforming into the complete image of Christ. Yesterday afternoon, additional blinders were removed in an hour and a half conversation with one of the men I serve with at Walk Thru the Bible.

So, this morning in my journal, I began confessing afresh deep hidden values which I am seeing more and more clearly are not the perfect will of God. They have been with me all my life, but the closer I draw to the Savior, the more sinful they

"WE MUST FACE THE FACT THAT WE HAVE A PERSONAL RESPONSIBILITY FOR OUR WALK OF HOLINESS. ONE SUNDAY OUR PASTOR IN HIS SERMON SAID WORDS TO THIS EFFECT: 'YOU CAN PUT AWAY THAT HABIT THAT HAS MASTERED YOU IF YOU TRULY DESIRE TO DO SO.' BECAUSE HE WAS REFERRING TO A PARTICULAR HABIT WHICH WAS NO PROBLEM TO ME, I QUICKLY AGREED WITH HIM IN MY MIND. BUT THEN THE HOLY SPIRIT SAID TO ME, 'AND YOU CAN PUT AWAY THE SINFUL HABITS THAT PLAGUE YOU IF YOU WILL ACCEPT YOUR PERSONAL RESPONSIBILITY FOR THEM.' ACKNOWLEDGING THAT I DID HAVE THIS RESPONSIBILITY TURNED OUT TO BE A MILESTONE FOR ME IN MY OWN PURSUIT OF HOLINESS."

—Jerry Bridges

appear to me! One of my closest friends takes a full day each month and spends it entirely with the Lord for evaluation, confession, worship, and planning.

5. The Yearly Cycle

Last, the "year method" is one of the most helpful to many of us. Many Christian leaders I know invest considerable time between Christmas and New Year's each year reading through their entire journal and prayer journal in order to surface what the hand of the Lord has been doing during the entire year. Once again, I have found this perspective entirely fresh and invigorating—remarkably demonstrating what some of the Lord's agenda has been in my life. As you read through the last year of your life, areas which were confessed and forsaken earlier in the year no longer surface later in the year. Areas which are still in the "fog" earlier in the year are now seen quite clearly. It's amazing how much perspective develops through 12 months of hindsight! The more hindsight, the greater the insight.

As you can see, this "cleansing" is no little or light matter. For those of us who pursue the Lord with all our heart, soul, and might, confession and cleansing is a way of life. Per-haps one closing thought to best prepare you on your personal pilgrimage: The closer you walk with the Lord, the more sinful you will realize you are! Therefore, although you may be sinning a great deal less because of the Lord's work in your life, you will sense your sinfulness much more deeply. May your heart for the Lord and His holiness draw you into holiness in all of your conduct.

Right now, why not set this book aside for a while, take the Ten-Step path, finish it, and send me that *"DONE!"* card—I'm praying for 10,000 men and women who will become "holiness card-carriers" with me!

6

THE TRUTH
ABOUT YOUR TEMPTATIONS

"No man knows how bad he is until he has tried to be good. There is a silly idea about that good people don't know what temptation means."

—C.S. Lewis

You are about to walk into the camp of your greatest enemy. As you walk through his ranks, you will be shocked when you read his greatest weapon against your desire to become a person of holiness. If you're like the others who have preceded you in learning what is revealed in this chapter, your life may never be the same. And when your eyes are fully opened, you will discern his weapons at every turn and know exactly what to do to defeat him and his deceitful plans against you.

What is the enemy's number one strategy used on every person who has ever lived to cause you to fall into sin? It is the ten-letter word "temptation." If you could destroy your enemy's ability to use temptations in your life, he would be instantly powerless.

Think about how temptations actually work in your life for a moment. How does a person like yourself who is born-again and loves the Lord ever move from being holy to unholy? What is the primary path or strategy which moves a believer from holiness to unholiness, obedience to disobedience, and righteousness to unrighteousness?

As you'll soon discover, the same strategy of temptations is unleashed millions and millions of times every day on the unsuspecting masses. Is this strategy effective? Well, for the vast majority, the use of a temptation or a series of temptations strategically timed and placed is all that's needed to bring down a person walking in holiness. The last time you "fell" into sin, you were actually "pushed" by the same hands of temptation that have always "pushed" or "pulled" you to sin.

Another word to describe a temptation is "incentive." An incentive is something that motivates or incites a person to do something. In the business world, incentives are used widely. For instance, when you walk into a store and two competing soft drinks are on sale, and one advertises, "Buy one bottle and get another free!" what are you motivated (or tempted) to do?

Or, if your boss walks over to you and announces that there is an unexpected overrun on the "red" product line, and during this week he will give a bonus for every case of "red products" you sell, when you call on your customers that week, do you think you would consciously promote the "red" product line?

As a parent, you encourage your children to keep their rooms clean and strive for good grades with some kind of reward or incentive. Are incentives wrong? Not if they encourage the right behavior done in the correct manner. As you read through the Bible, you can't miss the fact that God Himself uses incentives frequently to motivate.

However, incentives can be used not only for good ends, but also for evil ends. Do you know what the Bible calls an evil incentive?—a temptation. The primary purpose of every temptation is to motivate an individual to sin. Unlike good incentives, evil incentives use deceit and manipulation to motivate you to sin. Do you think your enemy sends you formal announcement that he is going to send a temptation to you this afternoon at 3:13 and if you foolishly fall for it, it will ruin your reputation, your family, your children, and your job?

Think how valuable it would be for you to understand this whole process of temptation. In this chapter, the truth about temptations will be unmasked and unveiled, taking away any assumptions

you may have about what they
are and how they work. In the
next chapter, the focus changes
as the seven stages of every
temptation are revealed from

> "TEMPTATION: THE FIEND AT
> MY ELBOW."
>
> —William Shakespeare

one unique passage in the Bible. You'll learn how to discern
instantly which of those seven stages you are in at any given
moment, and how to break that temptation at the one point it is
most vulnerable.

The more you understand the truth about temptations, and
learn to discern the stages of a temptation you are experiencing, the
more you will be free to immediately break any power of that temptation and remain in holiness.

THE KEY PASSAGE ABOUT TEMPTATIONS

When you want to grasp a truth of God's Word, always begin by
searching the Bible for the "key passage" which contains the most
truth about that topic and then mine it for its secrets. When the
subject of temptation is studied, the key biblical passage is 1 Corinthians 10. Read 1 Corinthians 10:12-13 carefully before moving to
the seven statements of truth about temptation and their applica-
tions:

> Therefore let him who thinks he stands take heed lest he
> fall. No temptation has overtaken you except such as is
> common to man; but God is faithful, who will not allow
> you to be tempted beyond what you are able, but with
> the temptation will also make the way of escape, that
> you may be able to bear it.

1. Temptations Are the Primary Reason You Desire to Sin

The linkage is unmistakable—the "fall" into sin is always preceded by the temptation which has "overtaken you." The temptation
is always the motivation to sin. If the temptation did not exist, you
wouldn't have a motivation to commit that sin. Before every sin you
commit hides the temptation.

When you open to the very first pages of the Bible, what do you find Satan doing? Tempting Adam and Eve to disobey God's direction not to eat from the tree of the knowledge of good and evil. Notice the subtle temptations or incentives he used on Eve:

"You will not surely die"—Satan tempts Eve to doubt the clear warning of God not to eat because they will die. In other words, the temptation must deal with known truth which is in opposition to the sin, or the sin may not be committed. If Eve didn't fall to this temptation to doubt that death would really take place in her life, she might never have given in to the temptation. *Temptations always minimize the real negative dangers and maximize the imagined positive benefits.*

"Your eyes will be opened"—Satan subtly implies that Eve's eyes must be closed and how wonderful to have them opened! And, by the way, who made your eyes "not opened" in the first place? What a subtle attack on the character of the Lord who must have purposely kept them blinded! Link this second temptation to doubt the character of God with the first to doubt the word of God. *Temptations always breed doubt about the word and character of God.*

"You will be like God"—Satan incites Eve's imagination with the thought of becoming "like God." What could be more exciting than to be "like" God? The temptation makes an incredible leap at this point. At that very moment, Adam and Eve were more "like God" than any living being anywhere in all the universe and throughout all of eternity! Adam and Eve were supernaturally created by God in His very image and likeness!

They already were "like God"! But, by eating of the tree, they chose to become the most "unlike God" that was possible! What was the method, then, of "being like God"? Think about it—the way Satan proposed they would become like God was to do the exact opposite of what God just told them! Only by choosing to disobey God could they become "like God." The root lie of a temptation is massive in proportion. Every single temptation is rooted in at least one massive lie which is promoted as the answer for what the person is looking for.

"You will know good and evil"—Satan knows how tempting "forbidden knowledge" is to the human. What could be more power-ful than secret knowledge? How incredibly deceitful is this temptation! Adam and Eve already knew the fullness of "good" knowledge as they were in the Garden of Eden, walking with the Almighty! Why would they ever desire to "know" evil since evil never brings good but always destroys good? All of life is wrapped around the pursuit of "good" so why rip it apart with that which destroys "good"?

Here the tempter uses desire or "lust" for something expressly outside the boundaries created for man. Man wasn't created to break through the safety fence separating him from good and evil. The Lord provided abundant good and then protected it with the absence of evil. By choosing to know that which the Lord purpose-fully chose to withhold, Adam and Eve fell into the same sin of Satan himself, the desire to independently rule and overthrow the sovereign limitations that God set. Temptation always incites lust to know and experience "evil" which is forbidden by God, in the false pursuit of that which is "good"!

Why did Satan use these temptations? Because without any temptation or motivation, why would Adam or Eve ever have considered disobeying the Lord? Do you see the critical role of temptation in life? Without it, what could the motivation be to choose to sin?

Likewise, consider what Satan did in seeking to defeat Jesus: He offered three powerful temptations. Note how Jesus rebuked Satan and revealed the very nature of his attack: "You shall not *tempt* the Lord your God."

Never again miss this strategy that Satan uses throughout your entire life. Whatever sin you commit is always preceded by a "temptation" which you believed, felt motivation, and then acted upon by disobeying God and willfully sinning.

2. Temptations Are Particularly Dangerous When You Think You Can't Fall

First Corinthians 10:12 begins with a strong warning about temptations: "*Therefore let him who thinks he stands take heed lest he fall.*" Perhaps this warning is placed first because it reveals the exact opposite of what a person would "normally" think about temptations. Which would be better: to think you can't fall into sin or to think that you can fall into sin? The stronger you think or feel you are—"I would never commit that sin!" or "I could never do that!" or "How could that person ever do such a thing?" or "I feel so close to the Lord that I know I won't sin today" represent giant flashing warning lights and screeching sirens of impending danger. Why shouldn't we seek to feel strong and powerful in the face of any temptation?

> "MY TEMPTATIONS HAVE BEEN MY 'MASTERS IN DIVINITY.'"
>
> —Martin Luther

"Pride goes before destruction, and a haughty spirit before a fall" (Proverbs 16:18). When we think we can't fall, pride reigns. When pride reigns, destruction will soon follow. Whenever we see arrogance, whether blatant or carefully hidden, we can be sure that a "fall" is already enroute. What then is the correct attitude and action in the face of temptation which leads us to victory and not destruction, to a position of standing rather than falling? These verses reveal the answer of watchfulness, prayer, and active dependence upon the Lord:

- "Watch and pray, lest you enter into temptation. The spirit indeed is willing, but the flesh is weak" (Matthew 26:41).

- "When He came to the place, He said to them, 'Pray that you may not enter into temptation'" (Luke 22:40).

- "Then the Lord knows how to deliver the godly out of temptations..." (2 Peter 2:9).

Our focus must always be upon our weakness and upon His strength. Pray daily that the Lord would keep you away from temptation, and if it comes, that He would strengthen you in and through it.

3. Temptations Seek to Overtake You

Temptations aren't inactive but active. Temptations don't flee from you, they seek to "overtake" you. To experience a temptation is to feel "overtaken": "Therefore let him who thinks he stands take heed lest he fall. *No temptation has overtaken you....*"

Even in the most spiritual of activities, temptations can step forward and grab you with power and persistency. The word that Paul uses here, "overtaken," presents the notion of someone seizing and holding you fast, as an enemy would.

Paul teaches that temptations are active and have an almost independent reality. They come and overtake—they seize—they assail—they grasp—they attempt to hold us down until we finally sin. You'll notice from every temptation in the Bible as well as in your own experience that when you have given in to temptation, it no longer exists. Temptations only exist on one side of sin: before it! *Before every sin lies its temptation. If you defeat the temptation, you will not commit the sin!*

4. Temptations You Experience Are Never Unique but Always Common

Without exception, if you have sinned repeatedly in a given area of sin, you will always conclude that those temptations aren't of the "normal" size and strength, but truly unusual and uncommon. But what is the truth about your temptations? "No temptation has overtaken you *except such as is common to man.*"

After one meeting where I spoke on personal holiness to men, I was approached by a younger man obviously under conviction. He shared that he was desirous of major changes in his life, but was having great difficulty. Soon he revealed that he was living with a woman and had lived with numerous women during the past ten years. I asked him why he didn't stop his immoral and ungodly lifestyle, and he said he wished he could but was powerless in the face of his sexual temptations.

I looked at him and said, "You know, your sex drive must be really strong!"

Immediately he responded, "Well...I'm glad you understand. My sex drive is so powerful that my temptations are just huge."

I nodded in affirmation, "Probably many times larger than the normal man's." He blushed sheepishly at being discovered and nodded in agreement. Finally, it appeared, he had found someone who understood—his sin wasn't really *his* fault—it was those giant temptations that attacked him.

I asked him if it would make any difference to him if those giant temptations were brought down to normal size. "Wow!" he exclaimed, "I'd give anything to have normal temptations. Why, I'd finally be able to say no and stop."

Then I turned around and scanned the room that was quickly emptying as the men left for work and continued, "So, if your temptations were just like Chuck's, Bob's, Forest's, and the others, what would you do?"

He turned quickly, "What do you mean, what would I do? About what?"

"About living in your immoral and sinful lifestyle. Would you then obey the Lord and depart from your immoral lifestyle? Only, of course, if your sexual temptations were brought way down to the 'normal' size, like everyone else's."

That sounded good to him so he nodded his head with nearly carefree abandonment. It was obvious he knew the answer; no one could fix his problem, so why worry.

Then I turned and asked him to read this very verse out loud: "No temptation has overtaken you *except* such as is common to man..." (1 Corinthians 10:13). What a shock to discover that his temptations were completely normal and were nothing more than the garden-variety of temptation growing in every man's life. He had believed the lie: "I'm helpless against the type of temptations I face that no one else faces. If my temptations were 'common' I certainly could stop." I started pointing to the men still lingering around the room and said, "He has the exact same temptation as you do—only he said no and you said yes."

In the next few moments, I watched this young man wrestle against the tragic lie he had believed. That lie had buried him under the heavy load of massive and crippling self-deception. And when that lie was brought directly into the light of the Bible, it fell powerless at his feet. With tears in his eyes, he kept saying, "My temptations are no different. I've been deceived. I'm going to break free today. I'm saying no to my sexual temptations. I'm leaving here…and walking in holiness."

Truth always sets us free;
the lie always holds us in bondage.

If you are in bondage to a sin;
it's simply because you believe a lie.

Regardless of what you may have thought about the temptations you face—especially about those temptations where you sin repeatedly—the Bible teaches that they are absolutely no different than the ones faced by all your neighbors. Think about the lies we tell ourselves:

- "It was just too strong, I couldn't help myself!"
- "I'm different; no one faces my temptations!"
- "It's in my family line—the 'genes' made me do it!"
- "I've always done it—it's too late to stop now."
- "The devil made me do it."
- "I don't worry about temptation; I'm too strong."
- "It's not my fault; I was tempted beyond my ability."

- "I prayed about the temptation, but couldn't stop."

- "It's God's fault; He knew I was too weak."

- "Lay off—no one's perfect."

If you look closely at the key verse (1 Corinthians 10:13), you'll quickly notice the word "except": "No temptation has overtaken you *except* such as is common to man." This verse not only teaches that there are no "uncommon temptations," but adds fuller truth— temptation that "has overtaken you" is specifically "common"! When you sin, just remember, the temptation could only have been a common one.

The literal meaning of "common" is "what belongs to men" and "after the manner of all men." All temptations are normal and therefore totally resistible. How then can we explain how we "feel" when those "uncommon" temptations assail us the next time? Perhaps a little dog may hold the secret to the answer.

Remember the wizard who ruled in the land of Oz? Everyone was fearful to the point of trembling about the strength and power of the wizard. Until a tiny, scruffy dog pulled back the sacred curtain! There Dorothy and her friends saw an old, weak little man disguising his voice and surrounding himself with special effects. Do you remember what happened next as they saw the truth about this "powerful wizard"? They looked at each other in complete anger and shock and began to laugh! Instantly the truth set them free. *When the deception of the temptation comes into the light, the temptation loses its power. The truth always sets one free.*

Pull back the curtain on your temptation and you'll find two things to be true: First, your temptation is the common type growing wild across the human landscape; second, your temptation is full of hot air and will always disappear into thin air when you simply say no.

5. Temptations Aren't Allowed to Go Beyond Your Ability Because of God's Faithfulness

All the times you think the Lord isn't around would certainly include the times you are tempted to sin! But the Bible reveals that the Lord is intricately involved in every temptation—not through sending it—but through making sure you can endure it without giving in to sin. "But God is faithful," the verse points out, *"who will not allow you to be tempted beyond what you are able."*

These words from the pen of Paul provide wonderful encouragement and guaranteed hope in the face of every temptation. Instead of feeling that you are "helpless" in the face of temptations, 1 Corinthians 10:12-13 communicates that you are definitely "helped" in every temptation. Helped by none other than the Lord God of the universe.

Make sure your mind wraps around this truth. Instead of avoiding you when you are tempted, the Lord approaches you to protect and aid you. He's

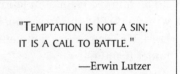

"TEMPTATION IS NOT A SIN; IT IS A CALL TO BATTLE."

—Erwin Lutzer

right there at your side, right in the battle, making sure that you aren't forced to cave in to any temptation. The preceding principle clarified that every temptation you face is "common" or natural to everyone else. This principle switches the focus from the "temptation" to the one being "tempted."

Although every temptation is common, each of us is very different. For instance, one may be tempted in the area of gluttony, another in pornography, another in gossip, while another in anger. What may tempt one, may not even tempt another. For instance, let's say that you and your friend are grocery shopping together. You are tempted in gluttony so you struggle in the dessert aisle and your friend faces a different temptation and struggles at the magazine rack. But does that mean you also struggle at the magazine rack? Probably not. You see, different temptations tempt different people.

Therefore, I may face temptations which are common, but because I may be extremely weak in a particular area, I may fall beneath a temptation in an area where you won't. In this verse, the Lord clarifies the truth about His role in personally protecting you from temptations which could overpower you individually: *God will not allow you to be tempted beyond what you are personally able to handle.*

Therefore, the Lord places a divine governor on temptations according to your unique ability to handle a specific temptation. Can you imagine that! Just think of what that means about how intimately the Lord is committed to you and your victory over temptation! Never again believe the lie that the Lord becomes angry or distant when you are in the middle of the temptation, because the truth is that the Lord becomes extremely involved at the very point of temptation. He draws a bold line in the sand and commands that the temptation can go this far, but no farther.

Why does the Lord draw this bold line for you and me? Because if He didn't, certain temptations would literally overpower us and we wouldn't be able to say no. In the wisdom and knowledge of the Lord, He limits every temptation to less than our ability to endure under it and not sin.

Therefore, never in your life in the past, present, or future, will the Lord permit you to face a temptation which will be too hard for you.

One afternoon while writing this chapter, I took a break and walked around in the neighborhood with my wife, Darlene. As we walked along, we passed a massive oak tree towering far above our heads. We marveled at the strength and majesty of this tree and how it had withstood decades of storms and winds. I asked Darlene if she thought there could ever be a storm fierce enough to blow over this massive tree. She nodded, thinking of the incredibly powerful tornadoes which destroy everything in their paths. But will there ever be a "temptation tornado" which will literally destroy you, and crush your strongest commitment to holiness? Never. The Lord protects us and limits the power of every temptation. Though Satan could easily force us to sin, the Lord limits his freedom in pushing us over the red line as we face a temptation.

Why do you think the Lord intervenes on your behalf hundreds and perhaps even thousands of times in your life? The first four words of this verse answer the question: *"But God is faithful...."* Faithfulness means to remain steadfast in affection and allegiance and to remain firm in keeping the promises made in the relationship. Faithfulness carries with it loyalty, constancy, and firm resistance to anything which would result in betrayal or desertion.

What is God faithful to in this context? God is faithful to you. God is faithful to His Word. God is faithful to His purposes. God is faithful to His promises. God is faithful to equity and fairness. How faithful would the Lord be to you if He commanded you to be "holy in all your conduct" while at the same moment permitting temptations to force you to sin when you did everything in your power not to sin?

Depend fully upon the sovereign limitation of your temptations as the Lord is unswervingly faithful. But what happens when we are repeatedly unfaithful—and we choose to sin in the face of a temptation over and over and over and over again? Obviously, the Lord must have a limit to His faithfulness depending upon how "faithful" we are to Him, right? In other words, God's character of "faithfulness" has limitations? Check out 2 Timothy 2:13 for the answer: *"If we are faithless, He remains faithful; He cannot deny Himself."*

Therefore, the truth about your temptation is that the Lord God will never leave you or forsake you in the face of a temptation. He will always—in every circumstance and at every time—sovereignly limit your temptations so they never exceed your ability to say no. No wonder God says to be "holy in all your conduct"—He has made sure to provide everything you need but limit everything you don't need.

Some implications surface immediately from this truth:

First, God limits the temptations I face according to my abilities, not someone else's. God doesn't limit my temptations by your life, but by mine. Regardless of what may be true about anyone else's temptations, you always know the Lord has His full attention focused upon you and your ability. The Lord sovereignly limits your temptations with only you in mind. That means that if you and your friends faced a large and unexpected temptation together, the Lord would limit that particular temptation differently for each individual. The same temptation is limited by the Lord according to the varying abilities of the individuals.

Second, God limits the temptations but doesn't necessarily increase our strength. Right before you is a massive barbell with 500 pounds of weights. The Lord instructs you to pick the barbell up. You bend your knees and struggle with everything in you but you cannot budge it. What does the Lord do? Miraculously add massive muscles? No. The Bible doesn't teach in this verse that "God is faithful, who will increase your abilities so you will be able to withstand the temptation"; instead, "God is faithful, who will not allow you to be tempted beyond what you are able."

God enables you to obey Him by taking weights off the barbell until He knows you can lift it. What He doesn't do is add 400 pounds of strength so you can now lift it. Therefore, never expect the Lord to miraculously strengthen you, but rather expect Him to miraculously limit the temptation's weight. By the way, after you sit down, the next person walks up to that same barbell. Guess what the Lord does for him or her?

Third, God limits the temptations by my abilities in every different situation. Your ability to withstand a temptation is not only different from everyone else's, but also changes according to what is happening in your life at the time. Let's say someone close to you died, you experienced a major business failure, and you had been sick for an extended time. Would you say that your normal ability to withstand a specific temptation would be as strong as usual? Obviously not. So, guess what the Lord does? Since your ability to withstand a temptation is now much lower, the Lord limits much more. Whatever your ability is at any given moment for any reason defines the limitation the Lord places upon your temptation.

I don't know how you feel about the Lord as you understand His incredible faithfulness to you, but His compassion and mercy in protecting me literally overwhelms me. No wonder the Lord can command us to be holy in all our conduct! He makes sure that we can!

6. Temptations Are Always Accompanied by the Lord's Way of Escape

Of all the remarkable revelations in these two verses about our temptations, none is more striking than this provision by God: "But

God is faithful, who will not allow you to be tempted beyond what you are able, but with the temptation *will also make the way of escape....*"

> "LEARN TO SAY 'NO'; IT WILL BE OF MORE USE TO YOU THAN TO BE ABLE TO READ LATIN."
>
> —Charles Haddon Spurgeon

After considering God's first provision, you may feel like I do—what else could God possibly need to do beyond what He has already done? But, as you think through this current principle, perhaps you will be amazed by His second action.

God's first provision in the face of temptation is a limitation: *He will not allow you to be tempted beyond what you are able.* God's second provision in the face of temptation is a provision: *He will provide the way of escape out of the temptation.*

God's faithfulness to us stimulates Him to two different and distinct actions. First, He doesn't allow any temptation to break through our ability, and second, He provides the way of escape for us so that we can experience freedom from temptation without sinning. In the face of your temptation, the Lord says both "No!" to the temptation and "Yes!" to you. His supreme goal is your complete and total victory over every temptation without even the smallest sin.

Just as Christ experienced throughout His life, all of us experience innumerable temptations to sin. As Christ, we are called to endure those temptations so that we are "without sin." "For we do not have a High Priest who cannot sympathize with our weaknesses, but was in all points tempted as we are, yet without sin" (Hebrews 4:15). Jesus was tempted the same way we are tempted, but He always said no. He always chose the way of escape.

Study these words carefully: "but with the temptation will also make the way of escape." The introductory word "but" leads into this unexpected contrast with the preceding comment. God limits our temptations, but God also makes the way of escape. Just because the temptation is limited doesn't necessarily mean we can escape it. What happens if every escape route has been blocked by our vicious enemy?

Question: How often does God "make the way of escape"?
Answer: "*With* the temptation" God makes the way of escape.

In other words, a new way of escape is constructed by God "with the temptation" you face. Previous escape routes that worked in another place won't be of any help to you when you are backed to the edge of a cliff. Because every temptation is different, the escape route must also be different. God doesn't "find" a way of escape for you; God "makes" a way of escape for you. In other words, when a temptation seeks to overtake you, God sovereignly and uniquely invents and then constructs your "safe delivery route" out of that temptation.

In case you're doubting whether this verse actually teaches a literal escape route, just glance once more at the word before "way of escape" and you'll immediately notice the word "the" and not the word "a." This verse doesn't make a vague generalization that "with temptations there are escapes available" but "with *the* temptation" God will make "*the* way of escape." The escape is supernaturally provided for your natural temptation. God reaches down into the temptation you're facing and personally "makes the way of escape" just for you.

The word "escape" refers to a secret mountain pass out of a box canyon. Imagine an army trapped in the mountains without any possible way out, when suddenly a path is discovered and the whole army escapes without harm. Read how the Apostle Peter described what the Apostle Paul just taught: "…*The Lord knows how to deliver the godly out of temptations…*" (2 Peter 2:9).

The practical application nearly shouts at us. How faithful is the Lord to us in the face of our temptations? Absolutely faithful. He limits and then He provides. He doesn't permit that temptation to run us over, but intervenes by making an original and unique escape route for you right out of that particular temptation.

The more the truth about your temptations becomes clear in your heart and mind, the more His command "Be holy in all your conduct" looks absolutely realistic.

7. Temptations Cannot Extend Beyond What You Can Bear

This final principle demonstrates the Lord's heart in His involvement in your temptation. Because He seeks a holy church, He provides for holiness in every situation imaginable. As you've seen, the Lord limits and provides to enable you "to bear it."

"But God is faithful, who will not allow you to be tempted beyond what you are able, but with the temptation will also make the way of escape, *that you may be able to bear it.*"

The greatest lie about your temptations is, "I can't say no to this temptation no matter how hard I try."

Now you know that couldn't be true or else the Lord God is utterly faithless. Never again succumb to this defeating lie, because the moment you entertain it even for a split second, you've already started down the slippery slide toward sin.

As you have seen, the Bible openly teaches that regardless of the temptation, you will always be able to bear it without being forced to sin. That doesn't mean standing strong will always be easy, because sometimes it won't.

Jesus faced the most difficult of all temptations and notice the degree of His struggle: "For consider Him [Jesus] who endured such hostility from sinners...you have not yet *resisted to bloodshed, striving against sin*" (Hebrews 12:3-4). Sometime during your life, you may face temptations so fierce that you will "resist to bloodshed, striving against sin." But, if you do, remember the Lord will not permit that temptation to extend beyond what you are able to endure.

The way of escape always exists, but the Lord may not always reveal it to you quickly or even when you ask Him. In most cases, the way of escape is right before you—like "flee sexual immorality," which means literally that the way of escape is standing in your shoes—and moving them in the opposite direction! Other times, however, the way of escape can require your "resisting" all the way even to your physical death. The ultimate truth is that it is more important to stand strong against the temptation to sin even if it may cost you your life. The "way of escape" for an innumerable host of martyred believers throughout history and even this world today has been to stand strong in the face of the most threatening temptation, even to the point of death.

Although many have paid with their lives, others who knew Christ and His call upon their lives ran into the darkness, denying the Lord who redeemed them in order to save their lives. Do you know the lie they listened to and embraced? "I can't do this—this is too hard." My friend, even death is not too hard, because the Lord will never permit any temptation which will ever exceed your ability to endure without sin. Those who ran into the darkness ran only because they believed the lie. *As long as you are being tempted, you are always able to resist—remaining holy in all your conduct.*

THE TRUTH ABOUT TEMPTATION

Two weeks after teaching a group of men this truth about temptations, I unexpectedly bumped into one of them in a nearby store. You should have heard him go on and on about what the Lord had done in his life during the past two weeks:

"I couldn't believe," he shared, "how deceived I have been all my life about my temptations. I saw them as these towering giants that I was powerless against. After a while, I gave up trying to fight the temptations because I thought I couldn't experience victory anyway. Then I learned the truth about my temptations in 1 Corinthians 10 and it's like all the air seeped out of them and I saw the truth for the first time. Now I know that God stops my temptations dead in their tracks before they can 'overwhelm' me. Now I know that God isn't mad at me when I'm tempted—and I shouldn't hide from Him— He's my true deliverer, providing the way of escape every time. What a God we have!"

He was talking a mile a minute, "So you'll never guess what has happened in the past two weeks. Those same temptations which used to knock me right over no longer do. In fact, I can hardly believe it, but during the last couple weeks, I rested on the truth about my temptations and didn't sin like I have been doing for years! This stuff really works! I think for the first time, I actually have hope that I can become holy in all my conduct before I die!"

The next time you feel like you're beginning to weaken in the face of temptation's LIE, speak these words of powerful TRUTH and you'll be amazed how the temptations flee into the darkness—right where they came from, and right where they belong. You see, the truth will always set you free!

> *I realize I am in the middle of a temptation to sin.*
> *I hereby commit to the Lord to depend upon the Holy*
> * Spirit and not sin.*
> *I know the Lord is limiting this temptation, and it can't be*
> * too hard for me.*
> *I know the Lord is making the way out of this temptation*
> * for me.*
> *I am able to bear this temptation until it is over.*
> *I choose to obey the Lord's command to be "holy in all*
> * my conduct."*
> *Thank You, Lord, for Your Faithfulness to me!*

7

TEMPTATION TOOLS
FOR VICTORY

*"The holy man is not one who cannot sin. A holy man is
one who* will *not sin."*

—A. W. Tozer

Now that you know the Lord intervenes in every single
temptation you face, this chapter will open your eyes to
exactly what you should do when facing those temptations. Although the Lord limits your temptation and makes the way
of escape, you still must face and overcome your own temptations.
You must fight your own battles through to victory. Although we
pray to the Lord and depend upon His Spirit, the Bible is very clear
that *we* must "be strong" and "put on the armor." The Bible reminds
us "*we* wrestle" and "*we* must withstand" and "*we* must stand."
Everything the Lord does in the time of temptation makes it so we
can stand.

This chapter equips you with powerful tools you can use to
defeat your temptations. If you are committed to becoming a person of holiness, you must become an *expert* in defeating your temptations. You must know how temptations work against you
uniquely, and then know exactly what to do to enjoy true victory,
one battle at a time. I can promise you one thing as you work

through this chapter: You'll never look at your temptations as you do right now, and you'll defeat your temptations more and more as you become skilled in using these weapons.

One last thought, however, before embarking. Just think of the joy and freedom that will be yours as you become a skilled "temptation warrior"—battling through temptations with the Lord's provision and your diligence. I want you to know these tools absolutely work—I use them regularly in my life. When I compare my life before using the temptation tools and after, there is a dramatic and enduring difference. Holiness lies on the other side of victory over temptation!

YOUR "TEMPTABILITY QUOTIENT"

Do you have a tool to do a "quick read" on yourself to determine how vulnerable to attack you are at any given moment? Temptations are specially timed. Temptations are carefully aimed. Temptations maximize their power by attacking at the greatest moment of vulnerability. From the prophet Moses to King David, temptations have succeeded in pulling down the mighty among us by assailing us at our *point of weakness* and at the *moment of weakness*. Study the men and women of the Bible and their bouts with temptation and you'll see the same trend. Temptations attack where and when the believer is weakest and least expecting.

When did Satan tempt Jesus? After 40 days without food and in the midst of physical weakness and complete isolation. When are you weakest and most vulnerable to temptation? The "Temptability Quotient" (TQ) is a remarkable little tool that will take all of two minutes to use after you've tried it once. The goal of the TQ is to alert you to how vulnerable you are at this very moment to temptation's attack. There are ten different categories, with the negative side on the left and the positive side on the right. At every moment of your life you are on the scale from the low number 1 to the high number 10 in these ten categories. Take a moment to circle the number which best represents you at this very moment:

1. Physically Exhausted / Tired	1 2 3 4 5 6 7 8 9 10	Energetic / Strong
2. Emotionally Discouraged / Down	1 2 3 4 5 6 7 8 9 10	Encouraged / Up
3. Mentally Bored / Discontent	1 2 3 4 5 6 7 8 9 10	Challenged / Content
4. Spiritually Depleted / Empty	1 2 3 4 5 6 7 8 9 10	Growing / Full
5. Geographically Distant / Alone	1 2 3 4 5 6 7 8 9 10	Near / Together
6. Relationally Alienated / Cold	1 2 3 4 5 6 7 8 9 10	Close / Warm
7. Internally Hopeless / Sad	1 2 3 4 5 6 7 8 9 10	Hopeful / Happy
8. Personally Insecure / Unsure	1 2 3 4 5 6 7 8 9 10	Secure / Confident
9. Secretly Bitter / Angry	1 2 3 4 5 6 7 8 9 10	Forgiving / Accepting
10. Deeply Wounded / Hurt	1 2 3 4 5 6 7 8 9 10	Appreciated / Loved
Today my "Temptability Quotient" is	_____	

After circling where you are right now in these categories, add up the total and you'll find your quotient. Here's how to interpret your score:

90-100   You're already glorified in heaven!

80-89   Very strong, but be alert to subtle pride and arrogance.

70-79   Strong, keep your dependence up with the Lord.

60-69   Adequate, though watch your trend—you're on the line.

50-59   Weak, you're emotionally vulnerable.

40-49   Danger! Guard yourself intensely—you're floundering.

30-39   Extreme danger! Call your best Christian friend and yell "help."

20-29   In the critical ward—probably already fell to major sins.

10-19   They're wheeling you into the morgue. Move your toe....

0-9   This is a bad dream, pinch yourself and try again!

If you are below 70, you'd better raise the "yellow flag" because the surf's up and the undertow is much worse than it looks on the surface. If you fall below 60, you are definitely in turbulent and troubled waters and heading for a wipeout. I share with my wife Darlene if I fall below 60—although she usually already senses that because we are so close: "Sweetheart, I'm feeling really vulnerable and not too stable—would you send a few extra prayers up in the next couple of days? And, if I'm a little impatient or not too sensitive, remember that it's not you, but me."

If you fall below 50, you'd better call in some heavy artillery. Just a word to your best friend—like "I'm not doing so hot" or "I'm struggling"—can open the door and encourage him or her to come into your life and lend much needed support. Make sure, however, you don't share these kinds of things with those of the opposite gender (except your spouse), as you are walking directly into a well-worn temptation trap. Never do it. Never! Do you know how many of my friends have gotten into trouble because they shared these deep personal issues with a person of the opposite sex? Many. Protect yourself from further temptation—go to someone of the same sex.

How often should you take your TQ pulse? Probably once a week for 12 weeks in a row. Why not copy the chart, put it in your Bible and take the quiz during announcements in church each Sunday morning? (Or in your car in case you're one of those who listens to church announcements!) If that won't work, select another place and time in which you can go every single week so it becomes a quick and natural procedure. Record your weekly score on the TQ "trend line chart" and monitor your progress. It will only take a second, but it will radically open your eyes.

THE TQ TREND LINE

Weekly TQ Score	1	2	3	4	5	6	7	8	9	10	11	12
90 - 100												
80 - 89												
70 - 79												
60 - 69												
50 - 59												
40 - 49												
30 - 39												
20 - 29												
10 - 19												
0 - 9												

As you've noticed, the TQ trend line has three categories with different shades:

■ The Healthy Zone

□ The Semi-danger Zone (this is really the transition zone)

■ The Crisis Zone

All of us move up and down through these zones. For instance, right now I'm at 59—and watching myself very carefully as well as praying for the Lord to "keep temptation away from me" and "please strengthen me in the inner man as I yield to Your Holy Spirit." Last week my score was 76 and the week before 83. So guess what? My trend line raises concern. If next week my TQ falls below 50, I'm going to exercise considerable effort before the Lord, alert at least one of my friends, and intensely focus on restoring my life to health and strength.

The value of this trend line is that it gives you immediate discernment of the direction you are heading. Think carefully about this: *I don't know of one believer who fell into major sin whose trend line wasn't in the "Crisis Zone" for at least three weeks in a row!*

Because you are committed to a life of holiness, you must become more alert to your own life and the condition you are in. The lower the TQ score, the greater your concern should be. The longer the TQ score falls below 50, the greater the concern. Two weeks of 50 or below should make you scream "FIRE!" and cause rapid change in your life.

Don't disregard your own condition another week! If you have a group working through this study together, start sharing with each other what your TQ Score is each week. In fact, share your TQ trend line for greater benefit. Don't feel your chart will be the only one beneath 95! Please remember,

> "WE ARE NO MORE RESPONSIBLE FOR THE EVIL THOUGHTS THAT PASS THROUGH OUR MINDS THAN A SCARECROW FOR THE BIRDS WHICH FLY OVER THE SEEDPLOT HE HAS TO GUARD. THE SOLE RESPONSIBILITY IN EACH CASE IS TO PREVENT THEM FROM SETTLING."
>
> —John Churton Collins

your score isn't a sign of sin, it's a sign of what's been happening in your life. Many times, the events of your life are totally out of your control. Don't be discouraged by your score, but use your score to alert you to your condition in the face of temptations!

As the TQ becomes a part of your life, you'll soon be able to look at the schedule for next week and almost predict what you'll be facing. Take measures then to offset what you anticipate and take charge of your life. Ask God to lead and strengthen you. As you do you will become stronger against temptations and for holiness.

UNRAVELING THE BLAME GAME

It is important you understand the exact steps that every temptation moves through in order to get you to sin. It's absolutely amazing, but the Lord reveals in His Word the exact steps the enemy uses on us every time! You'll soon see for yourself—the Bible once again comes to our rescue by openly teaching us our enemy's strategies.

Every temptation moves through seven stages as outlined in James 1:13-17. Just imagine knowing which stage you are in during a temptation, and the power of knowing what to expect next. This information is incredibly valuable, and that's why the Lord gave it to us!

Carefully read these verses, asking the Lord to open your eyes to everything He revealed for your victory over temptations:

> Let no one say when he is tempted,
>   "I am tempted by God";
>   for God cannot be tempted by evil,
>   nor does He Himself tempt anyone.
> But each one is tempted when he is drawn
>   away by his own desires and enticed.
> Then, when desire has conceived,
>   it gives birth to sin;
>   and sin, when it is full-grown,
>   brings forth death.
> Do not be deceived, my beloved brethren.
>   Every good gift and every perfect gift is from above,
>   and comes down from the Father of lights,
>   with whom there is no variation or shadow of turning.

When James wrote of the seven stages of every temptation, he wrapped his words with a direct attack upon the deepest lie there is about temptations: *"Let no one say...'I am tempted by God.'"* Do you know where every human being will eventually find him- or herself after the true consequences of a sin committed finally hits home? Blaming. Blaming someone else. Blaming something else. Until finally, there is no one to blame but God Himself.

How each of us hates to accept the full blame for the sin we commit! Even from the very beginning, everyone blamed someone else for their sin. When God said to Adam, "Have you eaten from the tree of which I commanded you that you should not eat?" Adam answered "The woman...she gave me of the tree, and I ate." Then, when God said to Eve, "What is this you have done?" Eve replied to God, "The serpent deceived me, and I ate."

Blame means to not accept full responsibility for one's actions by accusing another for the fault. In the marketplace, blame is called "passing the buck" until there is no one left to pass it on further, so we say, "The buck stops here." As the president of an organization, I'm familiar with those words. But when we have sinned and there are very painful or destructive consequences, the "buck" can often pass all the way to the very top. God must be the one responsible!

Did you notice the words that I didn't fully quote when Adam spoke to God? Here's what Adam really said: "The woman *whom You gave to be with me*, she gave me of the tree, and I ate." Who got the ultimate blame for Adam's sin? God. It's as though Adam was saying, "God—*You* gave me the woman, and if You hadn't, then I wouldn't have sinned. God, *You are the ultimate cause of my sin*, not me. You ultimately sent the temptation by giving me Eve. Therefore, don't hold me accountable for I am ultimately innocent."

Have you ever heard yourself blame God for your sin? "Why, if only God would have stopped him" or "If God knows everything, then He knew I'd sin when this happened; therefore, He should have stopped it sooner" or "I prayed and God didn't take away the temptation at work, so it's not my fault I sinned." Sounds all too familiar, doesn't it?

Now you know exactly why James started his profound revelation about temptation with the words: "Let no one say...'I am tempted by God.'" God is never the source of any temptation. Whenever you find yourself thinking, "If God had only..." or "It's not my fault because..." you know you are treading on the "blame fault line," which only results in massive earthquakes in your life. The Bible is clear: The Lord doesn't tempt anyone—not directly nor indirectly. Never.

GOD: THE GIVER OF ALL GOOD THINGS

But this passage goes even further and reveals something that is absolutely amazing. If God isn't the cause of the temptation, what exactly is He the cause of? Read carefully the last few lines of that passage: "Every good gift and every perfect gift is from above, and comes down from the Father of lights, with whom there is no variation or shadow of turning."

If you're familiar with the Book of James, you may always have wondered what these words have to do with temptations. The answer: absolutely everything! You see, temptations only seek our sin, and our sin seeks our destruction (as you'll see shortly). If God lies behind temptations, He must ultimately be a mean God who enjoys and plans for our pain and suffering. Is that the character of God? Well, tragically, I'm afraid that in the dark corners of our hearts, that's how we all think until we know the truth. Here's how it sounds: "If God loved me, He would not have let that temptation come into my life" or "If God really cared about me, He would know how weak I am and He certainly would have helped—even a little—by keeping that temptation away from me."

Do you realize what we are doing? Attacking the motives of God! Ripping His heart to shreds. He could have stopped the temptation and then we wouldn't have sinned. And since He didn't, His heart must be cold, hard, and even ruthless.

James must have anticipated our wicked hearts and twisted thoughts and so he

> "TO PRAY AGAINST TEMPTATION, AND YET TO RUSH INTO OCCASION, IS TO THRUST YOUR FINGERS INTO THE FIRE, AND THEN PRAY THEY MIGHT NOT BE BURNT."
>
> —Thomas Secker

revealed the real truth about God and my temptations. Instead of sending darts of destruction, listen to what God does send: "Every good gift and every perfect gift." Get it clearly in your mind: *God is never the author of any evil temptation. God is always the author of every good thing in your life.* How would any of us ever know this fact about God unless the Bible revealed it to us? How could I have ever known that behind "every good gift and every perfect gift" is the hand of God? We normally would think that "good things" that happen to us are the result of our hard work or just "happen." But that isn't even remotely true.

How is it true that we can think God must be behind every evil temptation but cannot believe that God must be behind every single good gift? It's almost like James anticipates our unbelief—and uses the word "every" two times in the space of only five words. "Every"—I mean "EVERY!" is his big idea. *Every good gift*—and *every perfect gift*—is from above. A "gift" may be delivered through a human delivery person, but if it is "good" or if it is "perfect" than you can be absolutely sure that it ultimately came "down from the Father"!

So what is the true motive and the method of God? Only good and perfect gifts come from His hands. Never evil temptations. Don't forget what Paul taught about God's involvement in our temptations from the previous chapter: God sovereignly limits every temptation that comes our way and God sovereignly makes the way of escape for us. Not only does He provide everything to get out of evil, but He gives us everything that is good! Whenever we've committed a sin with terrible consequences, we are immediately tempted to believe that God's heart isn't filled with love. We are tempted to think it's filled with evil intentions. Note how the serpent wove that doubt about God's character in the Garden with Eve: "Then the serpent said to the woman, 'You will not surely die. For God knows that in the day you eat of it your eyes will be opened, and you will be like God, knowing good and evil'" (Genesis 3:4-5).

Look deeply behind those subtle and deceitful words of the serpent and you can see the two powerful lies he slips into Eve's unsuspecting mind: First, the serpent says *God's character is flawed*

> "OFTENTIMES GREAT AND OPEN TEMPTATIONS ARE THE MOST HARMLESS BECAUSE THEY COME WITH BANNERS FLYING AND BANDS PLAYING AND ALL THE MUNITIONS OF WAR IN FULL VIEW, SO THAT WE KNOW WE ARE IN THE MIDST OF ENEMIES THAT MEAN US DAMAGE, AND WE GET READY TO MEET AND RESIST THEM. OUR PECULIAR DANGERS ARE THOSE THAT SURPRISE US AND WORK TREACHERY IN OUR FORT."
>
> —Henry Ward Beecher

because He lied. God may have said "…you shall surely die" but the real truth is "you will not surely die." Therefore, argued the serpent, God may lie again—you can never trust Him or His word.

Second, *God's motive is flawed* because He's purposefully keeping something back from you that you could have and really should have: "For God knows [and He never told you, did He…] that in the day you eat of it your eyes will be opened, and you will be like God, knowing good and evil." Therefore, God isn't committed to you and your good, but is selfish and holds back what's rightfully yours. Do you see how timeless his strategy is? To defame and defraud God's character and motive has always been the enemy's strategy. Why? Because the moment doubt enters your heart about God, you fling open the door to innumerable temptations.

Did God tell the truth? Absolutely, they both died just like He said. Was God motivated for their good? Absolutely, Adam and Eve didn't become like God, but became like the enemy of God. With the "knowledge of evil" came every evil thing into their lives. As you consider the meaning of that verse, you'll see that James once again anticipated what we would be thinking: "Every good gift and every perfect gift is from above, and comes down from the Father of lights, with whom there is no variation or shadow of turning" (James 1:17).

Will there ever be a time when these two truths about the character and motive of God aren't true? Could God ever become so angry or frustrated or upset with us that His heart would turn against us and He'd purposefully send a temptation to sin? James describes the Lord as One "whom there is no variation or shadow of turning." God has not, does not, and will not send temptations to you.

The third lie about temptation is that we cannot know or understand them because they are mysterious and hidden beyond human understanding. Nothing could be further from the truth! Not only are "temptations" understandable, but the more you pay attention to your temptations, the more you'll understand them and have power over them. In time, you will even anticipate when and where temptations may be lurking behind the shadows. We are not to be ignorant of the devices or methods of temptations!

The Lord is never the sender of any temptation to anyone.
The Lord is always the sender of every good and perfect gift.
The Lord has revealed openly how temptations work.

Now it's time to really get a handle on how to defeat your temptations—right where they are most vulnerable!

THE SEVEN STAGES OF EVERY TEMPTATION

Sometimes you stumble upon a literal gold mine of rich truth in which the more you dig, the greater the treasure you discover. James 1:14-15 only has three dozen words, but they completely unveil the inner workings of every temptation: "But each one is tempted when he is drawn away by his own desires and enticed. Then, when desire has conceived, it gives birth to sin; and sin, when it is full-grown, brings forth death."

The Number	The Scripture	The Stage
Stage 1	"...when he is drawn away	THE LOOK
Stage 2	by his own desires	THE LUST
Stage 3	and enticed. Then	THE LURE
Stage 4	when desire has conceived,	THE CONCEPTION
Stage 5	it gives birth to sin;	THE BIRTH
Stage 6	and sin, when it is full-grown,	THE GROWTH
Stage 7	brings forth death."	THE DEATH

Verse 14 introduces the subject with *"But each one is tempted…"* and launches into the seven different steps outlined below in summary form:

STAGE 1: THE LOOK—"WHEN HE IS DRAWN AWAY"

You are tempted "when" something takes place—if it didn't take place, you couldn't enter into temptation. "Each is tempted *when* he is drawn away." The words "drawn away" are borrowed from the fishing and hunting context in which an unsuspecting fish is slowly drawn out of its original retreat under a bank or in a hole or when an animal is tricked into the area in which traps are set. The picture is of a person being distracted with something which draws their attention away from what it is currently focused on.

Think about being "drawn away"—it is the subtle if not imperceptible link between being in a safe or protected state of minding your own business, then sliding into the risky state of the earliest stage of a temptation. Unless you are *drawn away* from what you are doing, you can't be *drawn into* a temptation.

Consider how this happens: a noise, someone walks past you, a telephone call, a "distracting thought" that seems to come from nowhere, a letter, a person who cuts right in front of you enroute to the office, a unique smell which instantly brings back old memories of previous sins, a wallet laying in the middle of the woods, your neighbor puts in a beautiful new pool next to your ugly backyard, the cashier mistakenly gives you $20 too much change, someone shares a tasty piece of gossip, the married co-worker in the next office starts dropping tempting hints about what could happen on the upcoming business trip.

This first stage is called "The Look" because it fulfills the role of the doorway into the land of temptation. Without being "drawn away," a temptation cannot even touch you. Skilled temptation warriors learn how to discern almost instantly when they are being drawn away—and instantly draw back! If you don't enter that doorway, you cannot be tempted!

The Secret to Stage #1: *Draw back instantly when you sense you've been drawn away!*

STAGE 2: THE LUST—"BY HIS OWN DESIRES"

Conduct a "temptation check" for a moment. Think about yourself and the major sources of temptations you face. For instance, how often have you heard someone say, "that bottle tempts me" or "that money on the counter was too strong of a temptation" or "my boss is the most unfair person I know and makes me work such long hours that I'm going to get even and steal from the company to even up the score" or "if my spouse would be more romantic, I wouldn't be so tempted to find satisfaction somewhere else" or "they cut my overtime at work and I just had to lie on my income tax to get a bigger refund so that we could pay our bills" or "she came on so strong to me on Saturday night after the big game, I just didn't have the power to resist the temptation."

Whether you're tempted to sin by anger, theft, immorality, hatred, selfishness, envy, drunkenness, pornography, or lying, see if you can't put your finger on the biggest sources of your temptation:

1. The major "person" who tempts me: _____
2. The major "situation" which tempts me: _____
3. The major "thing" which tempts me: _____
4. The major "place" where I am tempted: _____
5. The major "thought" which tempts me: _____

Just imagine if all those things that tempt you would just disappear! How wonderful life would be, right? Holiness would become a snap if those sources of your temptations disappeared. Right?

Wrong. Try these shocking words on for size: "But each one is tempted when he is drawn away *by his own desires* and enticed." What is the source of every single temptation you ever face? You. Me??? Yes, you. The only reason a temptation can tempt you is because of your own desires. If you didn't have the "desire" somewhere in your life, that thing or person or situation couldn't even faze you. The only reason you walk through that doorway is you hear your "name" being called! Your hidden desires draw you away each time. In fact, every time. Without your desire, why on earth would you pursue anything?

Right now I'm in the midst of a month-long diet to lose ten unwanted pounds. It's 3:32 in the afternoon and hunger is beginning to knock on the walls of my stomach. Let's say my wife comes downstairs with a little snack of chocolate chip cookies and hot coffee. How tempted would I be?

Now, let's take that example one step further. Say I just finished a huge meal and had a big second piece of that fresh blueberry pie. Then we go sit down in my den and Darlene brings two of those cookies. Would I be tempted then? What made the difference in my vulnerability to temptation?

Temptations only tempt you because of what's inside of you, not what's outside of you.

What a powerful revelation from God's Word! Therefore, when the young man I counseled recently said, "But she tempts me soooo bad!" what's really the truth? Or for the teenager who said, "I couldn't help myself, that money on the counter was too tempting." The woman wasn't the source of the temptation, his lustful heart was. That unguarded money wasn't the source of the temptation, his covetous heart was.

When the Bible says "by his own desire," the word "desire" merely means anything which attracts you, anything for which you have an earnest desire. When you desire food, that's good; but if you permit that desire for food to cross the barrier of self-control, you sin with gluttony. Every single desire is God-given. God placed all of man's desires within him as a sovereign act of creation. With each of those desires, man has the freedom to use the appropriate means to have each of those desires gratified without sin.

Each temptation always preys upon a God-given desire and seeks to push it into sin in one of two directions. First, by pushing the God-given desire to exceed its normal limits into excess. Second, by pushing the God-given desire to find fulfillment in "off-limits" areas.

The care of every one of your temptations is your heart. If you're tempted, never again blame anything or anyone, just hold up the mirror and point your finger at the person who's looking back at you. And, by the way, every time you feel tempted, you now know what desire is lurking in your heart at that very moment.

The Secret to Stage 2: *Every temptation can only tempt because of my personal desire.*

> "HOLINESS IS NOT FREEDOM FROM TEMPTATION, BUT POWER TO OVERCOME TEMPTATION."
>
> —G. Campbell Morgan

STAGE 3: THE LURE—"AND ENTICED"

This third stage is called "The Lure" because that's exactly what "entice" really means. If you've ever fished, you know the strategic importance of having the right lure and how it moves or has "action" through the water. This is the stage when the desire in you grows from a little urge to a burning desire. This is when you are allured and flattered and cunningly brought closer and closer to the heart of the temptation.

To entice means to attract artfully or skillfully by arousing hope or desire. Don't forget that although a particular thing can only tempt you because of your internal desire, that same thing can definitely work on your desire by fanning it hotter and hotter.

An interesting verse in Proverbs demonstrates both sides of the enticement, internal and external: "Do not lust after her beauty in your heart (your internal enticement), nor let her allure you with her eyelids" (her external enticement)(6:25).

What's the purpose of all enticement? To enlarge your desire so that it influences your thoughts and choices. This is the stage where you really "want" to do something. As your desire becomes stronger, you become less and less aware of everything else in your life and become incredibly focused upon that one thing you desire. Intense desire blinds doesn't it? The clearest passage in Proverbs about how enticement increases desire is in 7:10-22:

> And there a woman met him, with the attire of a harlot,
>   and a crafty heart.
> She was loud and rebellious, her feet would not stay at
>   home. At times she was outside, at times in the open

> square, lurking at every corner.
> So she caught him and kissed him; with an impudent
>   face she said to him...
> "Come, let us take our fill of love until morning; let us
>   delight ourselves with love. For my husband is not at
>   home; he has gone on a long journey...."
> With her enticing speech she caused him to yield,
>   with her flattering lips she seduced him.
> Immediately he went after her, as an ox goes to
>   the slaughter....

All that stage 3 does is throw dry wood on the smoldering fire of your desire. Wood can be thrown either by your internal heart or by the external actions of others. Every action of the external enticement is focused on just one thing—your desire growing until you don't care what it costs to get the thing you desire. In areas of temptation where you have not sinned at all or very little, it usually takes a long time of repetitive enticement to enlarge your desire enough so that you choose to sin.

However, if you have sinned in a specific area over and over, when that same temptation pokes its deceitful head above the horizon, your desire flashes so quickly that it may seem like you never passed through the "enticement" stage—but in reality, your desire didn't need to be stoked, it had a head of its own and was already precommitted to sin.

Enticement can be stopped. If the temptation is external, run away. If the temptation is internal, stop the self-talk immediately. The quicker you douse the growing flames, the easier to tame and control your desires. When your desires are controlled, the temptation fades.

The Secret to Stage 3: *Quench improper desire by stopping all internal and fleeing external enticements.*

STAGE 4: THE CONCEPTION—"WHEN DESIRE HAS CONCEIVED"

What an immense chasm exists between our "desire" and fulfilling that desire through "sin." Every temptation has one and only one goal: your sin. First the temptation draws you away, then your desire responds to it, then your desire grows through enticement, and fourth, your desire finally "conceives" the decision to sin. Note carefully the flow of this verse: "But each one is tempted when he is drawn away by his own desires and enticed. *Then, when desire has conceived*, it gives birth to sin...."

When does enticement end and "conception" begin in the stages of temptation? The moment you make the decision to fulfill your desire by sinning, enticement sits down, its work finished. Enticement is the powerful link from desire to decision.

Desire 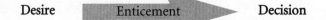 **Decision**

Enticement can only begin when desire has been aroused. How can you entice something which is sleeping or preoccupied? The flow of enticement drives desire right up that ramp until it feels like it literally overpowers your decision-making powers. That's why when you make the decision to commit the sin, you almost feel relieved or experience some type of emotional release. The pressure backs off and now it's time to sin.

The further along the enticement moves, the more it transitions through three specific phases. The longer the enticement stage, the easier it is to identify which of the enticement phases you are experiencing.

Enticement Phase 1: Emotional focus—"feelings"
Enticement Phase 2: Mental focus—"thoughts"
Enticement Phase 3: Volitional focus—"choices"

The three phases of your feelings, thoughts, and choices overlap and influence each other. We move from "desires" to "defending" to "deciding" we will sin.

The Three Phases of Enticement

Desire (Feelings) ➡ Defend (Thoughts) ➡ Decide (Choices)

During the Desire Phase, you experience growing emotional attraction to the temptation and you "feel" more and more strongly that you want to do it. The desire eventually pushes on your thoughts seeking justification or rationalization for giving into the sin.

During the Defend Phase, you start rationalizing to yourself why committing this sin is really justified. Two defense tactics are always used, the negative and the positive. To commit the sin, you must lessen the reasons not to do it (negative) and increase the reasons to do it (positive). Emotions never have the power to cause the person to sin, the mind and will are always involved and must give their permission and affirmation.

You slowly move the weights on the *Decision Balance* to shift your thoughts from reasons not to do something to reasons to do it. Sometimes you actually throw the reasons not to do something right off the balances or just stuff them deep within the caverns of your mind. Other times you may transition a reason not to do something into a reason to do something either by dredging up bad memories of past hurts a person may have done to you, or by inventing for them bad motives in your imagination.

The most powerful of all reasons to commit a sin is when you take a negative reason not to sin and turn it around into a positive reason to sin. It's amazing how creative we all are when our emotions are pushing at us. For instance, many married persons who are tempted to have an adulterous affair start with the negative reason that "they are married" and "I made my vows" and then destroy those reasons with memories of all the bad things their spouse did to them, ending up with the positive reason that "they are only getting exactly what they deserve, the dirty, rotten rat!"

During the Decide Phase, you make your choice. This is the last stage of the conception phase when you decide to commit the sin and begin planning when and how you will actually do it.

Remember the three phases of this stage as they are relatively easy to sense in your own life. First, you start being emotionally attracted to the sin; second, you start thinking of good reasons why you should commit the sin; third, you start planning how to do the sin. Although it may be difficult the first few times you try, learn how to read your own "pulse" in this issue. Just pay attention to where you are and you'll be amazed what you discover.

STAGE 4: THE SOFT SPOT OF TEMPTATION— "WHEN DESIRE HAS CONCEIVED"

As I counsel frequently, these three phases are helpful in discerning where a troubled believer is in their fall into sin. By asking one or two questions like "How would you commit this sin if you decided?" you'd be amazed what their answer will tell you. If they don't know, that's a good sign because they aren't in the "choice" stage.

This graph helps summarize the seven stages of temptation.

1	2	3	4	5	6	7
Look	Lust	Lure	Conception	Birth	Growth	Death
---------- EMOTION ----------		THOUGHT		WILL		
No Sin	No Sin	No Sin	Decide to Sin	Sin	More Sin	Most Sin

In looking at this chart, it's clear that victory over temptation is easier the earlier you end the temptation. As you begin to pay closer attention to your own feelings, thoughts, and choices, you will discern exactly where you are in these *seven stages*. This fourth stage is the weak spot in every temptation and the place where you must carefully focus your efforts. Remember the three phases:

The early phase: You are feeling strongly that you want to commit the sin.

The middle phase: You are thinking rapidly of reasons why you should do it.

The later phase: You are planning carefully how to get away with the sin.

Now, all three of those—feeling, thinking, and planning—occur right in you. They aren't subconscious feelings, thoughts, or plans, but conscious and right out in the open of your life. Although you may never have noticed them before, they are the lead actors of every temptation you have gone through.

So, what should you be asking yourself? First, *what am I feeling like I want to do?* On a scale of 1 to 10, how much do I really want to commit this sin? How long have I been feeling this way?

Second, *what am I thinking about this sin?* Am I trying to find reasons why this sin won't be that bad after all? Am I trying to justify myself because of other people's faults?

Third, *what am I planning to do with this sin?* Have I thought of when and where I'd commit this sin? Have I pictured it in my imagination?

Just by asking these simple questions, you'll immediately uncover exactly where you are on these three dangerous phases. If you can't think of any plans, but have just started a list of reasons, you are in the beginning of the middle phase.

Now, what should you do when you discover where you are? Realize that you haven't committed the sin yet so it's not too late. Recommit yourself to the truth and your obedience to the truth by affirming out loud such things as:

1. I am committed to live "holy in all my conduct."
2. I submit to the Lord and choose His will for my life.
3. I yield to the Holy Spirit and His work in my life.
4. I deny myself the lusts of the flesh.
5. I realize this is only a common temptation which everyone faces.
6. I believe the Lord is limiting this temptation to what I am able to bear.
7. I believe the Lord is making the way of escape for me right now.
8. I know the Lord is not the cause of this temptation.
9. I know the Lord is the giver of every good and perfect gift.

10. I know the Lord loves me and wants the best for me.
11. I know this sin not only displeases the Lord but will hurt me.
12. I have been drawn away by this temptation.
13. I have felt my desires pulling me toward this temptation.
14. I take every thought "captive for Christ" and stop all thoughts about this sin.
15. I affirm that I am fully aware of this temptation and am not deceived.
16. I know this temptation is aimed at my destruction.
17. I hereby choose to turn my back on this temptation.
18. I submit fully to Christ and resist the devil.
19. I present myself and all my members as weapons of righteousness.
20. I thank the Lord for His shed blood and my eternal salvation.

Just by praying and stating these truths—the "truth shall set you free"—you break the back of your lie! You'll be amazed how quickly the temptation will flee into the night when you bring out the Light!

The "Quick-Spit Principle" is a humorous but helpful insight taken from a fishing trip in Colorado I shared with my son, David. We had a guide who took us to a "hot" trout stream, where he guaranteed us we could catch all the trout we wanted. "It's so good," he told us, "every time you cast with one of my handcrafted lures, you're sure to catch a fish." He was quick to remind us that this was a "catch and release" section, so we could use only barbless hooks.

He took us out to his spot, positioned us along the edge of the stream, and directed us to cast the fly in one particular area, letting it drift with the current. I hit the spot dead on and watched the fly drift downstream. Nothing. As I prepared to recast, our guide said, "You missed him." I was surprised, and repeated the same cast. As I watched the fly float along, our guide suddenly said, "Missed another one." A few moments later he added, "Just missed another." I didn't know if he was psychic or just trying to lose his tip!

Frustrated, I handed my pole to our guide and suggested he step into the spot and show me what he meant. Then I stepped back and smiled smugly. His cast was in the exact same spot mine had been. Instantly, a big trout hit the fly! My son was doubled over in laughter as the guide handed me back the pole and reminded me there were many fish out there waiting for a chance at a fly, so I "couldn't miss one." I stepped forward, thinking he had "warmed up the spot," sensing it was my turn to catch the next one. My cast was in the exact same spot, and I leaned into the wind, taut with anticipation. Although I'm not a fishing guide, I have caught many fish in my lifetime, and this was getting a little embarrassing.

About thirty seconds later I heard him say those impossible words again: "You missed another one." I couldn't believe it! I hadn't felt the slightest vibration in my pole. I thrust the pole toward the guide, and another trout made a fool out of me with his very next cast. I couldn't stand it any longer, and asked him to let me in on his secret. Then, for the first time, he smiled.

"The fish here are real smart. Because they live in a catch and release section of the river, they've been caught dozens—maybe *scores* of times. They watch that fly go by, touch it to the front part of their lips, and if there's anything hard, they spit it out immediately. It only takes a split second. The reason you haven't caught one yet isn't because they haven't taken the fly, but because you haven't developed the touch required to set the hook in that split second before they 'quick spit' it back into the water!"

As I reflected on that the rest of the day, it occurred to me that like those trout we need to develop an incredible sense of awareness. Temptation may be seeking to hook us, so we need to learn to spit it out so quickly it never gets "set" in our lives. Those trout were like those mentioned in the Book of Hebrews: "Because of practice [they] have their senses trained to discern good and evil" (Hebrews 5:14).

May you and I become those who are so practiced in the ways of holiness we immediately can discern when the desires of our heart are going after that which will cause us to sin. How can you defeat temptation? Practice your "quick spit"!

The Secret to Stage 4: *Decide ahead of time not to sin, never permit yourself to think of one good reason to commit the sin, and you'll never make the choice to sin.*

STAGE 5: THE BIRTH—"IT GIVES BIRTH TO SIN"

The instant the decision to sin has been made in the will of the person is the same second that sin's "sperm" breaks through the person's "egg" and the life of that decision to sin has been conceived. In most cases, after a person has conceived sin by deciding to sin, the sin is quickly committed or birthed. In some cases, a period of time exists between the "conception" and the "birth" of the sin, during which the believer has one last opportunity to change his mind and forego the sin. During this "window of opportunity," the Holy Spirit frequently works powerfully, pleading with the believer in order to stop the sin. Conviction floods the heart, and the Lord once more extends mercy by offering the believer one last opportunity for deliverance.

The Secret to Stage 5: *If you're enroute to commit the sin, force yourself to submit to the conviction of the Holy Spirit and abort the sin before it's too late.*

STAGE 6: THE GROWTH— "AND SIN, WHEN FULL-GROWN"

Every sin grows. If you've given into rage, rage grows; if you've given into lust, lust grows; if you've given into the love of money, the love of money grows. Sin is never satisfied with only one time. Sin is addictive.

Sin grows like a living organism from conception to birth to full-grown. Between birth and full-grown are all the intermediate stages as sin grows and develops. One sin grows and spreads to the next sin and the next. Sin is never satisfied with the same level of that same sin and degenerates into deeper and longer sin. Sin seeks to rule.

The Secret to Stage 6: *Every sin you commit digs your grave; never believe for a moment the lie "just let me sin this one more time" as every sin strengthens itself against you for the next time.*

STAGE 7: THE DEATH—"BRINGS FORTH DEATH"

The power and presence of sin grow steadily as the believer repeatedly chooses to sin. Over time and through repeated defeat in the face of this particular temptation, the believer slowly experiences a most destructive trend. In the earlier stages of practicing this sin, he could easily choose to stop the sin, but in the later stages, he can barely resist it—even with all of his determination and sincere prayers.

Although some believers today teach that a true believer cannot fall prey to the power of sin, the Bible teaches that you can and everyone's experience validates that it happens. The Bible repeatedly warns of the severe danger of coming under the rulership of sin as a believer. A whole book could be written on this subject, but here are a few passages to stimulate your own study:

> Therefore *do not let sin reign* in your mortal body, that you should obey it in its lusts....*For sin shall not have dominion over you*....Do you not know that to whom you present yourselves slaves to obey, you are that one's slaves whom you obey, whether of sin leading to death, or of obedience leading to righteousness?...For just as you presented your members as slaves of uncleanness, and of *lawlessness leading to more lawlessness*, so now present your members as slaves of righteousness for holiness (Romans 6:12,14a,16,19b).

As you read Romans 6, it's obvious by Paul's commands "not to let sin reign" that sin can certainly reign in a believer's life—that's why he gave this command. Sin can have "dominion" over any believer who consistently succumbs to its temptations. In addition, "lawlessness leads to more lawlessness," validating the concept that a certain amount of sin always grows to a larger amount of sin. Last, note the phrase "whether *sin to death* or of obedience to righteousness," which pictures a "death" that spreads like cancer in the life of the believer who lives under the dominion of a certain sin.

What does this "death" look like? It's a slow darkness that creeps like the early morning fog over the landscape of a person's life. Joy, peace, and assurance slowly depart, only to be replaced by depression, anxiety, and doubt. I have found that believers who experience an extended period of dominion under the harsh taskmaster of sin eventually begin to doubt everything until they doubt even their own salvation.

"How could anyone who is saved ever live a life of secret sin like I do?" The biblical answer: By continual presentation of your life to that sin, you not only can live a life of sin, you inevitably will. Continual sin always spreads darkness:

> He who says he is in the light, and hates his brother, *is in darkness until now.* He who loves his brother abides in the light, and there is no cause for stumbling in him. But he who hates his brother is in darkness and *walks in darkness,* and does not know where he is going, *because the darkness has blinded his eyes* (1 John 2:9-11).

The deeper into sin a believer goes, the deeper into darkness he falls. As the believer continues to practice sin over and over again, his eyes slowly become blinded. He cannot see that which he used to see quite easily. When you meet a believer who is "blinded" or "hardened" to obvious truth in a part of their life, you instantly know there could be a major sin in their life which has been practiced for some time. That person may be in terrible bondage.

As the bondage grows, even the thoughts of what to do in order to become free again are lost to this person. He can't see because of the cataracts of reigning sin. This fierce taskmaster of sin keeps pushing and pushing until the believer loses all self-control in that area of sin:

> And a servant of the Lord must not quarrel but be gentle to all, able to teach, patient, in humility correcting those who are in opposition, *if God perhaps will grant them repentance,* so that *they may know the truth,* and that

they may *come to their senses* and *escape the snare of the devil*, having been *taken captive by him to do his will* (2 Timothy 2:24-26).

What a shocking revelation! Although some may teach that this passage doesn't apply to believers, the context proves that it does. This isn't a "salvation" passage as the paragraph above it is clearly describing sinful behavior, not unbelief in Jesus as the Savior. Can a believer actually "be taken captive (by the devil) to do his will" in one area of his life? Absolutely. I can't tell you the number of times I have been involved with believers all across our world who come to me in frightened desperation seeking freedom from terrible bondage to sin. Their eternal salvation isn't the problem; instead, they have lost their "sense," fallen into the "snare of the devil," and are now "captive...to do his will."

They didn't lose their salvation because of that sin—they only need to be freed from it and they'll once again walk in holiness. That's why Paul tells the Romans who are under the dominion of sin to present themselves to the Lord and get under the dominion of righteousness. He doesn't tell them to get saved. Or get saved again. Paul doesn't tell Timothy to lead those who are in bondage to believe in Jesus Christ as their Savior. Instead he tells him "in humility correct" them so "God perhaps will grant them repentance" for their sin so they may "know the truth," come to their "senses," "escape the snare of the devil" in this area, and break his terrible captivity.

The Secret to Stage 7: *Regardless of the degree of bondage you are under, the work of Christ is sufficient to set you completely free.*

YOU CAN DEFEAT TEMPTATION

In ministry for the Lord, there's hardly anything more wonderful than watching this miracle of freedom from the dominion of sin actually take place in the life of a believer. It's wonderful! In the past three weeks, I dealt with two men in this very issue. The first took 4½ hours before we kneeled on the floor and wept as he finally came to his senses and wept bitterly before the Lord and broke the enemy's bond over him. The second one took less than an hour. You should have seen him and his wife the next morning. Absolutely transformed!

Were these men solid believers? Absolutely. Were they in bondage to the enemy in at least one particular area? Yes, and they were quick to admit that to me. Were their minds blinded? Certainly. Were they walking in darkness in this area of their life? Without question. Were they captive to the enemy's will in this area? Both men described themselves with the words "helpless" and "bondage."

The first was a pastor of 15 years. The second was a pastor of 45 years. The first had been in bondage for 18 months. The second had been in bondage for over 50 years. Don't ever believe that it can't happen to you, my friend. The result of a choice to willfully sin has terrible and destructive consequences which can literally destroy your life and the lives of many people around you.

But the incredible good news is that the precious blood of Jesus has set us completely free. In fact, 1 John 3:8b states it powerfully: "For this purpose the Son of God was manifested, that He might destroy the works of the devil." Freedom from all bondage to sin is provided by the death and resurrection of Jesus and is the full right and privilege of every believer. My friend, if you are in bondage to sin in your life right now, I want to encourage you. It is never too late to turn around, repent, come to your senses, and be released from the clutches of your enemy.

Your life can be fully cleansed. Your conscience can become clean. No sin, no bondage, and no devil can ever overpower our mighty Deliverer, the Lord Jesus! Go back to chapter five and carefully work your way through the Ten Steps of Deep Cleansing. If you still struggle, go see your pastor or another person of godliness. Reveal your sin and ask for their help.

The Lord always gives grace to those who humble themselves seeking His cleansing!

8

OUR CULTURE'S
TOUGHEST TEMPTATION

*"Sensuality is easily the biggest obstacle to godliness...
today and is wreaking havoc in the church. Godliness and
sensuality are mutually exclusive and those in the grasp
of sensuality can never rise to godliness while in its
sweaty grip."*

—R. Kent Hughes

In an evening meeting with a group of 40 men recently, I
asked what they felt were the three biggest temptations men
face today. A man in the first row instantly called out:
"Number 1: sex; number 2: sex; number 3: sex!" The room exploded
with laughter.

In a recent survey, Christian men were asked to list the sins they
struggled with most. When the results were compiled, sexual immorality of one type or another represented 62 percent of all the
sins listed. (The next most frequently named sin only garnered 12
percent.) For men, the problem of sexual immorality is five times
greater than the next biggest sin problem.

Lest you think this is a male-only problem, there is increasing
evidence that women are as tempted as men to sin sexually—from
fantasizing to physical immorality. Look at the popular "soaps"
watched by millions of women which move from one lurid sexual
encounter to another. When discussing this problem with a traveling salesman recently, he laughed out loud and spouted, "For every

sexual affair in my office, or one-night fling on a business trip, I've noticed there's always a *woman* just as involved as the *man!*" And two days ago, Darlene and I led a couples retreat during which one executive shared the challenge of younger women who regularly engage in sexual immorality with traveling salesmen or bosses in order to move up the corporate ladder.

Research has revealed the most popular sites on the Internet today are not business or communication, but pornography. Lest you think this is a "secular" problem which hasn't infiltrated the ranks of believers, spend a few moments talking to any Christian college student about how rampant and destructive this problem is on campus.

So before moving onto the topic of "positive holiness," I thought it would be helpful to zero in on the single greatest temptation problem in our society. Sexual immorality is clearly the most widespread and destructive of all sins in our culture, yet it is rarely preached about or openly discussed in Christian circles. Left unchallenged, it eventually rules and ruins the lives of those under its dominion. Soon men and women lose all hope of ever being "free" and "clean" again—and slide into the dark, solitary prison of defeat and despair.

DOES GOD UNDERSTAND YOUR SEX DRIVE?

Let me ask you a strategic question: Do you think the Lord really understands your sex drive? Do you believe He created you, including your sex drive, but something went wrong in the process? Perhaps God looks the other way and "winks" at immorality. Maybe when the Lord said, "Be holy in all your conduct," He decided to overlook the problem of sexual immorality. Or perhaps you think the Lord did indeed create man and woman with strong sex drives, but just enjoys watching them squirm. In that case, God must be one big tease—giving you something you strongly desire and then mockingly saying, "Don't!"

All those thoughts couldn't be further from the truth. The Lord invented sex and gave the sex drive to mankind as a wonderful gift for many good reasons. God fully knows and understands the desires and needs that accompany this gift, and He provided a most remarkable answer for its full enjoyment and fulfillment. Don't forget, when the Lord said, "Be holy in all your conduct" that He included the area of sexual immorality. You are to be holy in every single part of your life and behavior—including everything to do with your sexual life.

> "THERE ARE MANY OUTWARD TEMPTATIONS THAT BEST MEN, EXCITING AND STIMULATING THEM TO DO EVIL. BUT THE ROOT AND SPRING OF ALL THESE THINGS LIE IN THE HEART. TEMPTATIONS DO NOT PUT ANYTHING INTO A MAN THAT IS NOT THERE ALREADY."
>
> —John Owen

This is a delicate subject, so we need to keep three things in mind as we explore the topic. First, *we have to remain biblical.* The Bible doesn't leave us in the dark about this issue, but reveals the very mind and heart of God about sexuality and sexual immorality. The main passage in the New Testament on sexual immorality will be unashamedly presented as God's answer to the problem. I will not add current psychological or sociological comment to the Word of God in this discussion; instead, I will open the verses which contain the direct answer to the questions.

Second, *we need to be straightforward.* Of all chapters, these will be the most difficult to write, and perhaps to read. Sexuality is a very private matter. In struggling with how to deal with this sensitive issue, the Lord reminded me that what He said and how He said it in Scripture reveal exactly what He wants us to know. Nothing more and nothing less. Throughout these discussions, we are going to deal with one primary passage, written under inspiration of God through Paul to a local church. When this letter was received, it was read out loud to the whole congregation. Paul wrote these straightforward words to a mixed audience and the audience heard them in an open, public setting. Therefore, I will be as straightforward as the Bible is in these matters of our sexuality.

Third, *we need to be focused.* This book is about dealing with sexual temptation, not attacking the ills of immorality in our culture at large. If you feel that I am glossing over cultural issues, remember my focus: What does the Bible teach about sexual immorality? Space does not permit a broad and complete presentation of love in marriage, so this chapter is narrowly focused on precisely what one primary New Testament passage teaches on God's solution to sexual immorality.*

GOD'S STANDARD OF SEXUAL CONDUCT

Many people, including Christians, are not clear in their own minds what is "holy" behavior and what isn't in sexual areas. Years ago, when I was teaching a *7 Laws of the Learner* training conference at a hotel, I experienced first-hand the deep confusion regarding God's standards of sexuality in a most amazing way. On the second afternoon, many of the attendees were scattered around the hotel swimming pool talking and discussing what they were learning about how to teach so people actually learn. I joined a number of them, and we had quite a discussion going when I asked each of them to share their names, where they were from, and what brought them to the conference.

We went around the circle of faces, and eventually a young woman announced she was enjoying the conference, having flown in from another state with her boyfriend. She added her boyfriend couldn't be with us, since he was up in their room watching the baseball game. I smiled and asked her if he was attending the course as well but she said, "No, he's not a Christian yet but wanted to come with me."

As you can imagine, her words about sharing a room with her boyfriend at a Walk Thru the Bible conference presented a delicate moment. I asked her if they had spent the night together, and she unashamedly said they had and had been living together for almost two years. (I noticed that at that point, no one around that previously animated group seemed to be breathing any longer.)

"Are you a Christian yet, or still on the way to Christ?" I asked.

---

* For further personal study on the larger subject of marriage, I would recommend Walk Thru the Bible's 12-part video series, *The Biblical Portrait of Marriage*.

"Oh, I've been a Christian for almost five years and really growing." She named her home church and enthusiastically said she really enjoyed her Sunday school class.

I shot up a quick prayer for grace and asked, "How do you think God feels about you two living together?"

"It's fine!" she answered with a bright smile, "I think he's going to become a Christian, and when he does then we'll be married."

"If God said you shouldn't have sex or live together before you are married," I continued, "what do you think you would do?"

By her body language it was clear that idea had never struck her before. "Well, I would have to ask my boyfriend to leave. It would be hard, but I love God and would do what He asked. Why?"

I looked around our little group, but as you would expect, a Bible doesn't typically seem to accompany a pool in the middle of a hot afternoon. "How about going back up to your room and bringing back the Gideon Bible? I'll show you something very important about the will of God for you and your boyfriend—I think you'll be very interested."

Off she went. No one around our pool circle seemed to have anything to say. Some of the more discerning were praying, as this was obviously an unexpected divine appointment. In the next few moments, I showed her the key biblical passages and then had her read them out loud for everyone else. In short order she saw what the will of God was—no one had to tell her, because she read it with her own eyes right from the Bible.

Then, for the first time, she became uncomfortable. Not from any of us, but from the internal, convicting work of the Holy Spirit. She slowly looked up from the Bible and said, "Then what I'm doing is 'fornication'—and a big sin in God's eyes, right?"

I nodded and waited for the Holy Spirit to lead her.

"Well," and her eyes flooded with tears, "then my boyfriend has to leave. We can't live together until we are married. Right?" I nodded in sincere affirmation. How kind the Lord was to lead her so gently to His will.

I will never forget what she said next: "I grew up in a totally non-Christian home. I didn't know anyone who was a Christian. All my friends slept together, so I never thought much about it. But I've been a Christian for *five years,* going to church almost every week. *How come no one ever told me sleeping together before you were married was a sin?"*

At that moment, everyone around our group looked up. No one spoke as the conviction of the Lord moved from the sin of this young lady to the massive sin of believer's everywhere who have hidden the clear teachings of the Bible because of their fear of rejection or ridicule. Something deep inside of me broke when she asked that probing and painful question. Since then, I have not taken anything for granted. May the Lord grant this same conviction to all who know His Word.

Defining Sexual Immorality

What specifically is sexual sin? Listed below are the five major biblical descriptions of sexual sin.

1. Sexual immorality is sex before marriage with anyone. One unmistakable standard of the Bible regarding sexual behavior is that sex before marriage with anyone is clearly sin. Generally, sex between unmarried people is called the sin of fornication, between married individuals it is called the sin of adultery, between those of the same gender it is called the sin of homosexuality.

Sex before marriage with the person you marry is just as much fornication as sex with a person you don't marry. Engaged couples are not married until they are legally married by a civil or religious authority and until they consummate their marriage following their wedding service. Sexual relations by engaged couples prior to their marriage ceremony is fornication. Engaged couples who say "secret vows" to each other in order to engage in sexual relations before they are formally married are not married in the Lord's eyes and are still committing the sexual sin of fornication.

Every once in a while, I meet an umarried couple who have had sex and think that they must therefore be married in God's eyes. Sex before marriage is never called marriage in the Bible, it is always called the sin of fornication or adultery. The will of God is clear: no sexual relations with anyone until after marriage.

2. Sexual immorality is sexual intercourse after marriage with anyone but your spouse. After marriage, a sexual relationship with any person except the person you are married to is always called sexual immorality.

3. Sexual immorality is any sexual activity with anyone but your spouse. Sexual immorality includes anything one person does with another person (except his or her spouse) for the purpose of sexual pleasure or satisfaction. This includes sexual activities undertaken alone, with a child, a family member (incest), or a hired sexual partner (prostitute). All are immoral in the Lord's sight.

> "A RELATIONSHIP CAN BE SEXUAL LONG BEFORE IT BECOMES EROTIC. JUST BECAUSE I'M NOT TOUCHING A WOMAN, OR JUST BECAUSE I'M NOT ENVISIONING SPECIFIC EROTIC ENCOUNTERS, DOES NOT MEAN I'M NOT BECOMING SEXUALLY INVOLVED WITH HER. THE EROTIC IS USUALLY NOT THE BEGINNING BUT THE CULMINATION OF SEXUAL ATTRACTION."
>
> —Randy Alcorn

4. Sexual immorality is doing anything by oneself for the purpose of sexual arousal. This general principle is of great assistance in helping a believer define if he or she is moving into sexual immorality. The Bible directs the fulfillment of sexual desires toward the marriage partner. Purposefully seeking sexual arousal or satisfaction with anyone or anything except a spouse is not within the will of God. This would include the "900" sex lines, Internet sex sites, and massage parlors which exist for the purpose of sexual arousal. Close and intimate relationships after marriage with a person of the opposite sex can also lead to emotional and sexual infidelity and should be avoided.

5. Sexual immorality includes lustful thoughts. Jesus clearly defines "lustful thoughts" as sexual immorality in Matthew 5:28: "But I say to you that whoever looks at a woman to lust for her has already committed adultery with her in his heart." Pornography includes lewd magazines, racy novels, strip-tease establishments, movies and videos with nakedness or sexual immorality, and talk shows which promote sexual immorality. All are produced to stimulate sexual immorality.

Now that you know the Lord's standards of sexual conduct, how would you evaluate your sexual behavior in the sight of the Lord during the past few months? Have you been sexually pure or impure? Have you pursued either directly or indirectly sexual arousal or sexual pleasure with anyone or anything except your marriage partner? Or if you aren't married, are you practicing celibacy both mentally and physically?

If you are like many, you may be feeling more than challenged about the Lord's standards and your behavior. Often three major questions surface at this point:

- What is God's answer to my sex drive?
- How do I handle my struggles with self-control?
- When sexual temptations arrive, how can I defeat them?

In this chapter, you are going to read for yourself the remarkable—and perhaps shocking—revelation of the Bible's powerful answer to all three of these crucial questions.

THE LORD'S PRIMARY PROVISION FOR SEXUAL TEMPTATIONS

First Corinthians 7:2-5 (NASB) presents the Lord's remarkable answer to sexual temptations. Read through this passage slowly before studying the seven principles:

> But because of immoralities, let each man have his own wife, and let each woman have her own husband. Let the husband fulfill his duty to his wife, and likewise also the wife to her husband. The wife does not have authority over her own body, but the husband does; and likewise also the husband does not have authority over his own body, but the wife does. Stop depriving one another, except by agreement for a time that you may devote yourselves to prayer, and come together again lest Satan tempt you because of your lack of self-control.

1. The Lord Reveals That "Because of Sexual Immoralities," Each Person Should Marry

Paul writes, *"Because of immoralities,* let each man have his own wife and let each woman have her own husband." Think for a moment: If someone came up to you and asked you what the biblical answer to sexual immoralities is, what would you say? To pray? To read your Bible? To use self-control? All these are good ideas, but none of them is God's specific answer. The Lord's provision for immorality is to get married! This verse is the most direct revelation regarding God's plan to provide for our sex drives in a way that pleases Him. Therefore marriage is to be considered "holy" and set apart unto Him.

Marriage couldn't really be the answer to all kinds of sexual immoralities, could it? What about pornography? How could marriage solve the temptations on the Internet? What about the temptations you face in the marketplace and on the road? Don't miss the answer: *Marriage is the answer to "immoralities" of all different kinds.* Why? Because sexual immorality is always related to only one thing: your sex drive. Sexual immoralities are the multiple ways you seek to have your sex drive fulfilled. When your sex drive is satisfied, multiple immoralities are relieved.

Marriage is God's primary solution to life's sexual temptations. The words *"let each man have his own wife, and let each woman have her own husband"* are imperatives—positive commands which are to be obeyed unless God uniquely circumvents that norm with the rare "gift of singleness."

God commands people to get married because of sexual immoralities. This command isn't some general principle, but very personal as demonstrated with the words "let each man" and "let each woman." Immorality is a problem both to men and to women, and the solution is the same one for both: Get married!

At the time of the New Testament, marriages occurred during and around the age of puberty. Marriage permitted the blossoming sex drive to be fulfilled and not frustrated. Today, however, marriages are postponed until later in life due to various educational, vocational, and financial pressures. The longer a human being postpones marriage past puberty, the more sexual temptations he or she will naturally have to face.

The majority of young people, including Christians, are sexually immoral and commit fornication before marriage. Perhaps the most influencing reason for this immorality is the postponement of marriage. It appears that the average Christian has decided sexual fornication is to be preferred to marriage due to the cultural constraints on schooling and the personal pleasures of an independent, covetous lifestyle.

Should people get married if they cannot handle their God-given sex drives? God's Word clearly states, "...*if they cannot exercise self-control, let them marry. For it is better to marry than to burn with passion*" (1 Corinthians 7:9). In the present unnatural postponement of marriage, many individuals give in to their sexual temptations and choose to become sexually immoral in one way or another. This sexual release outside of marriage greatly lessens God's dramatic and universal timetable. By finding sexual satisfaction outside the marriage union, millions of singles are circumventing the God-given pressure for a mate, bypassing the normal marriage timetable.

I have spoken at many Christian singles conferences in my lifetime, and I can tell you that, tragically, the vast majority of singles are sexually active and therefore sexually immoral. Because they have found "release" for their God-given drives in a God-condemned manner, their personal marital clock has been radically affected.

Are there exceptions to this? Of course. But all research, whether Christian or secular, clearly demonstrates the exception is an all-too-rare situation. At what age do you think most Christian young people commit sexual fornication? Fourteen to nineteen. And at what age do you think most Christian young people marry today? Twenty-four to thirty.

I'll never forget a conversation I had with a friend at one of our Walk Thru the Bible conferences in Phoenix, Arizona. A morning session on sexual immorality had surfaced some intense interest and discussion, and on my way back to my room a long-time friend began walking beside me. "Bruce," he told me, "I just don't know what to tell these younger guys any more."

"What do you mean," I wondered out loud, surprised because he has been discipling men for almost half a century.

"Well," he continued, looking kind of sheepish, "some of these guys have real sexual problems—with temptations and immoral things—I don't know what to tell them." Then, after a pause, he added, "Bruce, I can't identify with all their problems. My wife has always met all my sexual needs, and, well, I just don't have any frustrations in that area."

I can still remember the impact of his honest and vulnerable words. I stopped right in the middle of that hallway and looked him directly in the eyes. "You have nailed the Bible's answer! You are not sexually immoral not only because of your commitment to Christ, but because you have practiced God's perfect plan against temptations to sexual immorality—sex in marriage!" Then I turned to this very verse, showed it to him, and said, "Show it to them, teach it to them, don't mince any words, and don't back down one inch. But...make sure you share how it's worked so wonderfully in your 50-year marriage!"

Marriage is God's primary solution to sexual immoralities.

2. The Lord Commands Married Partners to "Fulfill Their Sexual Duties"

Paul continues, "Let the husband *fulfill his duty* to his wife, and likewise also the wife to her husband" (1 Corinthians 7:3 NASB). The Lord anticipated this particular problem. Just because someone gets married, all sexual temptations are not immediately solved. Marriage is the only God-approved release for one's sex drive, but it doesn't become that release for many men and women. In fact, many married men and women are the most sexually immoral. You see, *marriage* isn't the answer...*sex within marriage is!* But what happens if the husband won't respond to his wife's sexual advances? Her sexual drive becomes frustrated and she is tempted toward sexual immoralities.

The Bible teaches that marriage is both a delight as well as a duty. A "duty" is a moral or legal responsibility of obligation that arises from one's position. It is the duty of each marital partner to

> "GOD INTENDS, AS THE STORY OF EVE'S CREATION FROM ADAM SHOWS, THAT THE 'ONE FLESH' EXPERIENCE SHOULD BE AN EXPRESSION AND A HEIGHTENING OF THE PARTNER'S SENSE THAT, BEING GIVEN TO EACH OTHER, THEY NOW BELONG TOGETHER, EACH NEEDING THE OTHER FOR COMPLETION AND WHOLENESS. CHILDREN ARE BORN FROM THEIR RELATIONSHIP, BUT THIS IS SECONDARY: WHAT IS BASIC IS THE ENRICHING OF THEIR RELATIONSHIP ITSELF THROUGH THEIR REPEATED 'KNOWING' OF EACH OTHER AS PERSONS WHO BELONG TO EACH OTHER EXCLUSIVELY AND WITHOUT RESERVE."
>
> —J. I. Packer

meet the sex drive of their partner. Note that the Bible reveals the duty is toward the spouse: The husband has a duty "to his wife" and the wife has a duty "to her husband." The thought behind these words isn't that the husband's duty is to have sex with his wife if he wants it, but it is his duty to respond to his wife if she wants to have sex, and vice versa.

The duty does not belong to the person who *initiates* the sex, but to the person who *responds*. For instance, let's say the husband makes sexual overtures to his wife—this verse teaches that it is the wife's duty to have sex. Why? Because in this case, the husband has a sexual drive seeking fulfillment, and it's her duty to make sure his needs are met.

Therefore, whenever your spouse initiates sex in your direction, make sure you keep in mind your marital duty.

It may surprise you to think of all the words God could have chosen to express what He wanted in the marriage context, and yet He chose "duty." This is clearly a word of responsibility and obligation. When you marry, you are under God-given obligation to meet your spouse's sexual needs.

That same sentence uses the word "fulfill": "Let the husband *fulfill* his duty to his wife, and likewise also the wife (fulfill) to her husband." To "fulfill" means to make full, to bring to completion, to measure up to the total, to develop the full potential. To "fulfill a promise" means to complete fully that which was promised. To "fulfill a duty" means to completely accomplish that duty. Since the "duty" is related to the spouse not committing sexual immorality, the actions of both partners should satisfy the sexual needs in such a way that each partner would say they are fully satisfied. "Completely satisfied" captures the meaning of the biblical words "fulfilled duty."

Which of the two marital partners must be the one to decide if the sexual drives or desires are completely satisfied? The one initiating sex. *In other words, the only way a husband can know if he has "fulfilled his duty" as a husband is to ask his wife, "Are your sexual needs fully satisfied?"*

After counseling hundreds of couples over the past thirty years, I can promise you that it is the rare married couple who understands and practices this biblical principle. The "duty" of sex is never for yourself but always for your spouse. The sense of duty being fulfilled is in reference to your partner's needs. The Bible conclusively puts the responsibility to satisfy sexual needs under the "duty" of the marriage partner. *In general terms, the married partner should view his or her duty as being whatever it takes (which is not illegal or immoral) to satisfy the sexual needs of his or her partner.*

I'll never forget talking to a man in a parking lot after a *Personal Holiness Conference*. His marriage had ended in divorce after he committed adultery numerous times and his wife discovered it. He was a broken man, and his eyes filled with tears as he said, "...if only my wife had believed what the Bible teaches about sex in marriage my life might not be the total wreck it is today. She protected and ruled her body, using it as a carrot or a stick in my life. Oh, I know committing adultery isn't my wife's fault, it's mine. But if she would have had sex with me more than once a month, this might never have happened. She turned me away hundreds of times in our marriage, until I didn't even bother to risk the pain of rejection again. I looked elsewhere. The amazing thing is, I didn't *want* to go anywhere else. I loved my wife—but she decided if I had sex with another woman it proved I didn't love her. So she divorced me. I think how life could have been so very different if she had known and believed Scripture."

There are always extenuating circumstances in a divorce, but I wonder if that wife knows the part she played in her husband's immorality. She directly withheld from her husband the only acceptable fulfillment of his sexual needs. That's the point of this passage—because of sexual immorality, she was to fulfill her duty. They both sinned gravely by disobeying the Lord's clear command.

3. The Lord Gave the Authority Over Your Physical Body to Your Spouse

> "The wife *does not have authority over her own body*, but the husband does. And likewise the husband does not have authority over his own body, but the wife does" (1 Corinthians 7:4).

When you understand what God said in this verse, you may be shocked. When I fully came to grips with it, I began to understand the Lord's intense hatred for sexual immorality, and the extensive provision He made for our sexual purity. This verse reveals the remarkable extent to which a husband and wife are to fulfill their duty regarding the sexual needs and desires of their partners.

God sovereignly takes something away at the point of marriage and gives it as a heavenly wedding present to your spouse. The Lord doesn't ask you if He can take it, and the Lord doesn't ask you if you want it. Sovereignly, the Lord takes the authority you have had over your own body and removes it from you for as long as you live. He gives the right over your body to your spouse. There can be no confusion as to how serious He is about your sexual immorality and His provision for your sexual satisfaction.

Where is the only place your partner can express his or her sexual needs and be holy? With you, and only with you. Not with another person. Not even alone. The Bible only reveals one place that holiness can be completely fulfilled regarding sexual desires: by sex within marriage.

To make sure you are never withholding the only God-given provision to sex, God takes your body away from you and gives it as a gift to your spouse. Literally, *your spouse owns your body*. And because God gave your body to your spouse, your spouse only shows graciousness by asking you for it. Your spouse doesn't "borrow" your body, doesn't need to "beg" for your body, doesn't even need to be "affectionate" for your body. In raw and uncomplicated terms, God gave my body to my wife, and I had nothing to say about it. The term "authority" in this passage literally means "has rights over" or "has exclusive claim to." As one highly respected authority wrote on this verse: "Married persons no longer control their own bodies but must surrender authority over them to their spouses."

Success and victory in marriage are always a result of following the clear teachings of the Bible on a regular and enduring basis. It's a most comforting and encouraging thought to realize this idea wasn't man's or Satan's, but was only the Lord's. Nor was this the Lord's idea only for your spouse's pleasure and protection, but equally for yours. Not only did the Lord give you sexual drives and desires, but He also protects you from the trauma and destruction of sexual infidelity. His major protection for you against all kinds of sexual immorality is His gift to you of your spouse's body for your sexual satisfaction.

This clear teaching from the Bible goes directly against the independent, self-orientation of our modern culture. The thought that God gave your body to your spouse for his or her sexual satisfaction surfaces several reactions which must be carefully thought through in the life of each couple. After discussions on this topic with many couples, three misconceptions seem to inevitably surface.

First, some people think that *sex is inherently dirty, sinful, or given solely for children*. The Bible consistently teaches that sex is a gift from God, that you are to relish your sexual life as a couple independent to having children, and that to be naked before your spouse is nothing to be ashamed about. The Lord wouldn't exhort you to "fulfill your sexual duty" and "give your body to your spouse" if sex within marriage was in any manner wrong or less than holy. Marriage is "holy" because the Lord has set aside that relationship from every other relationship in the world.

A second misconception is that *sex is either a reward or punishment.* The Lord already gave authority over your body to your spouse, so sex is not to be withheld as a punishment or bestowed as a reward. Sex is not to be offered solely because a spouse has been kind, given a nice gift, come home on time, cleaned the house, not overspent the charge card, or for some reason "deserves" your sex. Neither can sex be withheld due to a spouse being unkind, harsh, forgetful, late messy, or a spendthrift. God takes sex out of the "reward and punishment" arena and places it within your spouse's authority to enjoy or not to enjoy.

A third misconception about sex is that *it is an optional part of marriage depending upon one's moods or preferences.* Most married people tend to consider sexual intimacy within their authority, rather than within their spouse's. Many don't initiate sexual intimacy due to a fear of rejection—yet this passage bluntly takes the option of rejection away. The proverbial excuses about "headaches" or "I'm too tired" or "come on, we just had sex last night!" fall under the false mindset that my body is my own and I can do with it as I please. When the Christian married person fully embraces this delegation of authority, their marriage undergoes an amazing and wonderful transition.

As you can see, this passage carries profound implications. Christian marriages are to reflect the Lord's wishes and be characterized by selfless love. No wonder there is such widespread immorality—the Lord's primary solution for sexual immorality is so widely abandoned! It the will of God that marries men and women experience satisfaction and fulfillment in their sexual lives. It is *not* the will of God that married men and women experience frustration and disappointment in their sexual lives.

4. The Lord Commands You to "Stop Depriving One Another" of Sex

> *Stop depriving one another,* except by agreement for a time that you may devote yourselves to prayer, and come together again lest Satan tempt you because of your lack of self-control (1 Corinthians 7:5 NASB).

Just imagine this happening at 6:00 P.M. as you arrive home from work. As you walk in the back door, you announce, "Wow, am I hungry! I can't wait until dinner." Your spouse looks up and says, "What are you talking about?

> "THE SEXUAL PROHIBITIONS OF GOD'S WORD WEREN'T GIVEN TO SPOIL MAN'S FUN, BUT TO PRESERVE HEALTH AND SEXUAL VITALITY."
>
> —William Backus

I made you breakfast and you ate it. Then you went out for lunch, and you ate again. Now you want me to make dinner for you. What are you, some kind of glutton or what?"

If this were you, how would you feel at that moment? As you turned to answer, what if your spouse continued, "And besides that, you're always thinking of yourself. Your hunger. Your timetable. You are so selfish!"

Now, that illustration would obviously never happen. Why not? Because everyone knows just because you've eaten breakfast and lunch, that food doesn't even begin to fill you at supper time. No one would call you selfish regarding your God-given desire for food at meal times, would they? So if a man had sex the night before, why does he somehow feel "selfish" for desiring it two nights in a row? And why should we look down upon a woman who desires sex more than her husband?

Is the need for food God-given and good?

Is the need for sex God-given and therefore good?

The answer must be equally "yes" to both questions.

Why then is there so much trouble and confusion and emotional frustration surrounding the sex drive and none around the food drive? As far as I can tell, there are three reasons.

First, the food drive can be fulfilled without anyone else's participation. Only three minutes ago, I went upstairs and made myself a good cup of coffee and a piece of toast. Guess what? It didn't require any attention from anyone. The sex drive, on the other hand, requires the active participation of another person every single time it is to be fulfilled according to God's Word.

Second, the food drive has been put into everyone exactly the same. Everyone gets hungry at least three times a day. In our culture, everyone knows and expects to eat at breakfast, lunch, and dinner. And, unless something unusual is happening, everyone gets hungry at about the same time. The Lord created man, woman, and child to all get hungry at relatively the same frequency. The sex drive, on the other hand, has often been placed into most men at a much higher frequency than most women. This difference represents a sovereign choice by our Creator God. The Lord forced all marriages to experience a certain disequilibrium regarding our built-in sexual clocks.

I can't tell you the number of men who feel "selfish" because of their God-given sex drives.

The need for sex in varying frequencies has nothing to do with men or women but everything to do with God. Men are no more "selfish" by needing sex more frequently than women are more "selfless" by needing sex less frequently.

"Selfishness" should not be applied to the sexual drive any more than "selfishness" should be applied to desiring to eat three times a day.

Whenever this series is taught, initially a few of the women in the audience become defensive: "If I let my husband have sex as often as he wanted, we'd have sex every single night!" Just read that sentence one more time, but now from the Lord's perspective. Return for a moment to the illustration of the desire for food. Let's say when the wife came home from the office for dinner, though it was her husband's time to cook, he not only hadn't prepared anything, but had locked up all the food too. What would she be tempted to do that evening? Right—go searching in the cupboards for food. Let's say her husband told her, "If you eat food elsewhere, you'll be unfaithful to me and it will prove you don't love me."

Do you know what would soon happen? That wife would stop looking for food in her own home and start looking for it on the way home in someone else's kitchen. She may even start stashing food beneath her bed or in the deep corners of her lower dresser drawers.

I realize the difficulty for many in this biblical passage. For men who have denied their wives sexual advances and kept back their bodies from their wives over and over again, this verse has drastic implications: "Stop depriving one another...lest Satan tempt you because of your lack of self-control" (1 Corinthians 7:5 NASB).

There are two very different perspectives about the sex drive within marriage. One perspective is that the Christian way to handle your sex drive is to exercise considerable self-control, deprive yourself frequently, and have sex as often as your spouse is open to it. The other perspective is that you exercise considerable self-fulfillment, deprive yourself very infrequently (usually because of travel or sickness), and have sex as often as you would like it.

Do you see the drastic difference in the two perspectives? In casual voting at seminars and conferences, Christian audiences have told me that over 80 percent of all Christian marriages practice the concept of "deprive yourself frequently." But what does the Bible teach about "depriving" yourself of sex within the marriage context?" "Stop depriving one another" (1 Corinthians 7:5 NASB).

Instead of teaching "Deprive yourself by self-control," the Bible says, "Stop depriving one another!" The biblical answer to sexual immorality isn't to learn how to be content by depriving yourself, but by being content through enjoying sex with your spouse. The Lord doesn't want you to live in sexual frustration or sexual inhibition within the boundaries of married life.

The word translated "deprive" literally means "do not rob one another" or "do not defraud one another." Commentators agree that defrauding can occur in marriage because one partner can actually cheat their spouse of what is properly his or hers. If a spouse withholds their body when a partner seeks sex, it is biblical fraud. Because the Lord gave a person's body to his or her spouse, by withholding that which is not theirs to withhold, they are defrauding the other.

I'll never forget what happened after teaching this to about 500 Christian leaders. Afterwards, many were in tears because of repentance. One dignified 65-year-old woman came to me after everyone had left. Her eyes were bloodshot and her pain no longer hidden.

She said, "I had no idea how I have been defrauding my husband all of our married life. I told him 'no' for every reason under the sun just to get him not to have sex with me. Finally he stopped asking and I fear he's gone elsewhere. I have sinned greatly against God and against my husband. Is it too late?"

Oh, what a precious time we had together that evening as the rain poured outside and the cleansing waters of God's Word washed over her life. When she turned to leave, she was a different woman. As she left she said, "My husband may have a heart attack, but starting tonight, I'm going to more than fulfill my duty to meet his sexual needs!"

5. The Lord Reveals You May "Deprive" Each Other of Sex with Only Four Conditions

"Stop depriving one another, *except by agreement for a time that you may devote yourselves to prayer*, and come together again lest Satan tempt you because of your lack of self-control" (1 Corinthians 7:5 NASB).

What are the exceptions? Does Scripture actually tell me I have to have sex every time my partner wants it? Fortunately, the Bible doesn't leave us in the dark about this most important issue and outlines four conditions whereby one marriage partner can deny the other of sex.

First, sex can be "deprived" when you both "agree." You can't decide by yourself to deprive your spouse of sex. Both of you must agree not to have sex in order to fit into this exception.

Here's how this may work in real life. Let's say that last night your spouse rolled over in bed and made sexual advances. Because of a long and exhausting day, you said, "I'm really tired tonight. Would it be all right with you if we waited until tomorrow night? If not, sweetheart, you know that tonight is okay too. *What would you like?*" Biblically speaking, who has the final say about this decision? Does the "tired partner" or the "initiating partner?" The "initiating partner" always has the final say, due to the fact that you are under divine obligation to fulfill your duty and your spouse has authority over your body. If your spouse wants sex even after hearing your request, he or she still has the "authority" over your body to have sex.

However, just because your body belongs to your spouse doesn't mean you don't have the freedom to negotiate! When the initiating partner hears a willing but tired attitude of acceptance rather than rejection—understanding should be forthcoming. The Bible doesn't leave room for depriving your spouse of sexual intimacy except by mutual consent.

> "WE ARE HALF-HEARTED CREATURES, FOOLING AROUND WITH DRINK AND SEX AND AMBITION, WHEN INFINITE JOY IS OFFERED US. LIKE AN IGNORANT CHILD WHO WANTS TO GO ON MAKING MUD PIES IN A SLUM BECAUSE HE CANNOT IMAGINE WHAT IS MEANT BY THE OFFER OF A HOLIDAY AT THE SEA, WE ARE FAR TOO EASILY PLEASED."
>
> —C.S. Lewis

Second, sex can be "deprived" when you both agree to delay it for a time. Whenever a couple mutually agrees to deprive one another sexual intimacy, the two must agree when they will have sex. To agree to "not tonight" would not be following the biblical pattern. Scripture uses a very specific Greek word for "time" here which means a "specific period of time."

Third, sex can be "deprived" when you devote yourself to prayer. Thus we read, "Stop depriving one another, except by agreement for a time *that you may devote yourselves to prayer.*" This certainly presents a clear and rather unusual reason for depriving yourself of sexual relations in modern society. The only biblical purpose for depriving yourselves of sex is to devote yourselves to prayer—sharing a spiritual focus in your marriage.

Fourth, sex can only be deprived until the two of you agree to come together again. Do you realize how quickly the Bible brings us back to the issue that sexual intimacy is to be the norm and never the exception? It's almost as if the author can't get this exception out quickly enough to return to the "norm of married life."

6. The Lord Warns That If You Deprive Each Other, You Open Yourself to Satan

"Stop depriving one another, except by agreement for a time that you may devote yourselves to prayer, and *come together again lest Satan tempt you* because of your lack of self-control" (1 Corinthians 7:5 NASB).

This verse blatantly states that in sexual matters you must *come together after an agreed-upon time of sexual abstinence or you will open yourself unnecessarily to satanic attack in sexual areas.* Sexual temptations can be incredibly powerful due to the drive God has put into the human being. After a period of time without sex, you are to come together again—if you don't, Satan will come against you with sexual temptations toward immorality. The longer sex is postponed and the marital partners have not yet come together, the greater the risk of satanic temptation.

7. The Lord Warns That You "Lack" Self-Control
When You Deprive Each Other of Sex

What happens to married individuals when they don't have sex for a period of days? The Bible reveals that Satan tempts you because of one reason: "your lack of self-control." By withholding sex from each other, you are weakening sexual self-control.

Somewhere in the mind of the average person is the very significant and dangerous misconception that there are no real consequences to "depriving" your spouse of sexual relations except immediate, short-lived frustration. This verse pictures the reality: Continued postponement of sexual relations within marriage places very real and unnecessary pressure on a person.

If I read this verse correctly, married individuals will be tempted more by Satan to commit sexual immorality if their sexual needs are denied than if they are met. From this passage we can conclude that the married partner who is depriving or defrauding the sexual needs of their spouse may be the primary opening for satanic temptation to be sexually immoral.

ENJOYING THE GIFT OF SEX

One of the realities of Walk Thru the Bible Ministries is travel away from home. With over 3000 Bible teaching faculty in over 70 nations and 50 languages, you can imagine the firsthand experience we have garnered in nearly 25 years of ministry. At each national training meeting our faculty comes together for additional training and ministry. Our dean of faculty and his staff share the seriousness of sexual temptation with all staff. In as discreet a manner as possible, he strongly encourages the faculty to share openly with their spouses the need for their sexual needs to be met *before leaving town* so as to lessen the amount of temptation they have to experience on the road.

I can't tell you the number of men who have circled back to me expressing their great appreciation for this forthright presentation—especially with their wives present. Sometimes even the most courageous among us find it difficult and rather uncomfortable to express these things. Some may still have a false sense of guilt regarding their desire to have sex before they leave on the road.

My wife and I were sharing in the hotel lobby during the middle of a week-long faculty training conference when one of our "veteran" faculty wives came up to us and asked if she could share something rather personal. She proceeded to tell how much she appreciated the "sex talk." And that even though she had been happily married to her husband (who was in full-time pastoral ministry) for more than 25 years, the concepts we shared about a man and woman's sex needs before travel were new and even surprising to her. She said that because she was a woman and had very different sexual needs, she never would have known unless someone else told her.

That woman, who was nearly 60, told us how disappointed she was that neither her mother nor any other older woman had ever communicated such a vital piece of information to her. She kind of smiled, broke eye contact with me and looked directly at Darlene as she said, "You know, Darlene, now that I know the truth, I never let my loving husband out of the house before a trip without the special gift that only I can give—even if he isn't in the mood! It's not just his present mood I'm concerned about, it's his mood tomorrow night, when I'm not around that concerns me. I want to remain the only person he's tempted to seek that gift from!"

PART THREE

DEVELOPING YOUR
HOLINESS HABITS

9

PURSUING
HOLINESS

"We cannot say 'no' to temptation without saying 'yes' to something far better."

—Erwin W. Lutzer

Every word to this point has been written to prepare you for this chapter. By now, you understand "holiness" means separation, must include separation "from" the secular and "to" the sacred, and must be defined by the standards of the Lord and His Word. By now, you understand "positional holiness" means how the Lord views you the moment you accept His Son's sacrificial death for your sins, "presentation holiness" means that because of the compassions and mercies of the Lord you have committed your whole life to Him and His service, and that part of "progressive holiness" is that you constantly cleanse yourself from all the Lord would consider to be unholy.

However, we've barely discussed what normally comes to mind when you think about holiness: Christlike conduct and character. The Bible describes a specific order to progressive holiness—see if you can notice the order from Ephesians 4:22-24:

> ...*that you put off*, concerning your former conduct, the old man which grows corrupt according to the deceitful lusts, and be renewed in the spirit of your mind, and that *you put on* the new man which was created according to God, in true righteousness and holiness.

Unfortunately, many believers miss this biblical pattern and experience continuing defeat and even despair regarding their sincere attempts at personal holiness. The Bible reveals a pattern to be followed: First unholiness is to be cleansed, and then holiness pursued. Although the Lord is obviously pleased with all actions of pursuing righteousness, the Bible alerts us to the fact that existing unholiness can hinder our progress in growing in areas of holiness.

In other words, tear out the dirty carpet before attempting to lay down the new carpet. "Put off" before you "put on." "Depart from iniquity" and then "pursue righteousness." Does this mean we should never pursue the positive characteristics of righteousness first? Obviously not. But perhaps the true biblical perspective would be this: *Pursue holiness by first cleansing all known unholiness; when all known unholiness is cleansed, then focus more directly on pursuing positive holiness.*

When believers seek the positive attributes of holiness while permitting major areas of sin to remain, the Lord may regard even our positive acts as sinful. Why? Because we may be rationalizing our existing sin by thinking that our devotional life or positive acts of service may cause the Lord to "forget" or at least "wink" at our existing sins.

Over and over again, throughout the prophets of the Old Testament, the Lord consistently reveals His divine displeasure at the nation of Israel for their habitual attempts at obedience while practicing major sin. The sin negates the obedience. In other words, positive holiness may be rejected by the Lord as unworthy due to negative holiness. Seeking the Lord in some areas while rebelling in others may defeat the whole process.

Listen to Christ's revelation in the Sermon on the Mount in Matthew 5:23-25 about which half of holiness should receive our first attention:

> "Therefore if you bring your gift to the altar, and there remember that your brother has something against you, leave your gift there before the altar, and go your way. *First* be reconciled to your brother, and *then* come and offer your gift."

By way of general principle, always seek to cleanse yourself from all areas of unholiness before focusing heavily on the areas of positive holiness. Don't get confused in this area. Both areas are equally in need of holiness! Although Christians think positive holiness is "better" than getting rid of negative holiness, the Bible doesn't teach that. In other words, pursue holiness first by cleansing yourself of sin and then by adding further obedience. The order is biblical, and from my experience, a central truth missing from the minds of most believers. Revival begins with repentance and cleansing and then breaks forth in closer intimacy with Christ and greater obedience to Him.

THE SECOND PART OF PROGRESSIVE HOLINESS

The first half of progressive holiness focuses on helping you eliminate all the negative from your life, whereas the second half focuses on helping you add all the positive areas. Both parts are processes rather than events, and both are lifelong and can never be completed once-for-all. Finish cleansing yourself from all known sin and honestly stand before the Lord with a clean conscience in all areas. Don't fall prey to the concept that "at no time can you be fully cleansed." The Bible commands you to work in that direction by "cleansing" or "departing" until the process is complete at that particular time. And don't fall prey to the other false concept that since you completed the process fully in both God's and your sight once, that you won't need to work through the same process repeatedly later in your life.

Reflect on these two parts of holiness a bit further:

Unholiness	Holiness
"Negative Holiness"	"Positive Holiness"
Complete First	Pursue Second
Sinful Acts of Unrighteousness	Godly Acts of Righteousness
"Purify Yourself"	"Pursue Righteousness"
Exclude All Unholiness	Include All Holiness
Put Off the "Old Man"	Put On the "New Man"
"Works of the Flesh"	"Fruit of the Spirit"
The "Self" Life	The "Spirit" Life
Disobedience	Obedience

As you look down these lists, recognize that although both are directly related to holiness, they are entirely different and distinct. In other words, one doesn't become biblically holy merely by erasing the sins from their life. Too many believers think "if I can just get rid of these sins in my life, then I'll be holy!" The Bible doesn't teach that holiness is merely an absence of something, it's also the presence of something else.

Consider this issue a bit more deeply: Why wouldn't you and I automatically become holy the moment we obeyed the Bible and cleansed ourselves from all unholiness? Because "underneath" it all, our hearts remain deceitfully wicked. Unlike many of the more modern and liberal theologians, the Bible is more than explicit that man does not have a "good" heart buried beneath everything, but a "wicked and deceitful" heart. Therefore, when we have obeyed the Bible by cleansing ourselves from all unrighteousness, we aren't then filled with all holiness—we are merely not unholy at that moment. We need to now clothe ourselves with Christ.

Holiness does not exist simply because of an absence of unholiness. That's why the Bible, when discussing holiness, nearly always exhorts Christians to take heed to both sides of the progressive holiness equation: Cleanse yourself and pursue righteousness. Put off the old man and put on the new man.

So do you "put on the new man" by simply "putting off the old man"? Absolutely not! Both the negative and the positive must be accomplished or the Lord would not describe us as *holy in all our conduct.* Conduct which is holy is characterized by the absence of sin and the presence of righteousness. The second half of progressive holiness is therefore the active and enduring pursuit of all which is Christlike.

THE DISTURBING TRUTH ABOUT PURSUING HOLINESS

Due to the massive amount of unholiness that exists in the Christian community today, you probably could predict there would be even less positive holiness existing in the lives of Christians. *As a general principle, the negative holiness (amount of preexisting, known sin) is always greater than the positive holiness (amount of preexisting, practiced righteousness).*

Of the two parts positive holiness is the more advanced. For enduring victory in progressive holiness, then, negative holiness (cleansing yourself from all iniquity) is a general prerequisite to positive holiness. That one principle may explain a lot about your spiritual life if you think about it for a moment. Perhaps a few implications may be helpful:

1. If a believer seeks to deepen their walk with the Lord, the first step is always to *seek cleansing first.* The reason why so many Christians fail over and over again with their devotional life is not a lack of discipline. Nor is it a lack of desire. Nor is it a lack of trying time after time. Instead, it is from the lack of personal cleansing of preexisting and numerous known sins. These sins act as huge and nearly insurmountable roadblocks on your personal pilgrimage to holiness.

2. The amount of habitual and ongoing positive holiness (I'll explain this more in depth later in the chapter) that regularly exists in a person's life is a *reliable revealer of the amount of sin* that currently exists in

> "NOTHING MAKES IT EASIER TO RESIST TEMPTATION THAN A PROPER UPBRINGING, A SOUND SET OF VALUES, AND WITNESSES."
>
> —Franklin P. Jones

that person's life. The less the positive holiness, the more the negative holiness. In other words, if a believer does not privately pray much, personally read the Bible much, sacrifice their money in the work of God, serve the Lord with their talents, praise and worship Him publicly and privately, invest their talents in eternal things, minister to the needy, or share the gospel with the lost, you can depend upon the fact that there are major areas of sin lying just below the surface in that person's life.

3. This general principle rules not only in the lives of individual Christians, but also *in a family, local church, or Christian organization.* One of the easiest ways to get a pulse on holiness is to monitor something as simple as prayer. By monitoring the amount of time and energy you personally invest in private prayer over a three-month period, you will have a good indication of the holiness of your conduct and character. People who don't pray much are not holy much. Churches who don't pray much are not holy much either.

I'll never forget moving to a new city and visiting a nearby recommended church. About 400 adults attended service each Sunday morning. On Wednesday night I visited the prayer meeting. In the sanctuary, the pastor preached. In a small back corner room I finally found the prayer meeting. Four godly women about my mother's age met weekly for the church prayer meeting. Guess what turned out to be true in the life of that local church? There wasn't much holiness, nor much life.

The next time you are together with someone who prays a lot, ask them if they have experienced many seasons of personal cleansing in their lives. They will probably smile and slowly nod in the affirmative. So how would you describe the amount of positive holiness in the lives of today's born-again believers? Here's what I've discovered in my own observations in the past 30 years of ministry around the world:

- When you don't count prayers at meals and at any church-related function, the average born-again believer prays less than 2 minutes per day.

- When you don't count reading the Bible at a Christian function with someone else present, the average born-again believer reads the Bible less than 3 minutes per day.

- When you read the public statistics, the average born-again Christian donates less than 3 percent of his total gross income to Christian causes.

Do these surprise or shock you? I doubt it. If you have been a Christian for any length of time, you undoubtedly sensed that such may be the case. You may have felt uncomfortable in those statistics as they may describe you too closely. This whole section has been written for you. Not only does the Lord desire you to break free from this shallow spiritual life, but deep down in your heart, so do you!

BY THEIR FRUITS YOU WILL KNOW THEM

Two weeks ago yesterday, I spent the afternoon with a senior student in one of our nation's most respected seminaries. I asked him how he enjoyed the past three years of graduate study preparing for the ministry. He quickly expressed appreciation for the many things he learned, but then he looked away and with a rather sad, pensiveness spoke these all-to-revealing words:

I'm glad I went to seminary, and I know I've learned a lot. But I have one major disappointment; I never was taught and never learned how to walk with God. I learned theology, Bible, missions, Christian education, evangelism, apologetics, and other important courses, and even had one semester course on the spiritual life. But you know, I never really learned how to pray, never learned how to meet God, and never learned how to walk with God. And I fear that although I've learned a great deal, can "do ministry" better than when I entered three years ago, I really am not a more holy person than when I began. In fact, my heart is less tender and I pray less than when the whole thing started.

Somehow, I was wrong. I thought seminary would teach me how to walk with God and lead me in the path of how to become a man who was holy. It didn't. *In fact, it never seriously tried.*

I sat down a little while ago and just figured it out. Although I go to one of the nation's top three evangelical seminaries—known for its emphasis on the spiritual life—my entire seminary career of three intense years invested less than 2 percent of that time on how to walk with God and become a man of holiness.

Then he turned back to me and asked the question I was afraid he was going to ask: "Do you think, Dr. Wilkinson, my seminary reflects the values of Jesus? Do you think that my seminary models the training that Jesus gave to His disciples? Do you think it's more important to learn Greek and theology than how to walk with God, how to pray, and how to be holy? Do you think that only 2 percent of the New Testament epistles is about walking with God, walking in the Spirit, praying, and living a life of holiness?"

What would you say to that young seminarian? As the source, so goes the river. As go the seminaries and Bible colleges, so go the pastors and missionaries; as the pastors and missionaries, so go the churches and Christian organizations; as churches and Christian organizations, so go the believers.

Perhaps one last observation would be helpful in this strategic matter. Let's say you were new in town and wanted to find out the reputation of a church you were interested in attending. But, instead of asking the staff or members, you randomly knocked on eight doors, which were all within walking distance of the church: two to the north, two to the south, two to the east, two to the west. What would people say when you said, "Could you please tell me about the church up the corner?"

If my experience is any monitor, don't try it. Because I did one day. You should have heard the earful I got. Of the church splits. The big arguments that the whole town knew about or the previous music director running away with the church secretary. And the pastor who kicked people out because it was his way or the highway. As I slowly walked off the front porch of the last person, the words of Jesus in Matthew 5:16 came to mind: "Let your light so shine before men, *that they may see your good works* and glorify your Father in heaven."

You see, holiness makes its mark in the marketplace and town square. Holiness spreads good works in every direction. Why? Because positive holiness influences behavior and controls actions. That's why Jesus spoke these words in Matthew 7:15-20:

> Beware of false prophets, who come to you in sheep's clothing, but inwardly they are ravenous wolves. You will know them by their fruits....A good tree cannot bear bad fruit, nor can a bad tree bear good fruit.... *Therefore, by their fruits you will know them.*

Did you see the Lord's logic? What is in a person must come out of a person. And, if there is goodness in a person, he must bear good fruit. "Good fruit" is nothing more than "good works" as those concepts are frequently used interchangeably in the New Testament. When a person is holy, his behavior overflows with good works. When a church is holy, its behavior overflows with good works and everyone within driving distance knows about it. Don't miss the fact that the people who were to see the believer's good works in Matthew were the non-Christians; therefore, the telltale biblical sign of the amount of positive holiness of a church can be gauged by asking the neighborhood, not the membership!

THE FRUITS OF THE CHURCH

Unfortunately, although there are notable exceptions, the vast majority of churches are only known for the evil works of divisions, immorality, power-hungry leadership, and financial problems. When the community cannot name even *one good work* of the church in the community, you can be sure the church is not overflowing with holiness. Biblical holiness always overflows into the community in the form of good works. If the community knows nothing of the good works, then the holiness is sorely lacking. Why? Because as Jesus pointed out, trees always bear fruit. Good trees must bear good fruit and evil trees must bear evil fruit. If the community knows of only evil fruit, the church cannot be holy in the Lord's eyes.

What then would a "holy" church really look like? Just this morning I finished reading about the life of a pastor who took over a fledgling church of 200 when he was 20. When he died at the age of 58, this ministry had touched literally the whole country. Look at the scope of "good works" this one church bore in their community:

1. 23 mission stations actively ministering throughout the community
2. 26 branch Sunday schools actively ministering throughout the community, especially in the downtown poor sections
3. Over 1000 members working in the slums and among the poor every Sunday evening
4. Stimulated large and lasting revivals in the whole area
5. Built a church that seated over 5000 and fully paid for it
6. Launched and constructed a large pastor's college to train pastors with over 100 pastors in training each year
7. Ran over 200 evening Bible classes each week throughout the area
8. Launched and developed a large Tract Society
9. Started a Christian book-selling organization which distributed massive numbers of Christian books through house-to-house visits, often resulting in home Bible studies throughout the community—in one year 926,290 homes were personally visited!
10. Started over 200 new local churches throughout the entire area

11. Constructed 17 houses for elderly widows and indigent women and donated all costs for the housing and food on an ongoing basis

12. Launched and constructed an orphanage for nearly 400 full time children, and supported it entirely without governmental funds

13. Started a book ministry and donated tens of thousands of Christian books, mailing them free of charge to missionaries and poor pastors all over the world

14. Launched the Ladies' Benevolent Society and made clothes for the orphaned children of the city

15. Baptized through its many ministries over 39,000 new converts in just 12 years

These are only 15 of 66 different ministries launched, funded, and actively served by the congregation of that one church! Can you imagine what the community felt about that one church and its humble servant, Charles H. Spurgeon? And, if you had seen that preacher on Sundays as he preached God's Word, you would have seen people coming to know Christ by the thousands as the years went by. As the people of God started living like the people of God, they bore good fruit like the plan of God.

Nearly every mark of positive holiness is missing in the vast majority of believers and local churches these days. May we repent before the Lord, cleanse our hearts and actions, and pursue His holiness with all of our heart, soul, and might. When we do, not only will heaven shout in celebration, but so too will the ungodly living nearby glorify God because they see works worthy of their praise:

Dear friends, I urge you, as aliens and strangers in the world, to abstain from sinful desires, which war against your soul. Live such good lives among the pagans that, though they accuse you of doing wrong, *they may see your good deeds and glorify God on the day he visits us* (1 Peter 2:11-12 NIV).

EVALUATE WHERE YOU STAND ON PURSUING HOLINESS

Sometimes there is great merit to examining oneself in order to evaluate progress. By now you should realize that the Bible reveals this third stage of holiness is progressive, beginning at your spiritual birth and concluding at your physical death. Between these two points lie the only opportunities you have in all of eternity to grow in holiness.

Check your *holiness pulse rate* by reading through these seven overlapping seasons of growing maturity and selecting the one you feel represents where you are in pursuing positive holiness at this time:

1. *Attempts fail repeatedly at a successful devotional life:* The first stage of pursuing holiness always seems to revolve around your devotional life. If you have experienced considerable difficulty in successfully launching and getting into the practice of regular devotions, you are still standing at the starting line of the walk of holiness. Consider returning to the earlier chapter and working through the painful but liberating "Ten-Step Cleanse."

Please do not believe the lie that the reason you don't have regular devotions is because you don't have the discipline or don't want to enough. The negative pull from existing sin in your life so weighs you down that you can only carry the load for a few days before giving up. But without regular time in the Word, you can't and won't grow in holiness.

2. *Actively serves the Lord in at least one, regular ministry:* This second stage of positive holiness may in your case precede the previous stage as it does for some Christians. The Lord always encourages His children to serve Him, and frequently this is an easier first step in moving toward Him. If you are still merely attending church and remaining on the fringes of the Lord's work, it's time to move closer to the center. Remember, the Lord saved you by His grace, but He saved you for His work: "For we are His workmanship, created in Christ Jesus for good works, which God prepared beforehand that we should walk in them" (Ephesians 2:10).

3. *Aspires deeply to live a much more holy life:* Somewhere during the progressive movement toward holiness, the believer comes

to a crossroads. In preparation, the Lord usually brings the believer to numerous mini-decisions that he can make either toward or away from holiness. If the believer continues to choose the pathway of obedience, then eventually the Lord will bring them right up to the "big decision" of whether or not they will knowingly and actively pursue holiness in their life.

Think back for a moment to our introduction about those men who were asked to describe themselves with a few words—and whether "holiness" would be on their 3" by 5" cards. Remember their aversion to the concept? Because "holiness" was not something they aspired to become, they remained locked in the ever-moving-but-never-getting-anywhere cul-de-sac of the spiritual life.

4. Abides with Christ through regular and meaningful devotions: By this time in the Christian's pilgrimage, he will have experienced a number of deep cleansings and personal humblings. His heart will have grown more fervent and his hunger for the Lord will have grown considerably. Because of his desire for the Lord, he is finally willing to pay the required price of deep cleansings in order to experience more of the Lord. As a result of those cleansings, the Lord permits this believer to enjoy a more meaningful and satisfying relationship with Him.

At this point a major transition occurs: Devotions move out of the "duty" category, which takes considerable determination and discipline, and into the "delight" category, which means the payback far exceeds the effort. The exertion seems small in relationship to what is achieved. Devotions grow to the high point in the believer's life at this point.

5. Advances faithfully in obeying the Lord in specific areas of Christlikeness: After the Lord has fed His child deeply through intimate devotions, He begins to call Him more pointedly to deeper obedience. At this point, the believer desires more of the Lord so deeply that he is more than willing to do whatever the Lord requires. Also, as the relationship with the Lord deepens, the believer becomes more attuned to His heart and walks more carefully, not desiring to wound or quench the Holy Spirit.

Now the believer transitions through another barrier in the spiritual life: Obedience is no longer the burden of duty because the Bible tells him to do something; rather, obedience is the joy of relationship because his closest friend and most compassionate Lord beckons him to be like Him. What a difference! It is during this season of spiritual life that the believer begins to look at the commands of the New Testament with new eyes. Commands that were once skimmed over now become personal directives from his loving Father. No longer does the believer rationalize whole areas of his life—indeed, he pursues with deep determination to "put on" such things as "tender mercies, kindness, humility, meekness, longsuffering; bearing with one another, and forgiving one another, if anyone has a complaint against another; even as Christ forgave you, so you also must do" (Colossians 3:12b-13).

6. *Accelerates the investment of time, talent, and treasure into the Lord's work:* By this time in the believer's progress toward personal holiness, so many threads of his life begin to weave together for the first time that the believer almost feels he is being carried along by the Lord (and he is!). As the believer's heart is broken, cleansed, and redirected, he begins viewing his life from heaven's perspective rather than earth's. What a dramatic difference the eternal perspective makes to the normal decisions of life. Whole areas of the believer's life which previously had high priority are now set aside as the believer realizes his lack of eternal significance.

Over years of time, the Lord continues inviting the believer to deeper and deeper levels of holiness. It's during this season that the believer realizes he is a steward of his life rather than the owner. As he submits to the Lord, he begins to redirect his time, talents, and treasure into the Lord's work. The believer's time becomes a precious commodity and he "redeems the time" as never before. The believer's talents are now seen as a "life stewardship" in which the Lord calls him to multiply his talents for eternity by 1000 percent as the Lord revealed in the parable of the talents in Luke 19. Finally, the believer releases the Lord's money (instead of hoarding it for either personal pleasure or fear of the future) and joyfully gives a growing percentage of his assets to the Lord and His service.

7. Abandons everything to know and serve Christ: I believe the "ultimate" level of positive holiness is the complete conformity into the image of Jesus Christ in every area of life. All that the believer desires in this final stage is to be one with Christ and to serve Him as Christ served His Father—completely, faithfully, and fervently. Paul recorded his seventh-stage attitude and actions in Philippians 3:8-14. Notice the depth of abandonment and intensity of intimacy and service:

> ...I also count all things loss for the excellence of the knowledge of Christ Jesus my Lord, for whom I have suffered the loss of all things, and count them as rubbish, *that I may gain Christ*...that I may know Him and the power of His resurrection....*I press on, that I may lay hold of that for which Christ Jesus has also laid hold of me*....Reaching forward to those things which are ahead, I press toward the goal for the prize of the upward call of God in Christ Jesus.

At this point, you may be wondering if Paul's attitude is really realistic. Should we seek to follow in His footsteps and ultimately display the same attitudes, actions, and aspirations? The Bible answers that very question in the next few verses:

> Therefore let us, as many as are mature, *have this mind;* and if in anything you think otherwise, God will reveal even this to you. *Brethren, join in following my example,* and note those who so walk, as you have us for a pattern. For many walk, of whom I have told you often, and now tell you even weeping, that they...set their mind on earthly things. For our citizenship is in heaven, from which we also eagerly wait for the Savior, the Lord Jesus Christ... (Philippians 3:15,17-20).

Take a moment and note where you are in your lifelong progress toward holiness.

Level #1	Level #2	Level #3	Level #4	Level #5	Level #6	Level #7
Attempts	Actively	Aspires	Abides	Advances	Accelerates	Abandons
and fails	serves the	deeply to	with Christ	in obeying	time,	everything
repeatedly	Lord in at	live a much	through	the Lord	talent, and	to know
at a	least one	more holy	regular	and	treasure	and serve
successful	regular	life	devotions	becoming	into Lord's	Christ
devotional	ministry			Christlike	work	
life						

SOW HOLINESS NOW IN ORDER TO REAP HOLINESS LATER

Holiness is not natural, it's supernatural. Holiness does not come as a result of one or two "crisis experiences"; it develops through years and years of godly living. The standards of holiness are clear and include "all your conduct" as Peter reminded us. Nestled deep within the words of Zacharias in Luke 1:74-75 is a remarkable prophecy regarding the work of Jesus for us:

> To grant us that we, being delivered from the hand of our enemies, *might serve Him without fear, in holiness and righteousness before Him all the days of our life.*

As you consider those two verses, you'll see that it may contain the most succinct and remarkable summary in all the Bible of our life's holiness goal: *"To serve the Lord in holiness before Him all the days of our life!"*

The longer I walk with the Lord, the more assured I am that one of the secrets of the spiritual life lies in the words, "all the days of our life." Not "all the weeks of our life" nor "all the months of our life" nor "all the years of our life." Holiness grows most through daily life, and therefore in this section, the majority of the practical emphasis will be upon specific daily practices that will generate guaranteed results in your pilgrimage to personal holiness in times of temptation.

Those words "guaranteed results" may sound a bit on the exaggerated side, but let me assure you they aren't an overstatement in any form or fashion. Instead, they are as certain as the unchanging laws of sowing and reaping. What one sows will inevitably be reaped. Sow seeds in the holiness garden and you'll reap the fruit of holiness. Not some of the time, not most of the time, but all of the time. How encouraging! That means if you but sow seeds of holiness, you will see them grow, blossom, and bear holiness fruit. There's no need for "blind hoping" as the Lord always causes these seeds to germinate. There are four things necessary to remember as we begin this section:

1. Remember the time between sowing and reaping requires ample patience.

Patience isn't typically needed in the sowing or the reaping, but primarily in the time *between* sowing and reaping. I remember when I planted my first vegetable seeds in our backyard as a young child. I would race downstairs each morning, run out the backdoor, and turn right to the small 3 foot by 10 foot garden—which felt like a giant field to my little fourth-grade mind. I checked it each day just to see if my tomatoes, eggplant, and radishes had come up yet. After three days passed, I wanted to dig them up just to make sure they were still there! Day after day nothing happened, and I became more and more discouraged. My wise father assured me over and over again that I must exercise patience, that they would come up when they were supposed to.

Perhaps Paul knew all too well of the tendency among believers to grow impatient and lose faith that their efforts would be rewarded when he wrote Galatians 6:7,9 (with a few scattered comments of my own for explanation):

> Do not be deceived, God is not mocked;
> for whatever a man sows, that he will also reap.
> And let us not grow weary while doing good [planting
>   holiness seeds],
> *for in due season* [precisely on schedule]

we shall reap [not may reap or hope to reap but
shall reap]
if we do not lose heart [become discouraged because
nothing has happened quickly enough and stop
sowing, watering, and weeding in the meantime].

Never doubt for a moment that if you continue in these holiness habits you will indeed enjoy a glorious and bountiful "harvest of holiness." The greater the harvest you desire, the more you must sow and continue to sow. God guarantees results in direct proportion to your sowing, but in a far greater amount. Do you know why? Because you always harvest many times more than you sow. Plant one tiny seed of watermelon, and plan to invite all your neighbors to help you eat of its harvest.

2. Remember the reliability of your harvest lies in the quality of your seed.

Plant tomato seeds and regardless of how much you may work and hope and seek, you cannot and will not grow cucumbers. If you seek holiness, then plant holiness seeds. Plant a poor strain or diseased tomato seeds and the results cannot be guaranteed. If you plant and water ineffective seeds, your payback will not be satisfying to you, rather it will be discouraging and defeating.

Too many Christians seem to rely upon unusual and emotional practices to develop holiness in their lives. These practices seem to have amazing bursts of tremendous success, but they are followed by the eventual slides resulting in deadening defeat. No matter where I travel across the world, I find many disillusioned believers who for one reason or another have dropped out from the holiness pilgrimage. A large proportion of them seem to have trusted in "poor seed" to bear fruit in their lives.

Instead of seeking the "good old standard packets of holiness seeds" used by the church throughout the centuries, a certain percentage of people seem drawn like a moth to a light to new and novel methods to grow in their holiness. After decades of observing this practice, may I strongly encourage you not to veer from the straight and narrow? If the holiness practice is not clearly taught or modeled in the Bible or practiced throughout centuries of church history (such as spiritual journaling for instance), don't seek it.

On a personal note, last night I went to bed after writing the above paragraph. This morning I was in the middle of reading famed John Bunyan's *The Heavenly Footman* from the mid-1600s. Notice his warning of the same dangerous trend:

> In the little time I have been a believer, I have observed that there is a great many running to and fro—some this way and some that way; yet it is to be feared that most of them are not on the right way. As a result, though they run as swift as the eagle can fly, they benefit nothing at all.
>
> There is one who runs after quaking, another after ranting; still another runs after baptism, and another after independency....Yet, it's possible that most all these... are running the wrong way....

As some of my friends over the years have walked down these paths, I have found myself interceding for them with the Lord and seeking the root of their error. Although there may be some exceptions, I have come to some personal conclusions: The vast majority of believers who get sidetracked and derailed in their search for true holiness usually have one of these three common traits:

First, *they exhibit a propensity for a "quick fix"* for an issue which does not have a "quick fix"—in other words, they are commonly unwilling to practice the "hard things" of holiness, always seeking for a simpler, easier, and quicker secret.

Second, *they exhibit a weakness for making decisions* on the basis of emotional experiences and "signs" in their lives which validate their unusual direction. In other words, they come to believe through numerous personal experiences that the Lord is supernaturally calling them to this unusual method. It's almost universal that those in this trap eventually defend their position by the words "but God told me..."

Third, *they exhibit a deeply hidden selfish ambition* driving them to find the "deep things of God" beyond their friends, family, and peers. Somewhere in this slide into delusion, they believe they have uncovered a "lost truth" or previously "unknown truth" about the spiritual life which God has entrusted to them. The reason that others do not appreciate their ideas, actions, or directions is simply because they haven't been initiated into this "deeper level of truth."

Friend, if you identify with any of these three, you are in dangerous waters and far greater storms will eventually arise on the waters of your life. Flee these waters! Get off this boat. Stop reading whatever literature you are reading. Stop attending whatever services you are attending. Stop listening to the "tapes" which promote this. Go back to the straight and narrow path of all who would find the blessings of holiness. Although you will undoubtedly have to transition through some less exciting waters for a period of time, your spiritual life will be delivered into the safe harbor.

3. Remember that between sowing and reaping you must continue to weed.

In the pursuit of holiness, don't forget the inevitability of the weed! If you are new in your pursuit of holiness, expect a great number of kinds of weeds to surface! Why? Because up to this time in your life, you left your "field" open to the will of the land. All kinds of thistles, weeds, and undesirables moved in and basically ruled your garden.

The first year of a garden, you must weed seemingly forever. "All this work," you may find yourself feeling, "just for a few tomatoes!" But, the next year, there will be less weeds and more fruit. And the following year, far less weeds and great quantities of fruit. As that patch of ground is reclaimed by your attention, and the seeds and roots of the undesired weeds are ripped out and burned, the ground slowly becomes totally devoted to your will and the seeds that you plant. Instead of fighting for the freedom to grow in your weed-filled garden, your fledgling plants will experience nearly complete freedom to grow without those powerful distractions, diversions, and disasters.

So you must realize your life may have been covered over with all kinds of weeds and brambles and thistles. Don't despair, just keep at it! Confess and cleanse yourself over and over again as new weeds of sin continue to appear. In time, less and less will appear due to the repeated cleansings of your garden. Do you think mature people of holiness have the same amount of weeds after a decade of careful and diligent spiritual gardening? Hardly. And you should see their crop!

4. Remember holiness requires sowing and reaping of multiple "holiness habits."

When our family first lived in the country we planted only two things in our garden: watermelons and sweet potatoes. What a crop we had that year, but what a lesson we learned! Three weeks after the harvest of each of these crops, we all felt if we saw another sweet potato or watermelon we would scream. We gave bags of potatoes and melons to all of our friends and told each other that next year we'd be much wiser in what we planted. Sowing only one or two things leads to boredom.

Do you know what seems to be the unexpected culprit of sincere believers' search for holiness? Boredom. Initially the believer feels guilt about feeling bored. How can anyone become bored with holiness? By limiting themselves to one or two types of holiness practices in their life. Become a highly diversified holiness practitioner.

For instance, think for a moment and name every method you currently use to pursue holiness with the Lord. Try to discipline yourself for a moment and fill in this little chart.

#1 Method that I pursue holiness	
#2 Method that I pursue holiness	
#3 Method that I pursue holiness	
#4 Method that I pursue holiness	
#5 Method that I pursue holiness	

What did you discover? Before turning in for the night last evening, Darlene and I talked for about an hour about our various methods of holiness, both personally and as a couple. What a list we came up with as we outlined the various holiness tools which are meaningful in our lives right now!

Too often believers just depend upon one or two methods to pursue the Lord and holiness in their lives. May I encourage you to discover at least a few and rotate your crop? Give your "land" rest from one method and move on to another. Remember, holiness methods are merely tools in your hand to help you achieve holiness in the Lord's sight. Whatever holiness tools work for you (which is either biblical or historically verifiable by the history of the church), are acceptable!

May your heart not only turn fully toward holiness, but may your habits begin to turn toward holiness as well! Come join me for the primary holiness habits you should master.

10

THE FOUNDATIONAL
HOLINESS HABITS

*"The serene, silent beauty of a holy life is the most power-
ful influence in the world, next to the might of the Spirit
of God."*

—Blaise Pascal

B ack at the turn of the century, Samuel Smiles expressed
the theme of this chapter:

Sow a thought and you reap an act;
Sow an act and you reap a habit;
Sow a habit and you reap a character;
Sow a character and you reap a destiny.

This life-linkage is unmistakable and unbreakable. We move
from thought to act to habit, and those habits create our character.
Never in your life are these steps out of order; never are they
skipped. Your destiny is ultimately controlled by the habits of your
life and thoughts. Right smack in the middle of that five-link chain
(thought to act to habit to character to destiny) is the concept of
"habit." A habit of life is a settled tendency or usual manner of
behavior which has been acquired by frequent repetition over time
so that it has become nearly or completely involuntary.

When a habit is built, a character is formed. When you think about it, character is the sum total of a person's habitual traits and qualities. When a major habit changes, that part of the person's character changes. For instance, if a person habitually lies, his character becomes untrustworthy. If he learns to habitually tell the truth, his character becomes fully trustworthy.

Let's say you are at a company party and one of your co-workers is behaving totally out of the norm. In describing her behavior to her perplexed boss, you say she was acting "out of character" which means she was not acting the way she habitually acts.

> *Change your habits and in time, you will change your character. Therefore, to enjoy a life of holiness, change your habits into habits of holiness.*

If you want to become a person whose character is holy, then you will have to identify and establish personal habits of holiness. The longer and deeper those habits are practiced, the more they will become a part of you—until finally they become the "whole" of you! Habits which become involuntary are called "character qualities."

When people seek to change their character, they must change their habits. To move from unholiness to holiness means, at least in one sense, habits of life have changed from negative habits of unholiness to positive habits of holiness. When they seriously pursue holiness, the reality of what becoming holy means must move beyond the generalities into specifics. Holiness isn't some vague dreamlike existence painted with a soft, glowing aura of heavenly clouds. Holiness is specific and objective and is to be fully mastered by all who name the name of the Lord Jesus. The Lord calls us to be "holy in all our conduct," and He has provided everything we need for righteousness and godliness.

Because the Bible teaches that holiness is both a *position* as well as a *progression*, we must continue to think clearly of how holiness really works. Holiness begins the moment we accept Jesus Christ as our personal Savior. At that time, the Lord separates us unto Himself as His child and a member of His family. From that point forward, the Lord calls all of us to be transformed from glory to glory into the exact image of Jesus Christ. As time goes on, all of us should be exemplifying the identical traits of Christ's character—love, joy, peace, longsuffering, kindness, goodness, faithfulness, gentleness, and self-control.

> "HOLINESS DOES NOT CONSIST IN MYSTIC SPECULATIONS, ENTHUSIASTIC FERVORS, OR UNCOMMANDED AUSTERITIES; IT CONSISTS IN THINKING AS GOD THINKS AND WILLING AS GOD WILLS."
>
> —Chuck Colson

Although our lives may demonstrate seasons of holiness acceleration for most of our lives, growth will be gradual and steady. Just as none of us can actually see the growth of a nearby plant or flower as it occurs, yet if we leave for the day and come back in the evening a bud may have opened into a beautiful rose, so is our growth in holiness small but significant. Leave time for its natural growth and you'll see a noticeable difference. In 2 Corinthians 7:1, Paul reminds us that we are to "cleanse ourselves from all filthiness...*perfecting holiness* in the fear of God." "Perfecting holiness" reflects the lifelong process of conforming ourselves into the image of Christ.

Remember, habits determine character. Character is not transformed unless habits of thought, belief, and behavior are changed. As you change your habits, your character will also change. You won't have to "hope" that somehow, in some way, your character will change, because you know it will change. Not instantly, but certainly. As you can't see that rose open its petals, so you won't be able to see your character blossom into Christ. But, circle back on your life in a few months and you may not recognize yourself!

How is it possible that holiness will result from these habits? Because the Bible repeatedly exhorts us to practice them—often with specific promises and benefits tied to them. Throughout the history of the church, Christians just like you and me have practiced these habits and have always enjoyed the same beneficial results. You don't have to hunt around for some magic words or secret initiation rite—these habits are obvious and equally within reach of all of us.

Try this experiment: Think of the most godly person you have ever met. Call him up and tell him you are right in the middle of this book and that I encouraged you to call and ask one question: "What have been the three secrets of your walk with God and godly lifestyle?" If my experience reflects the norm, you'll find they are the same main spiritual disciplines outlined in this chapter and the next one. Don't expect something new or exotic. Most importantly, you can only expect things to make a dramatic difference if you practice them regularly over a long period of time.

HOLINESS HABIT #1:
ESTABLISH YOUR DEVOTIONAL HABIT

What is currently the center of your life? Your work? Your marriage? Your family? Your church? Your leisure? Your money? Your business? Whatever is at the center of your life, you must move it into second position so the Lord and your time with Him reigns as the central focus of your life. The single most strategic change you can do to sow seeds of holiness and later reap holiness is to put your daily "devotional habit" first on your priority list at this very moment.

Half of the "devotional habit" is the word "devote," which means "to set apart for a special and often higher end." The focus of daily devotions isn't the specific procedures one follows, but one's intimate relationship to the Lord. Because you are devoted to the Lord, you choose to dedicate priority time each day to Him and Him alone. And because He is the most important person in the world to you, you do not allow anyone or anything to take precedence before Him. Here are a few tips to maximize your devotional habit.

1. Select Your "Devotional Habit" Place

The first key to successful devotions is to identify your favorite location in the house for your devotions. It should be comfortable, absolutely quiet, and as private as possible. In the Wilkinson home, "Darlene's Place" is in the front room in her green rocker, "Jessica's Place" is in her bedroom, and "Bruce's Place" is in the basement, in the back corner overlooking the backyard.

In that corner sits my favorite blue chair a good friend from Colorado gave to me unexpectedly one afternoon. Just in front of it along the wall is a bookcase filled with my "spiritual life" books, more recent journals, and my prayer journal. To the left is a lamp with a small table and at my right a large globe for praying for the world. For me, it's perfect.

As time passes, I have set apart this space to the Lord and dedicated it as the place where I rise to meet Him in the early morning. This place has become filled with praise, worship, meditation, and intimate friendship.

2. Schedule Your Normal "Devotional Habit" Time

I grew up as a staunch "evening person." I was sure it made no difference to the Lord what time I decided to have my devotions, and I can remember defending my position rather vigorously in my early Bible college days. One day many years ago, an older mentor and I were bantering this question around and he asked me if the spiritual giants of history had their primary devotions in the morning or evening. I had to admit that every one of them I was familiar with had them in the morning, but I was quick to point out that didn't prove anything.

When I said that, he folded his arms, smiled, and just sat there—not saying a word. Finally, when I had nothing else to say, he warmly but soberly said, "Bruce, until you stop defending your laziness and rise with the sun, you'll never meet Christ as you are seeking Him." With that, he rose and left.

That friend proved absolutely correct. The early morning hours are the *holiness hours*. Over time, things changed and I have become a committed morning person. The Lord and I like to meet while the sun is yet rising to join us.

> "THE GREATEST MIRACLE THAT GOD CAN DO TODAY IS TO TAKE AN UNHOLY MAN OUT OF AN UNHOLY WORLD, AND MAKE THAT MAN HOLY AND PUT HIM BACK INTO THAT UNHOLY WORLD AND KEEP HIM HOLY IN IT."
>
> —Leonard Ravenhill

This may mean you will have to alter your routine, get to bed earlier, or at times live with less sleep. To be honest with you, in most people's busy lives today, when priorities change such as this, sleep suffers until you learn to discipline yourself a bit more closely.

Whatever you eventually decide, *meet the Lord at the same time each day throughout the week*. As far as Saturday and Sunday are concerned, you should realistically select the time on these two weekend days. Personally, I don't get up early on Saturday but do most Sundays. Saturday frequently permits a more casual approach, and I'm not unsure that the Lord doesn't enjoy this leisurely approach as well.

Remember not to fall prey to the temptation to become legalistic in your walk with the Lord. Your devotions should flex with the ebb and flow of your life including emergencies, exhaustion, and unexpected situations. Just this weekend while ministering at the Billy Graham Cove in Asheville, North Carolina, I found myself counseling all day and very late into the evenings. On the last morning I was so emotionally and physically exhausted that I rose early Sunday morning, pulled a large stuffed chair up to the fireplace, and enjoyed the presence of the Lord in quietness. I didn't follow my normal schedule, didn't pray through my prayer list, didn't write in my journal, and didn't even read my Bible. What did I do? I just sat in the presence of the Lord for an hour—worshipping and enjoying Him. Remember, devotions are for man, not man for devotions.

3. Structure Your Normal "Devotional Habit" Agenda for Each Day and Year

Nothing seems to ruin good intentions faster than not knowing what to do when you semi-stagger in the early morning hours to your "devotional place"—and then spend those precious moments in frustration trying to figure out what to do.

Take the complexity out of life! Build a routine which you follow each morning. I have discovered that the best way is to construct a new routine for each year from what I discovered during the previous year. Then, when I finally sit in my big, blue chair with my orange juice and coffee, I don't waste a second. It's wonderful, but unfortunately, I have to admit that it took me years just to figure that out. I can still remember the frustration of searching through the Bible trying to figure out what to read, or what to pray, or just to get started. Now that never happens. It's wonderful!

> "THE CHAINS OF HABIT ARE TOO WEAK TO BE FELT UNTIL THEY ARE TOO STRONG TO BE BROKEN."
>
> —Samuel Johnson

What's the secret? Just figure out what seems to work for you right now—write it down on a card or sheet of paper, try it the next day, and revise it. The first time it may take a couple of weeks to really zero in, but relax and don't try to figure it all out the first time. Get started and then revise your list of steps until you are comfortable; then use them for the rest of the year. The point isn't how many things you do, but that whatever you do works for you.

TIPS FOR SUCCESS

The first thing you should do is the easiest, most motivating, and the thing that starts your engine best. Never tackle the hard things first, but prepare yourself. For instance, one of my wife's friends starts her morning by turning on a praise tape, closing her eyes, and worshipping the Lord for the first 10 minutes. For me, I read a spiritual biography or spiritual life book for a while—it gets my battery charged. Remember, the key is to start with whatever you find is the easiest, most enjoyable, and immediately encouraging. There's nothing more spiritual then to immediately start praying first. If I started with prayer, I'm afraid I would fall back to sleep half the time! Darlene however, starts her morning with prayer and praise, then reading her Bible, then her journal, and ends with additional prayer. The order isn't important to anyone but you.

Second, when you are ready to turn your heart toward the Lord, stop yourself and prepare yourself for Him. Close your eyes and quiet your heart. Bring all your thoughts into sharp focus upon the throne room in the heavenlies. Bring every thought captive and do not permit interfering or distracting thoughts to conquer your intention. If this is new to you, you will become more than a little frustrated as your mind seems to be like our new, untrained little puppy, yipping and running in every direction at once. For the first few months, this may take more than a few moments, but don't become frustrated. Eventually, bringing your heart into focus will only take a few seconds.

Third, follow your schedule point by point in the same order every day. Don't skip a step, no matter how much you're tempted. Discipline yourself and do not permit the "avoidance temptation" to conquer your resolve. This "avoidance" emotion can be quite strong, but must be absolutely conquered. Put your finger on the step you're working through in your devotions and don't move onto the next step until you have finished that step. When this happens to me, I take careful note of it and put a little star in the margin to alert me to the spiritual opposition.

Whatever you do, don't permit your focus to leave the Lord and what you are committed to do in this devotional step. As you remain focused on Jesus Christ, the opposition will always dissolve shortly right in front of your eyes. Don't doubt this principle. Just this morning on number 16 of my prayer list, I unexpectedly experienced this very thing and remembered that such opposition had occurred yesterday and the day before that. Why? I don't know, and don't necessarily need to know—so I upgraded my fervency and broke through. Tomorrow I'm going to come to this step with commitment and dependence upon the Lord that the opposition will flee into the darkness.

Fourth, don't ever allow anything to take the place of the two absolutes: prayer and the Word of God. Never allow any book, no matter how good, to take the place of reading His Word. Never allow yourself to skip or shorten the amount of time you pray before the Lord. Regardless of what you do in your devotional schedule, at least 50 percent of your total time should be focused on the "Big Two"—prayer and the Word.

Why not spend a moment, take a piece of paper, and develop your first devotional schedule right now. Start revising it after you try it tomorrow morning. If it's your first year, don't try more than three or four or you'll be exercising with too heavy weights. Value the habit more than the difficulty or depth at this point! Take these basics and put them in the order you think you would enjoy them best:

> Bible reading
> Prayer
> Praise
> Journaling
> Reading a Christian book

What happens if you miss a day? Or a week? Or even a month? Prepare yourself to restart this holiness habit and pick up exactly where you left off! Don't try to catch up—just skip what you missed. Never permit yourself to construct a mountain you must conquer to make yourself "pay" for neglecting the Lord. Christ paid for all your sins and all of mine. His payment was sufficient for the Father, so it also must be for you. Just apologize to the Lord as you would to another friend for avoiding their company and receive His forgiveness and warm embrace. He's missed your fellowship more than you missed His. Remember, no relationship flourishes long term if it is based merely upon guilt and responsibility.

Holiness Habit #2: Meditate on Scripture

Of all the specific holiness habits which build holiness and directly control your transformation into a person of holiness, reading the Word of God is the absolute highest priority. Although you may think that prayer is the secret to transformation, I do not believe the Bible teaches that. Rather, the Bible is the *primary transforming agent*. Obviously, the Holy Spirit is the ultimate transformer, but He uses the Word of God as His primary tool of transformation.

Notice how the Apostle Paul describes this transformation in Romans 12:2b: "...be transformed by the renewing of your mind." Transformation begins with the believer's mind, not his behavior. All of us behave exactly in accordance with what we believe. Although we may think our behavior doesn't reflect what we deeply believe, the Bible reveals it does. In fact, there is never an exception.

CHARLES SPURGEON WAS ONCE SENT A BLACKMAIL LETTER TO THE EFFECT THAT IF HE DID NOT GIVE MONEY TO THE AUTHORS, THEY WOULD PUBLISH SOME THINGS IN THE NEWSPAPERS THAT WOULD DEFAME HIM AND RUIN HIS PUBLIC MINISTRY. HE LEFT THEM A LETTER IN REPLY: "YOU AND YOUR LIKE ARE REQUESTED TO PUBLISH ALL YOU KNOW ABOUT ME ACROSS THE HEAVENS." HE KNEW HIS LIFE WAS BLAMELESS IN THE EYES OF MEN AND, THEREFORE, THEY COULD NOT TOUCH HIS CHARACTER.

If I sin, then at the time I sinned, I thought that, considering all the options, sinning would be in the best interest for me, or I wouldn't have sinned. When I truly believe that the best option for me is obedience, then I will choose obedience.

What I think determines what I do. What I believe determines how I behave. Since that is true, the critical issue is for my mind to be changed to think exactly what the Bible teaches. Usually, our minds are not changed instantly nor in a sudden flash, but little by little as we understand and believe more and more of the truth.

Paul revealed that transformation is a process by his choice of the word "renewing," which literally means "to make new again" and again and again. The believer must make his mind new over and over again until every thought from the "old" way of thinking has been rooted out and everything from the "new" (biblical) way of thinking has been firmly planted and rooted.

Transformation occurs by *renewing our mind* by the Bible and not merely by reading our Bible. Although reading the Bible certainly influences our life in many wonderful ways, our transformation only occurs as our mind is changed from believing a lie to believing the truth. If reading the Bible doesn't adjust the way we think, then the Bible won't magically transform our behavior. Never forget those famous words of D. L. Moody, "The Bible wasn't given for our information, but our transformation." Don't read the Bible only for information; read for transformation through the renewing of your mind.

1. Renew Your Mind by Annually Reading the Whole Bible or New Testament

The habit of reading through the Bible or New Testament every year is a wonderful practice that hundreds of thousands of committed believers practice each year. There's nothing better for general spiritual vitality than reading through large passages from the Bible day after day. As you would anticipate, Walk Thru the Bible is thoroughly committed to this practice. We have published more than 100 million devotional guides and numerous Bibles to help people read and renew their mind through the Word of God. We would be delighted to serve you by encouraging you with the daily Bible reading and meditation habit. Here are some of our better known devotionals:*

> *The Daily Walk*—read through the Bible in one year.
> *The Closer Walk*—work through the New Testament in a year.
> *The Family Walk*—equips you to train your children through family devotions.
> *The Youth Walk*—a hard-hitting, lifechanging devotional guide for youth.
> *The Quiet Walk*—a slower pace with more worship and meditation.
> *The Life Walk*—contemporary topics for busy adults.

2. Renew Your Mind by Meditating on Carefully Selected Verses

Unlike reading through large sections of the Bible, this habit carefully selects small passages which focus specifically on those areas you know need transformed in order to fully please the Lord.

How do you know which verses to meditate upon? Watch your behavior and monitor your attitudes, and whenever you find anything that isn't duplicating Jesus, that's your meditation agenda! Take that area of your life and find three to five different verses or sections in the Bible which deal directly with your problem area.

---

* You can call 1-800-877-5486 for further information on these devotionals.

Type or write out on some 3" by 5" cards these verses and start reading them out loud day after day. Dedicate at least one month to each area as you'll not be able to renew your mind fully with only a few days. Slowly meditate on these verses while asking the Lord to show you where you believe the lie which must be discarded and the truth which must take its place.

Each time you read these verses, put a mark on the bottom of the card and stay on target until one of two things has happened in your life. If you uncover the lie you believed up to this point in your life that was the power behind your sin, carefully and actively renew your mind in that area until you know your mind has literally changed and you see reality differently.

If your cluster of sins surrounding that particular "lie" is no longer a part of your life, you can stop meditating as you know your transformation worked! The point of scriptural meditation isn't that you meditate, but that you are completely transformed in that particular area. The process is only valuable to you, therefore, to the degree which it brings transformation to you!

So many well-meaning believers memorize Scripture without any transformation, thinking that somehow if they can just remember the verses, the transformation will automatically and supernaturally take place. Some of the most carnal Christians I know can quote the most Scriptures by memory! Memorizing Scriptures only puts them in your "memory banks" so you can meditate upon them so you can be transformed by them. If memorization is viewed as the desired target, then memorization becomes an end in itself rather than the means to the biblical end of transformation.

If you really want Scripture memory to transform your life, select an area of your life which you know needs transformation. Name that area needing transformation with a biblical word such as anger or stealing or lust or gossip. Then find the best three to five passages in the Bible about that biblical area which give clear statements of truth and directives for life and write them down on a 3" by 5" card. Carry them with you everywhere and read them out loud over and over again. Think through every single word and seek the "wisdom" that lies in that verse.

Pray and ask the Lord to reveal the "lies" you must believe in this area, then confess the sins you have committed in this area of your life, one at a time. Make sure to identify what you used to believe (the "lie") but now know isn't biblical, and state the biblical truth with its godly attitudes and behaviors: "The Bible teaches that..." Depend actively upon the Holy Spirit in applying and enabling you in your commitment to know the truth and enjoy freedom to obey the Lord.

The point isn't how many verses you have memorized, but how many areas of your life have been transformed! Stop collecting verses as "trophies" when the only trophy that heaven celebrates is your life of holiness.

3. Renew Your Mind by Turning the Scriptures into a Prayer

This is a wonderful habit of holiness for you to use on a regular basis. Take Scriptures which are particularly meaningful to you at the time and pray them back to the Lord. Easy passages to do this with are from Psalms, Proverbs, Ephesians, Colossians, and Philippians. As you pray these Scriptures to the Lord, a different part of your life will be influenced and transformed. Usually meditation touches your mind and prayerful meditation touches your mind and heart.

As you read and meditate on the Scripture, make sure you record personal notes and insights right in your biblical text. Put dates when the Lord especially communicated to you through a particular passage. One of my earliest Bible professors in Bible college showed us his Bible in class one day—it had lines and arrows and colors and circles and notes everywhere! I couldn't believe it and wondered if I should do that to my Bible. Now, over 30 years later, I would strongly encourage you to do that very thing. Whenever I reach over to pick up my Bible, I always simultaneously pick up that blue or red pen to mark what I learn right in the text.

Therefore, change the way you look at the Bible. The Bible is a priceless gift from the Lord for the entire body of Christ as well as for each one of us individually. The more you bring your life into the clear agenda of the Bible and use it for its intended purposes, the more you will experience the fulfillment of God's promise of your transformation into the very image of Jesus Christ:

> All Scripture is given by inspiration of God, and is profitable for doctrine, for reproof, for correction, for instruction in righteousness, that the man of God may be complete, thoroughly equipped for every good work (2 Timothy 3:16-17).

11

THE HABIT
OF JOURNALING

*"Holiness appeared to me to be of a sweet, pleasant,
charming, serene, calm nature; which brought an inexpressible purity, brightness, peacefulness, and ravishment to
the soul. In other words, that it made the soul like a field or
garden of God, with all manner of pleasant flowers."*

—Jonathan Edwards

First you lay, then you lift your head, then you rock back
and forth, then you crawl, then you stand, then you stag-
ger, then you walk, then you trot, then finally you run.

First you count, then you add, then you subtract, then you multiply, then you divide, then you work equations, then you work in
geometry, then finally you work in trigonometry.

In all areas of life, there are always "first steps" followed by
"intermediate steps" followed by "advanced steps." This chapter
presents two intermediate habits of holiness that build upon the
earlier foundational habits of holiness. As you might anticipate,
there are "expert" secrets and skills of holiness beyond this chapter,
but those will be covered in the next chapter. If you can practice and
eventually master all six habits of holiness, I can promise that your
life will experience a radical transformation into the wonderful
image of Jesus Christ.

HOLINESS HABIT #3: THE PRAYER JOURNAL

The third holiness habit that should become a "core competence" by a person pursuing holiness is prayer. Of all the spiritual disciplines, I believe that prayer is more preached about but less practiced than any other. Many people feel that prayer is at the same time the easiest and the most difficult.

If the Bible is the basic tool for renewing the *mind*, then prayer is the basic tool for renewing the *relationship* with the Lord. Prayer is the language of relationship and opens the portal of intimacy between the human and the Divine. Without a vital prayer life, your walk of holiness will only become a one-sided attempt at human improvement. Prayer is the glue of relationship and intertwines your heart with the Lord's.

Not only is prayer the language of relationship, but God designed prayer to be the primary tool to release supernatural answers to your wishes, hopes, desires, and life's impossible or emergency situations. Although some promote the concept that God doesn't intervene supernaturally today, the Bible overflows with commands to seek that very thing—a supernatural answer. What is a supernatural answer? When God hears and answers your prayer, you are the recipient of a purposeful change in the "natural" that God "supernaturally" made happen just for you.

When you have seen the Lord answer your prayers time after time, your confidence in the power of prayer will literally go through the proverbial roof. In fact, the more you see the Lord answer you, the more you will be encouraged to pray for hundreds of things you would never have dreamt of asking God to provide for you. The Bible is remarkably clear and completely consistent in what it says about prayer: "Most assuredly, I say to you, whatever you ask the Father in My name *He will give you*. Until now you have asked nothing in My name. Ask, and *you will receive*, that your joy may be full" (John 16:23b-24).

Does the Lord have any requirements for answering your prayers?

> If you abide in Me, and My words abide in you, you will ask *what you desire*, and it shall be done for you (John 15:7).

Notice the first word is "if," which usually precedes a condition to be fulfilled for the answer to be granted. Not only "abiding in Christ" is required in John 15:7 for the fulfillment of such

> "THE TRUE CHRISTIAN IDEAL IS NOT TO BE HAPPY BUT TO BE HOLY."
>
> —A. W. Tozer

an incredible promise of answered prayer, but so also He says, "My words abide in you." James 5:16b-18 links the prayers of a "righteous man" to their answers: "The effective, fervent prayer of a righteous man avails much. Elijah was a man with a nature like ours, and he prayed earnestly that it would not rain; and it did not rain on the land for three years and six months. And he prayed again, and the heaven gave rain, and the earth produced its fruit."

This passage is remarkable because its main thesis is that a New Testament believer can experience remarkable, yes supernatural answers to prayer—just like the prayer of the Old Testament prophet Elijah. His prayers literally stopped all normal rain for three years—God gives answers to those who are righteous and pray "fervently."

ASKING IN HIS NAME

There is no doubt why people are not seeing many answers to prayer these days. They are neither walking in an intimate relationship with Christ nor walking in obedience to His Word (holiness). Therefore, they cannot inherit the magnificent but conditional promises of God giving them what they desire—and the incredible joy that such answers bring to the believer. Don't miss these remarkable and direct statements of fact about prayer by Jesus Himself:

> And whatever you ask in My name, that I will do, that the Father may be glorified in the Son. If you ask anything in My name, I will do it (John 14:13-14).

> ...ask what you desire, and it shall be done for you (John 15:7b).

...that whatever you ask the Father in My name He may give you (John 15:16b).

Most assuredly, I say to you, whatever you ask the Father in My name He will give you. Until now you have asked nothing in My name. Ask, and you will receive, that your joy may be full (John 16:23b-24).

Do you know what the church of Jesus has done with these verses? Basically, cut them out of the New Testament. Why? Because Christians have decided they don't work—and if they don't work—then they can't be true! Is that the truth? No. If the clear and repeated teachings of the Bible aren't working in our lives, it's not because the Bible has suddenly become untrue, *but rather because we have stopped fulfilling the requirements for those promises.*

Return to those passages and search out the conditions that He sovereignly and universally attached to those promises. Fulfill those conditions, pray fervently in faith, and just watch the Lord keep His promises to you!

Not too long ago, I was in a deep discussion about this very issue with a close friend who is a prayer warrior. I'll never forget what happened in the next 20 minutes or so. This prayer warrior simply smiled and brought out his prayer journal from his nearby desk drawer. It was April 30, 1998. He flipped back page after page in his prayer journal until January 1, 1996 and counted right before my eyes 368 different prayers the Lord answered in those two years and four months. *God said yes to 368 specific requests to this man's prayers!*

I sat dumbfounded.

Can you imagine such a wonderful prayer life? He was beaming and at times laughed winsomely as he shared some of the more remarkable and miraculous answers to prayer he had experienced. Amazing! As he closed his prayer journal, I looked deeply into his joyful heart and realized that the Lord's promise regarding prayer had been fulfilled right in this man's very life!

Why all this discussion about the fact that God actually still answers prayers—lots of them? Because the Lord commands you to pray to Him for answers so He can give them to you and cause your joy to literally overflow like my friend's. Only problem? You must abide with Him and walk in holiness. Such a little price for such an overwhelming reward.

"...Keep my commandments...just as I have kept my Father's...that your joy may be full" (John 15:10-11).

Nearly everyone that advances beyond the most basic level of praying uses a prayer journal of one kind or another. I know that until I became committed to become a man of prayer and established my own regular prayer practice with my prayer journal, my prayer life produced more guilt than anything else!

The most practical prayer journal I have discovered is a 5½" by 8½" three-ring binder with plastic tabs—buy a bunch of different colors of paper and make your own notebook. You'll get some ideas in the pages that follow but here are three very practical tips on maximizing your prayer life in your pursuit of holiness.

STANDARDIZE YOUR PRAYER SCHEDULE

Routine is the great efficiency provider. By establishing a daily and weekly routine to follow when you pray, you destroy the three greatest hindrances to praying. The most common hindrance to prayer is not having a set place, time, and procedure to follow. When you schedule your focused prayer time to occur at one particular place in your devotional habit, praying becomes very natural. For instance, I discovered that prayer works best for me after I have spent time journaling and in God's Word rather than before, whereas Darlene does exactly the opposite. Again, just select the best order and after some initial experimentation, don't change it. Any frustration you feel is probably that "avoidance temptation" discussed earlier.

The second most common hindrance to prayer is not knowing what to pray when you want to pray. Without that established ahead of time, you will spend more time and energy trying to decide what to do. The third most common hindrance to praying is what I have called the "wandering mind," which seems to plague nearly everyone in the early stages of prayer. By establishing a fixed and written track to pray on, the opportunities for a "wandering mind" to derail you rapidly decrease and even disappear.

Listed below are some of the categories that you can select from to develop your own prayer schedule. Be careful, however, to start slowly and work in more categories one at a time after you have used a new one for at least a month successfully. If you are in the early stages of the prayer holiness habit, then make sure you only start with four to six prayer categories for a few months.

1. Sin

Confess all known sin and quietly wait before the Lord, making sure that your heart is clean before Him in all areas.

2. Self

Confess your independent nature, die to self, enthrone Christ. Humble yourself before Him, establishing Him as your Lord and Master this day. Present yourself to Him as a living sacrifice. Present the members of your body as weapons for His usage this day.

3. Sanctification Prayers

These are requests you will pray for the rest of your life regarding your desire to become more like Christ in specific areas. These are never fully answered as there is always more of Christ.

4. Specific Prayers

These are requests that are concrete and ones that you'll know for sure when they are answered by the Lord with a "yes" or "no" or "not now."

5. Spirit of God

Recommit to not grieve or quench the Holy Spirit. Ask the Holy Spirit to fill you for service this day. Depend upon Him for guidance, wisdom, strength, and leadership.

6. Spiritual Gifts

Thank the Lord for the gifts He sovereignly gave to you. Ask the Lord to deepen each of those gifts by name and cleanse you from any pride or selfish ambition you may have about His gifts in you. Petition the Lord to help you narrow the focus of your life so you focus more and more of your life on using those gifts for His glory.

7. Spiritual Vision

Ask the Lord for His vision for your life, your marriage, your family, and the places you serve Him, including your church. Set your mind in the heavenlies and seek to see your life from the Lord's perspective.

8. Spiritual Service

Pray for the specifics of that day, including all major responsibilities, meetings with individuals, important decisions, and so on.

9. Spiritual Warfare

Put on the whole armor of God one piece at a time, making sure nothing is out of place. Recommit to stand and resist the enemy. Ask the Lord to keep you away from temptation and the evil one and precommit to choose obedience.

10. Spiritual Strongholds

Confess all strongholds you are seeking to be fully cleansed from and experience renewal through Scripture meditation. Renew your mind in prayer by confessing all known unbiblical thoughts and actions. Ask the Lord to shower His mercy and grace upon you and work deeply in you.

11. Spiritual Wisdom

Ask for the mind of Christ and His thoughts for the challenges of the day. Ask for financial stewardship and generosity. Ask for wisdom from above which is pure, peaceable, and willing to yield.

12. Spiritual Thanksgiving

Thank the Lord for at least ten specific things you are thankful for since yesterday, with no overlap. Don't leave this section until your heart is rejoicing with gratitude.

13. Spiritual Goals

Pray for each major goal for the year, asking for the Lord's wisdom, patience, grace, and empowerment.

14. Spiritual Intercession

Pray for each member of your family, extended family members, people with whom you work, church friends, people that don't know the Lord yet, your pastor and other Christian leaders, the president of the United States, and people you are mentoring.

WRITE YOUR REQUESTS IN YOUR PRAYER JOURNAL

Motivation in prayer is undoubtedly one of the keys which must be unlocked for an enduring and fulfilling life of prayer. When God created us, He linked the motivation we feel to those things we feel are important to us and the people that we love. The more important something is to us, the more motivated we feel to move in that direction.

So, as I finish praying through specific requests from previous days, I now ask myself what I wish the Lord would answer for me today. Then, as things come to my mind that are important to me and wouldn't be in disagreement with His will or ways, I write those specific requests in my prayer journal. Then the next day, guess what prayer requests are the newest on the list? Right—the most timely and important to me. Since imitating this practice, motivation has never again been a problem in my prayer life!

As I pray through these specific requests, I see if the Lord has answered any of the requests since yesterday and then mark them off. What an exciting daily adventure!

After experimenting with various methods of recording these requests, here's the format which seems to work really well:

Number	Specific Request	Date Started	Date Answered	Number of Days	Yes / No
1					
2					
3					

Number: The number is the number of this request. For instance, if you started this today, you would probably think of five important prayer requests and you would number them like that. Then tomorrow if after you prayed through request numbers one through five, your next specific prayer request would be recorded as number six.

Specific Request: On this one line write the specific request you want the Lord to answer. It has to be very specific so you will know if the Lord has answered it or not. One of the later lessons in this area is not to put a date by which you want something answered unless there is a very real reason. So often, I have discovered that the Lord answered my prayers, but His timing was different than the date I had assigned, without any reason.

I was putting dates on my prayer requests merely because I didn't want to wait—and I learned that by putting dates on "undated" issues, I was trying to put the Lord in a box. Thus He would have to hurry up and answer my prayers according to my timetable. This was not God's plan.

Date Started/Date Answered: These are the dates when you first write your prayer request in your prayer journal and the date when you know the Lord's answer. Here are what the three look like on an earlier page: 3/4/96–9/5/96; 3/4/96–3/16/96; 9/23/96–4/30/98.

Number of Days: This is a bit personal, but I wanted to get a handle on how many days I had prayed before the Lord answered my prayers. I counted the number of days between the date I started praying the request and the date the Lord answered the request and put the number of days off to the right of that specific request.

Looking down an older page of prayer requests where every request was answered, here's what that page looked like: 181 days, 148 days, 12 days, 90 days, 120 days, 2 days, 54 days, 60 days, 75 days, 15 days, 15 days, 60 days, 90 days, 164 days, 15 days.

Yes/No: When the answer comes from the Lord, I always write His answer in the form of a "Yes" or a "No" or "0" if something unusual comes up and the answer is no longer possible. I put these on the far right side of the line with a box around them. What an encouragement! So, as I turn the pages, I look down the far right column looking for an empty box and pray specifically for that request. But, as you can imagine, every page has a number of "yes" and "no" boxes so just the daily process deeply encourages me to continue on in my prayer life. Looking back over God's most recent answers for my prayers, here's what the yes/no box looks like: yes, yes, yes, no, no, yes, yes, yes, yes, yes, yes, yes, yes, yes, no.

This prayer habit deepens your consecration to Him. Don't you think the miraculous answers to prayers that you record would utterly convince you that the Lord God is intimately involved in your life?

SET YOUR LIFETIME PRAYER GOAL

Every once in awhile, the business world surfaces a concept which becomes very helpful to those of us in ministry. One of the better concepts in recent years is something called "Benchmarking," a method of establishing the highest "standard" of excellence which then becomes the new standard to match one's performance by. At Walk Thru the Bible, the various ministries develop their own internal benchmarks. For instance, in the seminar ministry which is currently in its 23rd year, they researched the year which they performed the best in the following categories:

1. Total number of seminars in one year
2. Total number of attendance in one year
3. Total number coming to know Christ in one year
4. Total number expressing a lifechanging spiritual experience in one year

5. Total number committing to read the Bible regularly in one year
6. Total amount of revenue for all sources in one year
7. Total amount of margin available for new ministry in one year

These standards then become practical measurements that the seminar team prays and labors to improve upon and exceed each year. For instance, last year (1997) in the United States, Walk Thru the Bible established a new benchmark of 1600 seminars in just 12 months. This year, the vice president of seminars lifted that bar of excellence and is seeking to top 2000 seminars in just 12 months. As you can imagine, that standard has risen higher and higher because of a known standard against which to measure our previous performance.

> "UNLESS THERE IS WITHIN US THAT WHICH IS ABOVE US, WE SHALL SOON YIELD TO THAT WHICH IS ABOUT US."
>
> —P.T. Forsyth

What measure are you using in your prayer life? I believe it is wise for a steward to have three specific measures to evaluate his life. First, use the biblical measures whenever you can find one. Second, use the standard of performance that you achieved last year for the Lord and seek to improve it in both quality and quantity. Third, find the highest benchmark you can in that area and place that out in the far distance as the "finish line" you would love to approach before you meet the Lord at the end of your life.

In my life, I call the highest benchmark anyone has set in a particular area the "life benchmark." Obviously, Jesus Christ is the final life benchmark in many areas of my life, but in others, He wasn't called by the Father to achieve the same goals the Father assigned in my race. Remember, Jesus was able to say He finished the work that God assigned to Him and yet He never was called to write a book.

When seeking to uncover who is the greatest example of the person who received more answers to prayer than anyone else, I didn't have much difficulty. Although others have written classics

> "THERE IS NO DUTY WE PER-
> FORM FOR GOD THAT SIN
> DOES NOT OPPOSE. AND
> THE MORE SPIRITUALITY OR
> HOLINESS THERE IS IN WHAT
> WE DO, THE GREATER IS THE
> ENMITY TO IT. THUS THOSE
> WHO SEEK MOST FOR GOD
> EXPERIENCE THE STRONGER
> OPPOSITION."
>
> —John Owen

on prayer, others may have had more dramatic answers to prayer, I don't know of anyone who has even come close to the man who lived his life purposefully to prove that God answers prayer: George Mueller. Before he died, he had recorded over 10,000 specific answers to prayer that God granted him directly and personally during his lifetime.

Two weeks ago, Darlene, Jessica, and I had the pleasure of skiing for a week in Colorado and staying at a close friend's beautiful mountain cabin. As we rode those ski lifts for thousands of feet, literally into the clouds, we felt like we were walking on the underside of heaven itself! I'll never forget one snowy afternoon breaking through the clouds into the brilliant sunshine and staring at a magnificent scene of the entire mountain range. It was breathtaking.

When I consider the mountain George Mueller scaled in prayer before the Lord, I couldn't help but call this "Prayer Life Benchmark" anything less than "Mueller's Summit."

Why not join me in this exhilarating quest of following in the footsteps of this giant prayer warrior. Although I'm afraid I'm still in the far distant foothills, I'm committed to staying focused on the goal and not looking back. Maybe someday before I meet the Lord, by God's grace, I'll be able to break through those clouds and at least get a glimpse of that magnificent but distant "Mueller's Summit"—so get on your hiking boots, my friend, bend your knee, and write out Prayer Request #1.

HOLINESS HABIT #4: YOUR LIFE JOURNAL

My wife loves to write letters. As much as she loves writing them, I dislike writing them. If ten years ago you had told me that I would someday write a book about the values and practice of a daily life journal, I wouldn't have believed it. In fact, if the truth were known, I think over my lifetime I have started at least six or seven journals and then thrown them in the bottom dresser drawer out of sight and mind within three weeks of starting each new resolution! If I'm not mistaken, every single one of those false starts began with the date "January 1, 19—" and probably had the last record somewhere between February and March.

Ever started, restarted, and restarted again? And then finally gave up? When it came to writing a journal, I found it was considerably beyond my greatest good intentions. And, if you have been tracking with me throughout this presentation, the reason the life journal didn't work for me earlier in my life was due to the lack of other underlying spiritual disciplines that also didn't exist. I was trying to build the "fifth-floor spiritual discipline" without floors three and four!

Something happened when I was 38 that thankfully changed all that. I don't know how many journals I have written and completed since that date, but it would be safe to say dozens of them. This morning at 5 A.M., my journal was once again opened; I greatly profited and enjoyed the process.

In the middle of a rather difficult midlife crisis in 1985, I flew across the country to see a man who specialized in the development and growth of Christian leaders. After discussing on the phone my desire to quit the ministry and hearing my frustration and despair, he invited me to fly out and spend the afternoon with him.

What he shared with me that day marked my life forever. The first thing he asked was for me to share my life story. When I had reviewed it up until approximately two years from that date, he stopped me and asked if he could finish the story. I quizzed him on how he could do that, but he only smiled and waited for me to listen. As he began to speak, I couldn't believe my ears! The longer he spoke, the greater was my amazement as he expressed exactly what had been happening to me.

After he finished, I asked if there was any help for such a person as myself! He laughed and said, "You are right on schedule." Although I had no idea what those words meant, I sighed, deeply encouraged that perhaps things could turn out for the good after all.

Then he put his two hands up in front of me with his left higher than his right. He said that early in my Christian life, my inner walk with the Lord was strong (the left hand) and my competence in ministry for the Lord was weak (the lower right hand). I nodded in agreement. Then he shared that in time, through Bible college and then seminary, my competence grew quickly but my walk with the Lord probably suffered. As he described that, he slowly changed his hands so that the right hand representing competence raised over the left hand representing my inner walk of devotional holiness. I nodded in agreement, but began to sense growing conviction.

Then he said the reason I was so tempted to leave the ministry was because my sense of fulfillment from the ministry had been taken away by the Lord, and regardless of how hard I pushed myself into the work of the Lord, it couldn't bring the fulfillment and joy that it did earlier—the Lord wouldn't permit it. I can remember wondering how he knew that....Then he took the rest of the blinders off my needy eyes.

"What is happening at this time in your life is that the Lord knows that unless these two hands switch one more time back to the original order, you will never become the spiritual leader God has created you to be for Him in your life." Then he asked some very penetrating questions about the spiritual disciplines of my life. Although I practiced daily devotions, they were shallow. Though I read my Bible regularly, I didn't receive much help or food from it. And, although I prayed, I certainly didn't pray very long nor have many answers to my prayers.

Once again, he smiled and nodded in affirmation—with no condemnation in his voice or eyes. How I thank the Lord for him and his insight at that crisis point in my life. Then his lower hand representing my walk with the Lord began pushing against the competent one. He said the Lord deliberately and forcibly was bringing pressure on me by taking away any fulfillment from "doing" so that I could learn the deeper fulfillment from "being" once again.

He said there was a reason of conviction that the Lord brought in everyone's life in which He called them to walk with Him more than work for Him and that the switch must come. Then my afternoon mentor shared that I must go back to Atlanta and focus my best efforts on learning and practicing these spiritual disciplines. And did he ever nail me on this life journal idea! He

> "NO HORSE GETS ANYWHERE UNTIL HE IS HARNESSED. NO STEAM OR GAS EVER DRIVES ANYTHING UNTIL IT IS CON-FINED. NO NIAGARA IS EVER TURNED INTO LIGHT AND POWER UNTIL IT IS TUNNELED. NO LIFE EVER GROWS GREAT UNTIL IT IS FOCUSED, DEDI-CATED, DISCIPLINED."
>
> —Harry Emerson Fosdick

said the daily journal is an incredibly powerful tool to assist you in the pilgrimage back from doing to being.

That man was absolutely right. I dedicated myself to the Lord during those lifechanging months and have never looked back. How I praise the Lord that those "hands" switched back to correct priorities. Now walking with the Lord is the high point of my life, not working for Him. Finally ministry is birthed in "being," not in "doing."

TIPS ON YOUR LIFE JOURNAL

Obviously, a whole book could easily be written on each of these spiritual disciplines, including how to experience great victory through the practice of the life journal. Here are a few of the secrets I have discovered:

1. Write in your life journal every day you have devotions.
2. Devote a whole page in your life journal for each day.
3. Put your pen on the top of the page and don't take it off until the whole page is filled.
4. Give yourself about three months to get into the swing of it; don't be frustrated.
5. Release yourself to be completely honest, including your sin.

6. Remember that the life journal is meant to be the spiritual lever to your spiritual life.
7. Try as many different things as you can in your journal and continue whatever helps you the most.

What should you write in your journal? Here's a list of some of the categories I use in mine, but please remember that next year, I may have different ones—use whatever works for you during this time in your life. If it isn't working, just remain patient and continue trying while asking the Lord for wisdom in what to do. Keep at it! You might find it helpful to:

1. Journal your prayers to the Lord
2. Journal your insights from meditating on the Bible
3. Journal your confessions of sin (many people lock their journals)
4. Journal your frustrations and fears and discuss them with the Lord
5. Journal your private dreams and visions and desires
6. Journal your lessons from successes and failures
7. Journal your praise and worship to the Lord

There are some helpful Christian books on journaling that any good Christian bookstore could direct you to—but whatever you do, learn how to write with your heart in your journal. If you read my journal, you would soon know me from the inside out—just the way the Lord knows me. The men and women who have begun this holiness habit have become wonderfully "addicted" to the joy of the journal!

12

ADVANCING
TO HOLINESS

*"A holy life is a voice; it speaks when the tongue is silent,
and is either a constant attraction or a perpetual
reproof."*

—Robert Leighton

If you were to visit your local Christian bookstore and ask for
the section on the spiritual life or spiritual disciplines, you
would undoubtedly find numerous outstanding books on
more than 20 different disciplines of the spiritual life. Obviously, by
only discussing 6 in this book, your favorite may not even be mentioned. Don't think, however, that fasting, or a small-group Bible
study, or an accountability group, or solitude, service, mission trips,
spiritual retreats, aren't strategically important in your life, because
they are.

But after encouraging people around the world in their own
spiritual lives, I have come to discover that these six holiness habits
are the primary ones used by those believers who walk with the
Lord and touch the world with their lives. Additionally, these six
habits are presented in the specific order that I've observed believers begin to practice and finally master them.

Obviously when one is limited to only one book on personal
holiness, more has to be left out than can ever be included! People

like you and me just don't seem to be attracted to books of 3000 or 4000 pages....So, you'll have to read other books to learn of walking by the Spirit, union with Christ, spiritual warfare, the theology of the spiritual life, and spiritual mentoring. But in the next few pages, you'll learn of two advanced holiness habits.

HOLINESS HABIT #5: PRAISE AND WORSHIP

It's amazing—we call it the "worship service" and yet nearly everything takes place during that hour except genuine worship. Worship is defined as the reverent act of offering extravagant respect, admiration, or devotion to the highest object of esteem: our Lord. The root of "worship" comes from the concept of "worthiness" or "worth" and therefore when we say that we *worship* the Lord, we express to Him how we feel about His worth. *Praise and worship are nothing more and nothing less than expressing to the Lord God privately and publicly how we feel about His worth.*

Recently I was out of town speaking at a leadership conference; on Sunday morning I attended a nearby church worship service. During the key moment of "worship," the singing of the worship hymns, I dared to take a slow look at the congregation. I counted 20 adults in a row and found 6 of them singing. As I watched their faces and body language, I didn't observe that even one of those six remotely connected to the Lord during that worship song in order to ascribe to Him value and worth. Have you ever felt like that in a "worship service"?

Even as I write this sentence, memories flood my heart of an opposite experience that occurred only months earlier. On an international trip for Walk Thru the Bible, I had the privilege of speaking to a large church in Singapore and then flying the next week to speak in a large church in Malaysia. Do you know what happened in both services? The pastoral staff led the congregation in a one-hour praise-and-worship session before I was invited to preach the Word. In both countries, no one sat down during that one hour of praise and worship—and as I scanned that vast audience looking for reliable signs of true worship, I saw the exact opposite of that other church service. Intense "worth-giving" flooded the faces and echoed through the voices of thousands of people. How the Lord must have relished the adoration of His people!

Have you learned to praise and adore and worship the Lord yet? In America, two recent movements have brought praise and worship back into the church. The first is the charismatic movement and the second is Promise Keepers (PK). As I've spoken at numerous PK stadium events, I've seen it happen over and over again. Men who may have never truly worshipped the Lord at any time in their lives become initiated to the wonders of God-worship.

At first they sing hymns like they always do. Then they begin to sing from their hearts and mean the words. Then they begin to connect with the Lord while they are singing. Finally, they become enraptured with the Lord and cannot seem to stop praising Him. Once men have tasted the fruit of true biblical praise, they never want to go back to praiseless praise services and worshipless worship services.

But the tragedy is that they do. And even worse, most men and women never learn how to praise and worship on their own, without all the support of a praise gathering, a special worship conference, or a PK event. *The fifth holiness habit is your continual practice of public and private praise and worship.*

As far as we know, the Lord only bestowed the gift of praise and worship on two of His immense number of created living organisms: angels and mankind. Just because the Lord created our innate ability

"IF ONLY TEN AMONG US BE RIGHTEOUS, THE TEN WILL BECOME TWENTY, THE TWENTY FIFTY, THE FIFTY A HUNDRED, THE HUNDRED A THOUSAND, AND THE THOUSAND WILL BECOME THE ENTIRE CITY. AS WHEN TEN LAMPS ARE KINDLED, A WHOLE HOUSE MAY EASILY BE FILLED WITH LIGHT; SO IT IS WITH THE PROGRESS OF SPIRITUAL THINGS. IF BUT TEN AMONG US LEAD A HOLY LIFE, WE SHALL KINDLE A FIRE WHICH SHALL LIGHT UP THE ENTIRE CITY."

—Saint John Chrysostoam

and desire to worship, however, doesn't mean that we use it for the purpose He gave it.

Without learning and then practicing this incredible gift of praise, the believer will remain limited and experience life only on the horizontal plane. Millions of Christians "worship" year after year and never truly connect with the Lord on a deeply personal and radically transforming level.

A believer can have daily devotions and not praise and worship. A believer can attend church weekly and not praise and worship. A believer can pray regularly and not praise and worship. Praise and worship are unique experiences and represent the fifth holiness habit.

EXPRESSING HIS WORTHINESS

The first trait of biblical praise is to express to the Lord that He is worthy. I'm convinced that the primary reason why so few believers truly worship the Lord is simply due to their being so out of touch with His greatness and power. Although many feel that Christians don't praise and worship because they haven't been trained, I am convinced that just isn't the case. When any of us enter into the Lord's presence at death, we will immediately and intensely worship and praise the Lord. Whenever an individual in the Bible saw an angel in all of his glory, he instantly fell down and worshipped. Worship is the immediate and innate response to the presence and power of God. Individuals who know the Lord and His glory always worship. Individuals who don't worship are inevitably blinded by their own glory.

The reason praise and worship is the fifth habit of holiness instead of the first, second, or third is because believers don't worship on an ongoing and meaningful basis unless the other disciplines are in place. Without devotions, Bible meditation, and regular prayers, the believer lives such a self-life that they never break through to experience the true majesty of God.

Unless the person leading the worship service and especially the music knows how to lead the people to praise the Lord in worship, the congregation will be led in such a way which actually hinders worship rather than helping it. After ministering across the nation for 30 years in hundreds of settings, it is my observation that less than 10 percent of churches lead their congregation to personally praise and worship.

Remember, if the heart of the believer does not connect with the Lord in order to express His "worthiness," then biblical praise and worship do not occur regardless of the external things that do. For instance,

- Singing is not worship, singing is expressing words to musical tones.
- Singing quickly or slowly is not worship, that's called tempo.
- Singing loudly or quietly is not worship, that's called volume.

When then does praise and worship actually take place? When the individual (or group of individuals) connects with the Lord in order to express how wonderful He is. *Praise and worship is an intimate interaction where the believer "compliments" the Lord so personally and directly that he feels he is the only person in the Lord's presence at the time.*

If the believer does not seek personal "connection" with the Lord, biblical praise can't occur. That's why the Lord receives so little praise and worship even in the middle of the worship service of a large church. The congregation's focus is on the singing of the song rather than worshiping the Person to whom the song is being sung. The focus has to move off of the process of singing so that singing can be the vehicle that carries and delivers the heart's praise. Singing may be the easiest method in which to praise and worship. But, if the leader is demanding all the attention upon him or her, then the Lord cannot receive the attention—and when that happens, the music leader may actually become a hindrance rather than a help to worship.

Somewhere in the singing, the congregation must be transitioned from the act of singing into the act of praising. The words and the pace of the singing must become secondary so that the person can internally express praise and adoration.

Learning a new praise song can become a hindrance to praising the Lord, unless the leader can train the congregation to know it well enough that they can sing it to the Lord rather than focusing on the new words and melody. If you'll notice the newer praise songs, they have a simple melody and usually very simple words. Older believers have often criticized these praise songs as lacking depth, but in reality, I believe the primary purpose of singing is to praise and worship the Lord, not communicate deep doctrines. Obviously, many hymns of the faith overflow with significant theology, and some of them also encourage praise, but others actually hinder praise.

Singing is a valid part of church life and does not always need to transition to praise or worship. Sometimes hymns are tremendous teaching tools. But, if the heart of the believer does not actually express heart-praise to the Lord during the singing, then the singing was not praise. The Lord doesn't want to be serenaded. He wants to be worshipped.

So, I return to my original question, do you praise and worship the Lord? And if you do, are you a "worship co-dependent?" Do you only praise when you have an external environment where you are "set up" to worship? Let's say you are fortunate to attend a church which leads the congregation to truly praise the Lord—do you praise Him through the week when you are alone? If you don't, then it may be more true that you know how to be "led in praise" than actually know how to "praise the Lord."

Often, the part of the Sunday morning service where the pastor preaches is labeled in the bulletin as "Worship through Preaching." Once again, worship may or may not occur through preaching. I know that when I hear some of the men of God in the pulpits, they lift up the Lord so effectively that I cannot help myself—I must thank and praise the Lord! The higher the pastor lifts up the Lord, the more I spontaneously worship the Lord from my heart.

But, as is the case in the "praise service," so also in the "preaching service." In most pulpits, even those who are fortunate enough to have solid Bible-believing, Bible-preaching preachers, the Bible is genuinely preached but the Lord isn't lifted up so that the audience worships the Lord.

Sermon after sermon opens the meaning of the biblical text, but rarely does the pastor fulfill his greatest calling—to lead the heart of the congregation through the preaching of God's Word into the glorious presence of the Lord, so they are overwhelmed by His grace, greatness, and glory and respond to Him in sincere worship and praise.

Sermons must move through three distinct stages, from focusing on the pastor, to focusing on the Bible, to ultimately focusing on the Lord Himself. If the final "amen" is spoken before the needy hearts of His people touch the heart of their God, then unfortunately a tragic abortion has occurred in the preaching process.

> "THE BEAUTY OF HOLINESS HAS DONE MORE, AND WILL DO MORE, TO REGENERATE THE WORLD AND BRING IN EVERLASTING RIGHTEOUSNESS THAN ALL THE OTHER AGENCIES PUT TOGETHER. IT HAS DONE MORE TO SPREAD RELIGION IN THE WORLD, THAN ALL THAT HAS EVER BEEN PREACHED OR WRITTEN ON THE EVIDENCES OF CHRISTIANITY."
>
> —Thomas Chalmers

Preaching must link heaven and earth so powerfully that the preacher eventually becomes absolutely irrelevant in the minds of the people! People leave such preaching appreciative for the Word of God but even more than that, captivated by the God of the Word. Whenever the focus remains on the Scriptures rather than the Lord of the Scriptures, our response to Him is aborted in the process.

But now, may we change the focus from the music and preaching back to you? Because if that doesn't happen, I will not have been any service to you except to give you reasons to be tempted to sin through criticism, rationalization, or blame for your lack of praise and worship. Ultimately, the Lord calls you and me to worship and praise Him regardless of whether the minister of music or the senior pastor makes it easy or not.

PERSONAL WORSHIP

My greatest praise and worship occurs in my "devotional chair." *My most intense personal praise and worship occurs between Sundays and not on Sundays.* So should yours. Sunday is a time to come together to praise and worship corporately, but it shouldn't be the only time you praise and worship the Lord.

Why not? Because the Lord's greatness doesn't decrease when you walk out of the church service, so your response to Him shouldn't change! This is not a book on praise and worship, but on holiness. The habit of praise produces holiness in two directions. First, when you set yourself apart in order to ascribe to the Lord glory and strength, you dedicate yourself to that sacred purpose.

Second, when you lift the Lord up in your own mind and set Him apart and above everything and everyone else, you make Him holy in your heart. The more you lift the Lord up in your mind and set Him apart in His magnificence, the more you worship Him in the beauty of holiness. The more your heart praises His holiness, the more you will begin to live more deeply in that holiness.

Throughout this book, I have had to fight the natural desire to write about the Lord's holiness rather than ours. But this book is focused specifically upon your holiness, especially during times of temptation. Perhaps a slight glimpse into His holiness may be permissible.

When you cross the final threshold and enter the presence of the Lord, what will you find the 24 elders, the four living creatures, the hundreds and hundreds of millions of angels, and millions of believers all doing? The Lord revealed this answer directly to the Apostle John. Here's what the 24 elders and four living creatures sang:

> *"You are worthy* to take the scroll, and to open its seals; for You were slain, and have redeemed us to God by Your blood out of every tribe and tongue and people and nation, and have made us kings and priests to our God; and we shall reign on the earth."...And I heard the voice of many angels around the throne, the living creatures, and the elders; and the number of them was ten thousand times ten thousand, and thousands of thousands, saying with a loud voice: "Worthy is the Lamb

who was slain to receive power and riches and wisdom, and strength and honor and glory and blessing!" (Revelation 5:9-12).

This vision climaxes with this revelation. Don't miss who says this.

And every creature which is in heaven and on the earth and under the earth and such as are in the sea, and all that are in them, I heard saying: "Blessing and honor and glory and power Be to Him who sits on the throne, And to the Lamb, forever and ever!" (verse 13).

Did you ever wonder why everyone will be saying or singing the same thing through all of eternity? Only because when we see the Lord and know the truth about Him and what He has done and is doing and will do, we will not be able to stop our hearts from bursting with inexpressible and inexhaustible praise and worship.

The first words—"You are worthy!"

When you believe the truth about the true worthiness of the Lord, you will not be able to stop yourself in "worthy-shipping" Him. And when you want to express your heart filled with wonder and gratitude and adoration, you only want one Person to hear it— the Lord. When you care enough to connect and express to Him that He is worthy, you will have entered through the portal of praise.

FERVENT WITH THE LORD

The second trait of biblical praise is that you connect with the Lord fervently. The Bible gives remarkably diverse instructions about how we should praise and worship the Lord. These instructions are in all of our Bibles—and they are as straightforward as they can be. They aren't hidden in complicated passages, and you don't need Greek or Hebrew to understand. Instead, they lay on the surface more than almost any other major teaching of the Bible.

So what's the problem? Each denomination or fellowship inevitably selects a few passages that the Bible teaches about praise and worship and then summarily excludes and avoids the rest of the passages which are just as direct and straightforward and biblical as the ones they chose to affirm and practice. Not only that, but in order to justify their choice, each group eventually attacks the practices of the other groups whose "selected list" of "approved practices" of praise and worship are different.

When you travel around the world and minister in many different denominations and groups, your eyes are forced open to your own narrowmindedness! In the early days, I can remember actually sweating because I didn't know what to do with my hands. In some nations and nationalities, I can remember worrying because I didn't know what to do with my feet. In other situations, I can remember biting my lip until it almost bled because I didn't know what to say out loud when others shouted.

You see, I was raised in a great church in a wonderful tradition. Now looking back, I realize it was the "passive position of praise." The less the better. The quieter the more biblical. The darker the clothes, the holier. The slower the tempo, the deeper the praise. But I couldn't find instructions for this type of worship in Scripture. Finally I realized that I must find out exactly what the Lord instructed His people to do in praise and worship.

What I found was that God instructs us to worship Him *fervently*. How "fervent" are you in your praise and worship? Think through the past week and rate yourself on the "fervency" range of your praise and worship. If a "zero" means that you had no fervency, and "100" means that you experienced extremely fervent worship, where would you score yourself? How fervent are you when cheering your favorite football team? When celebrating a big business deal? And how fervent were you the last time read the Psalms?

If your praise and worship languish around the 10 to 30 mark, not only will the Lord not be too impressed, but neither will you return very often to the corridors of praise. Why? It bores you to tears. Compare that with the fervency of God's people in the Bible.

The biblical word for fervent praise is the Hebrew word "*hallelujah!*" Psalm 150 captures this attitude of fervent praise and worship—I call it the "*Hallelujah Chorus of the Old Testament*":

Praise the LORD!
Praise God in His sanctuary;
Praise Him in His mighty firmament!
Praise Him for His mighty acts;
Praise Him according to His excellent greatness!
Praise Him with the sound of the trumpet;
Praise Him with the lute and harp!
Praise Him with the timbrel and dance;
Praise Him with stringed instruments and flutes!
Praise Him with loud cymbals;
Praise Him with clashing cymbals!
Let everything that has breath praise the LORD.
Praise the LORD!

Notice the exclamation points and specific instructions in that psalm. When a person becomes fervent, his or her voice often raises, and the body becomes more animated. For a quick study on what fervency looks like, just watch a professional football or basketball game and listen to the people in the stands. Watch what they do, especially the closer the game's scores become and as it nears the end of the game. As you scan the audience, no one will be seated, no one will be quiet, and no one will have their hands in their pockets. Why? Because fervency must demonstrate itself *physically*.

Do you think the laws guiding fervency when expressed in an athletic game change when expressed in a religious service? When anyone becomes fervent in praising and worshipping the Lord, it is difficult, if not impossible, to remain seated. In addition, the more intense an individual praises the Lord, the more he begins to face heaven. Interestingly, when Christ prayed right before the famous feeding of the 5,000, notice his posture in prayer: "And He took the five loaves and the two fish, *and looking up to heaven*, He blessed and broke and gave the loaves to the disciples..." (Matthew 14:19b).

Obviously the Bible doesn't command a certain posture to praise all of the time, and there's nothing inherently better about "bowing your heads to pray" or "lifting your heads to pray." But if you'll notice not only yourself but everyone else, the more intense the prayer or praise, the more you'll involuntarily begin to face heaven.

Not only is it true with the face, but I've also discovered something amazing about the hands. The more intense the worship, the more our hands find a reason to move up. For a person who grew up with holiness being defined as "hand's down," I can't believe how far I've strayed (or come, depending on which side of the "hands" you sit on!). The trend is observable in a gathering of the Lord's people who intensely and fervently pray or praise. I've observed this over and over at Promise Keepers conferences. On Friday night, only a few scattered men have their hands up, and they probably feel a little out of place. On Saturday morning, about 30 to 40 percent raise their hands spontaneously when we sing "Amazing Grace." By the middle of the afternoon, when we are singing "Holy, Holy, Holy," you can't find a man whose hands and face are not reaching toward the heart of heaven.

I would guess most of the speakers don't raise their hands when they are back home, so why do they raise their hands at a PK event? The same reason they would raise their hands if the worship and praise became intensely focused on the Lord in any other setting.

Don't get me wrong, I'm not advocating hands up or hands down. I'm only sharing my observations about what "hands" seem to do in direct proportion to the fervency of prayer or praise: *"Therefore I exhort first of all that supplications, prayers,* intercessions, and giving of thanks be made for all men....I desire therefore that the men pray everywhere, lifting up holy hands, without wrath and doubting..."* (1 Timothy 3:1,8).

One other concept linked to fervency is the use of your posture. I can't find the command: "Sit and pray!" or "Sit and praise!" but I can find passages that tell us "standing" and "kneeling" are biblical. "Falling on your face" is biblical. ("Dancing" is even biblical, but after the "raising the hands," I'd better not be too biblical!) So when you want to follow the biblical model, don't spend so much time sitting in prayer or praise.

Some of the greatest men and women of God read their Bible only on their knees. Revelation records that the 24 elders in heaven "fall down" in worship before God.

Therefore ask yourself, *"How comfortable am I in widening my 'comfort zone' to the biblical norm in praising and praying before the*

Lord?" Can you whisper? Can you shout? Do you kneel? Do you lay prostrate? Do you weep? Can you clap loudly and really get into it? Do you ever dance before the Lord in the hidden recesses of your basement or among the deep forests or even in the imaginations of your worshipping heart? Can you join King David as he "dances before the Lord with all his might" (2 Samuel 6:14a) or obey the directives of the psalms when they instruct us to praise with instruments?

Wrapped up in this sort of freewheeling discussion about the "style of your praise" is an encouragement to loosen up a bit! Do you think when you get to heaven that heaven's choir will never clap their hands, stamp their feet, raise their voices, or shout "glory!"? If heaven provides liberties to express our praise more than a quiet and reserved whispered "amen" once every four years or so, perhaps we had better start practicing for the "real thing"!

How do you know when you've started hitting reality in your praise? When you behave with the Lord the same way you did when your son scored the winning touchdown at Homecoming! When *the boundaries of praise are enlarged, then the effectiveness of praise automatically and dramatically increases.* Just imagine if you broke through your inhibitions regarding your praise and prayers! The broader the style of worship, the fuller and more fulfilling the praise.

EXPRESS THE LORD'S "WORTHY-NESS"

How many different reasons do you have to praise and worship the Lord? The more reasons you have to praise, the more potential you have to praise Him. If you can only think of five or six things to praise the Lord for, you'll soon run out of honest and meaningful praise and worship. The more categories of praise you know and use, the more your life can be full of praise and worship. Consider some areas for which you can praise the Lord.

1. The creation of the Lord is an amazing and almost infinite category of praise. Everywhere you look you see the handiwork of the Master Creator. The more you know of any living organism, the more impressive His handiwork becomes! Everywhere you look, the Lord has left His creative genius not only for your enjoyment, but

> "HEROISM IS AN EXTRA-
> ORDINARY FEAT OF THE
> FLESH; HOLINESS IS AN
> ORDINARY ACT OF THE
> SPIRIT. ONE MAY BRING
> PERSONAL GLORY; THE
> OTHER ALWAYS GIVES
> GOD THE GLORY."
>
> —Chuck Colson

as a subtle invitation for you to extol His greatness.

2. *The compassions of the Lord* are threaded throughout human history and uniquely throughout your past, present, and future. As you purpose to see the Lord's handiwork throughout your life, you will never lack for meaningful reasons to express your praise and worship. Our awareness of the Lord's compassion should provide us with a new list every day. Jeremiah speaks to the issue in Lamentations 3:22-23: "Through the LORD's mercies we are not consumed, because His compassions fail not. They are new every morning; great is Your faithfulness."

Did you see the flow of his innate thought? He saw a new reality of God's compassions and mercies which immediately turned his thoughts directly to the Lord in the now famous praise: "Great is your faithfulness!"

3. *The character of the Lord* becomes the most treasured focus of praise and worship the longer you walk with the Lord in the habits of holiness. Why? Because the most precious thing about a person is not what they did or said but who they are. That's perhaps why Jeremiah didn't thank the Lord for some of the specific new compassions, but rather praised the greatness of His character of faithfulness.

Over the past decade of focused praise, I have noticed the trend of my increasing appreciation, respect, and "valuing" of the Lord's character above His conduct, promises, Word, mighty works, miracles, and prophecies. How I praise and extol Him for His tenderness, loyalty, compassion, patience, strength, wisdom, longsuffering, mercy, goodness, and kindness.

I have yet to meet a single believer who fervently and continually connects with the Lord in praise who did not already enjoy regular devotions, reading the Bible, and a substantial prayer life.

Here's what King David revealed about this incredible source of joy and pleasures that never end: "In Your presence is fullness of joy; at Your right hand are pleasures forevermore" (Psalm 16:11).

May each of us experience this "fullness of joy" through our worship of the Lord on this side of the eternal veil and enjoy right now the foretaste of the "pleasures forevermore"!

HOLINESS HABIT #6: FASTING

As you look across any shopping mall, visit any restaurant, or walk through the low-fat and diet aisles of a supermarket, you can quickly tell that we are not a generation who believes and practices the regular fast. How many believers do you know personally who have fasted for at least two days more than twice in their entire lifetime? Fasting is a lost art for most believers today. But, when you quickly survey the Scriptures for who practiced, notice who you discover: Moses, the nation of Israel, Samuel, David, Elijah, the Ninevites, Nehemiah, King Darius, Daniel, Anna, Jesus, John the Baptist and his disciples, the Pharisees, the apostles, Paul, and the early Christians.

What exactly is a spiritual fast? A fast is the practice of denial of something for a specific time by an individual, couple, family, church, city, or nation for a spiritual reason. Why does spiritual fasting work? In the Lord's sovereignty, He decided that whenever a person denies himself of food or sleep or speaking (silence) or the presence of others (solitude) for spiritual purposes, the spiritual consequences will be multiplied. Remember, for instance, the difficulty the disciples were experiencing in Matthew 17:14ff. when they tried to heal the epileptic who had the demon. When they asked the Lord to explain what they did wrong, they must have been shocked with His answer: "This kind does not go out except by prayer and fasting."

Normal prayer and normal procedures for demonic problems weren't powerful enough to expel this particular kind of demon. However, when you add fasting to your prayer, he will leave. The Lord multiplies the power of prayer when His people fast and pray.

Believers choose to fast when battling an area in their lives which is important to them. Most people who fast don't do it because they enjoy it—because fasting isn't pleasurable nor attractive—but because it aids them in some way. Some fast in order to break free from a stubborn sin, in order to thank the Lord for a major answer to their prayers, and in order to focus all their attention upon their relationship with the Lord.

You can fast in order to receive the Lord's guidance in an important decision or matter, to repent and humble yourself before the Lord, or to seek the Lord's protection from war, tragedy, or destruction. Some believers even fast in order to beseech the Lord to send revival. But you won't fast unless you really need the answer to your prayers, and know that the Lord is the One who can meet your need. You won't fast unless you really believe the Lord is powerful enough and interested enough in you to answer your prayers and intervene in the situation you face. You also won't fast unless you have come to the conclusion that by denying yourself in order to humble yourself before the Lord, your prayers will have a greater degree of influence with the Lord.

Crisis often thrusts people into fasts. If a terrible car accident put the person you loved the most in a life-threatening situation, many would stop eating just to continue praying fervently for the Lord's miraculous intervention.

How often should you fast? As often as you would like. But don't let anyone purposefully know that you are on a fast. Whatever you do, don't stand up in a prayer meeting and ask for prayer as you endure your fast! As Jesus instructed, put on your best clothes and "happiest face" and veil your fasting from the eyes of men. What should you do when you are out to lunch or dinner? Share that you aren't eating for "personal reasons" but you would love to enjoy their company.

Some people participate in an *annual fast*, selecting the same period of time each year and building a habit in their lives. Others participate in a *weekly fast*, selecting the same 24 hours each week to fast on a regular basis. A practical period is to start by fasting through the Sunday evening meal and Monday's breakfast and lunch, then eating again on Monday evening.

You can also try a *quick fast* whenever something really important arises and you are intently seeking the Lord's help. Purposefully skip one meal and get away by yourself for that time in order to focus directly on the Lord. Some even participate in a *Daniel fast*, eating nothing but fruits and vegetables for a week. They partake of no coffee, soft drinks, bread, or dessert for seven days. Darlene and I have found that every single Daniel fast brought a tremendous breakthrough on the sixth day—and we never want to stop on the seventh because of what the Lord is doing in our lives. The Daniel fast works well within a family context and permits you to deal with social responsibilities a bit more easily.

One spiritually mature pastor has been practicing a 40-day total fast for 14 years in a row. Two months ago, I discovered that a large portion of his church joins him on this spiritual fast each year, and the number is growing. How wonderful! You should hear the stories of the miraculous breakthroughs occurring in the lives of the individuals and the church as a whole.

Fasting is an advanced holiness habit but repays those who practice it with rich rewards in their walk with the Lord and holiness of life. If you aren't practicing any fasts in your life, why not try a Daniel fast for a solid week? I can promise you from personal experience, you'll be thrilled you did!

LIVING A LIFE OF HOLINESS

In conclusion, may I speak to you personally? As you think about your life today, how are you doing with these holiness habits? Take a moment before reading any further and do a bit of reflection. Mark the following chart where you feel you best fit. When you are done, add the total score just to get a handle on your progress with the *"holiness habits"* at this point in your life.

Regardless of where your holiness habits score may be at this moment, don't be discouraged! The main issue isn't where you are today as much as where you will be tomorrow, this time next year, and in ten years. Take a broader look and realize you are a steward of your whole life and are challenged by the Lord to continue the development of your progressive holiness.

Of these holiness habits, which one do you feel would make the most difference in your life if you were further down the road of

Holiness Habit:	Haven't Started	Usually Fail at Attempts	Sporadic Successes	Usually Practiced	Habitually Enjoyed
Holiness Score	0	5	10	15	20
1. Devotions					
2. Scripture					
3. Prayer					
4. Journal					
5. Worship					
6. Fasting					
Total					

mastery? That's the one you should start with first! Don't try to implement everything all at once because it is a guaranteed way to failure. Take the one you desire the most and spend the next 30 days specifically focusing on it. All of us who have experienced major victories in our lives regarding these daily habits have discovered that it takes at least a month if not a quarter of a year to build a solid habit. Fight the tendency to work on the advanced habits before developing a strong success rate in the foundational habits.

Fight the natural tendency to want to fix everything today. Deny this temptation as it nearly always is from your fleshly pride wanting to be perfect. Instead, enjoy victory and lasting lifechange by succeeding in one habit at a time. After you practice it regularly and it doesn't require major effort, select the second (the one you desire the strongest) and work on it for another quarter. Just think what your life will be like in a couple of years!

Finally, let me offer a few parting words of encouragement. *First, live under grace not under law:* Don't become a legalistic slave to your holiness habits. Give yourself breathing room and don't be afraid to take a day or two off now or then. On Sunday, I have an entirely different routine, and by Monday morning, I'm more than ready to get back at it. You haven't committed a major sin by missing a day or even a few days—leave a little bit of room for the unexpected bumps that life brings us. The Lord more than understands!

Second, enjoy yourself more by adding variety to your schedule: If you are experiencing a little boredom or if it's getting harder to get up in the morning, then try something: share with the Lord that you are

> "THE TRIUMPHANT CHRISTIAN DOES NOT FIGHT FOR VICTORY; HE CELEBRATES A VICTORY ALREADY WON. THE VICTORIOUS LIFE IS CHRIST'S BUSINESS, NOT YOURS."
>
> —Reginald Wallis

going to sleep in tomorrow morning because you thought you'd be better company after a little extra rest. Go to bed as early as you can and sleep in as late as you can. It's amazing what a few extra hours of sleep can do for a tired holiness warrior! Then, to recharge your batteries, go find a really motivating Christian book or tape and fit it into your devotional schedule. I started doing this years ago, and by changing my reading diet regularly, my interest and motivation hasn't been a problem.

Third, anticipate the joy of discipline-less holiness habits: After practicing these holiness habits for a while, the payback you receive will be so large and so meaningful to you, you won't want to miss it! Gone will be those days of having to use all the self-discipline you can find to get up early and meet the Lord. Instead, your internal motivation will pull you right out of bed.

If you think about it for a moment, discipline is required when you don't want to do something or you have an existing habit that is the opposite of what you are now seeking to do. When you have developed strong and meaningful holiness habits, you'll move into a different sphere of living—where devotions, prayer, journaling, worship, and meditation come naturally.

What causes something to come "naturally"? Habits. What happens to your character when your habits are holy in nature? You become holy. So start developing these habits today, and move toward personal holiness.

RESOURCES FOR PERSONAL HOLINESS

Victory over Temptation, edited by Bruce Wilkinson

How can we make our lives holy when we're surrounded by so much sin? Part of the answer is to fill our minds with holy, mature thinking. In this encouraging, day-by-day journey, you'll find practical wisdom on how you can live for God and avoid the temptation of the world. It is filled with articles by such authors as Max Lucado, Charles Swindoll, Jack Hayford, Chuck Colson, R.C. Sproul, Gary Smalley, and John Trent. You'll want to read a different article each day as you move closer to personal holiness—and closer to God. By exploring how other men of God achieved victory over temptation, you will be encouraged and strengthened in your Christian walk. Includes study questions. 256 pp., $9.99.

Personal Holiness in Times of Temptation Video Course

Here is the down-to-earth, biblically based help you've been praying for. This video, a four-part series by Dr. Bruce Wilkinson exploring holiness, temptation, sexuality, and victory, was recorded live at a Walk Thru the Bible seminar. It has proved tremendously helpful to Bible studies and men's groups around the country. Includes course workbook. $19.99. (Extra workbooks are $6 apiece.)

Personal Holiness Audio Cassette Series

$19.95 for the same information as above on four cassettes, with six life-changing daily devotionals for each session. This series also includes the Transformers—Scripture and prayer cards you can take with you to support and inspire you throughout the day.

Personal Holiness Church Kit

This box includes a leader's guide, bulletin inserts, poster, video, and six workbooks for your men's group to get started with an in-depth study of holiness. $59.95.

All resources can be ordered from:
Walk Thru the Bible Ministries
1-800-763-5433